# Studies in the Dead Sea Scrolls and Related Literature

*Peter W. Flint, Martin G. Abegg Jr., and Florentino García Martínez,*
*General Editors*

The Dead Sea Scrolls have been the object of intense interest in recent years, not least because of the release of previously unpublished texts from Qumran Cave 4 since the fall of 1991. With the wealth of new documents that have come to light, the field of Qumran studies has undergone a renaissance. Scholars have begun to question the established conclusions of the last generation; some widely held beliefs have withstood scrutiny, but others have required revision or even dismissal. New proposals and competing hypotheses, many of them of an uncritical and sensational nature, vie for attention. Idiosyncratic and misleading views of the Scrolls still abound, especially in the popular press, while the results of solid scholarship have yet to make their full impact. At the same time, the scholarly task of establishing reliable critical editions of the texts is nearing completion. The opportunity is ripe, therefore, for directing renewed attention to the task of analysis and interpretation.

Studies in the Dead Sea Scrolls and Related Literature is a new series designed to address this need. In particular, the series aims to make the latest and best Dead Sea Scrolls scholarship accessible to scholars, students, and the thinking public. The volumes that are projected — both monographs and collected essays — will seek to clarify how the Scrolls revise and help shape our understanding of the formation of the Bible and the historical development of Judaism and Christianity. Various offerings in the series will explore the reciprocally illuminating relationships of several disciplines related to the Scrolls, including the canon and text of the Hebrew Bible, the richly varied forms of Second Temple Judaism, and the New Testament. While the Dead Sea Scrolls constitute the main focus, several of these studies will also include perspectives on the Old and New Testaments and other ancient writings — hence the title of the series. It is hoped that these volumes will contribute to a deeper appreciation of the world of early Judaism and Christianity and of their continuing legacy today.

Peter W. Flint
Martin G. Abegg Jr.
Florentino García Martínez

# THE ARCHAEOLOGY OF QUMRAN
# AND THE DEAD SEA SCROLLS

*Jodi Magness*

WILLIAM B. EERDMANS PUBLISHING COMPANY
GRAND RAPIDS, MICHIGAN / CAMBRIDGE, U.K.

© 2002 Wm. B. Eerdmans Publishing Co.

Wm. B. Eerdmans Publishing Co.
255 Jefferson Ave. S.E., Grand Rapids, Michigan 49503 /
P.O. Box 163, Cambridge CB3 9PU U.K.

Printed in the United States of America

07  06  05  04  03  02      7  6  5  4  3  2  1


Library of Congress Cataloging-in-Publication Data

The archaeology of Qumran and the Dead Sea Scrolls / Jodi Magness.
p.      cm.      — (Studies in the Dead Sea Scrolls and Related Literature)
Includes bibliographical references and index.
ISBN 0-8028-4589-4
1. Qumran community.
2. Excavations (Archaeology) — West Bank.
3. Qumran site (West Bank).
4. Dead Sea scrolls — Criticism, interpretation, etc.
I. Title.   II. Series.


BM175.Q6 M34   2002
296.1'55 — dc21

2002067924


www.eerdmans.com

# Contents

CONTENTS

# Acknowledgments

It is a pleasure to acknowledge the assistance and support of the individuals and institutions who made this project possible. First I would like to thank the institutions that provided financial support during my sabbatical year, giving me the time and resources I needed to write this book. In addition to my sabbatical salary from Tufts University, the Faculty Research Awards Committee at Tufts provided $1500 to help defray the publication costs of this book. I was supported by two fellowships in 2000-2001: a Fellowship for College Teachers and Independent Scholars from the National Endowment for the Humanities, and a Skirball Visiting Fellowship from the Oxford Centre for Hebrew and Jewish Studies. My cottage at Yarnton (the "Orangery") provided an idyllic setting that was most conducive to writing. I benefitted from the many scholarly contacts that I made in Oxford. I am especially grateful for the hospitality and advice provided by Martin Goodman (my academic host), Geza Vermès, Fergus Millar, and James Howard-Johnston. I enjoyed the company of the other fellows and residents at the OCHJS, including Alan Steinweis, Mitchell Hart, and Nina Caputo. I would also like to thank Glenda Abramson, Joan Sinclair, Sheila Phillips, and the other staff for making my stay at Yarnton so enjoyable and productive.

Many friends and colleagues have provided valuable assistance on matters relating to the archaeology of Qumran. I am especially grateful for the advice and support provided by Hanan Eshel, Magen Broshi, Susan Sheridan, Armin Lange, Emanuel Tov, David Amit, Joan Taylor, Joseph Lauer, Sidnie Crawford, Joseph Zias, Stephen Goranson, Nurit Feig, Andrea Berlin, and Shani Berrin. Joanne Besonen provided invaluable assistance with the index.

Last but not least, I am thankful for the love and support of my parents,

Herbert and Marlene Magness, and my husband, Jim Haberman. Jim not only tolerates my long hours at the office and library and summer trips to the Middle East, but lovingly and enthusiastically supports everything I do. I am truly blessed.

# Illustrations

In addition to photographs by the author, figures were provided by the following sources:

Nahman Avigad, *Discovering Jerusalem* (Nashville: Thomas Nelson, 1983) [Figs. 51-54]

Pesach Bar-Adon, "Another Settlement of the Judean Desert Sect at 'En el-Ghuweir on the Shores of the Dead Sea," *Bulletin of the American Schools of Oriental Research* 227 (1977): 1-25 [Fig. 66]

Dominique Barthélemy and J. T. Milik, *Qumran Cave 1* (Oxford: Clarendon Press, 1955): Grace M. Crowfoot, "The Linen Textiles," 28-38 [Figs. 61-62]; Roland de Vaux, "La Poterie," 8-13 [Figs. 21, 61-62]

Pierre Benoit et al., *Les Grottes de Murabba'at* (Oxford: Clarendon Press, 1961): Roland de Vaux, "Archeologie," 3-63 [Fig. 57]

Jane Cahill et al., "It Had to Happen," *Biblical Archaeology Review* 17/3 (1991): 64-69 [Fig. 43]

Jean-Baptiste Humbert and Alain Chambon, *Fouilles de Khirbet Qumrân et de Aïn Feshka* 1 (Fribourg: Éditions universitaires, 1994) [Figs. 6-8, 11-12, 15-16, 20, 23-26, 30, 32-35, 37, 40-41, 46, 48, 64-65]

Carl H. Kraeling, *The Synagogue* (New Haven: Yale University Press, 1979) [Fig. 60]

Stephan Steingräber, ed., *Etruscan Painting* (New York: Harcourt Brace Jovanovich, 1985) [Fig. 36]

Roland de Vaux, *Archaeology and the Dead Sea Scrolls* (Oxford: Oxford University Press, 1961) [Figs. 5, 13]

Roland de Vaux, "Fouilles de Khirbet Qumrân: Rapport préliminaire sur les 3e, 4e, et 5e campagnes," *Revue Biblique* 63 (1956): 533-77 [Fig. 22]

Roland de Vaux, "Une hachette essénienne?" *Vetus Testamentum* 9 (1956): 399-407 [Fig. 45]

Yigael Yadin, *The Finds from the Bar-Kokhba Period in the Cave of Letters* (Jerusalem: Israel Exploration Society, 1963) [Figs. 55, 58-59, 63]

Yigael Yadin, *Masada: Herod's Fortress and the Zealots' Last Stand,* copyright © 1966 by Yigael Yadin. Used by permission of Random House, Inc. [Fig. 56]

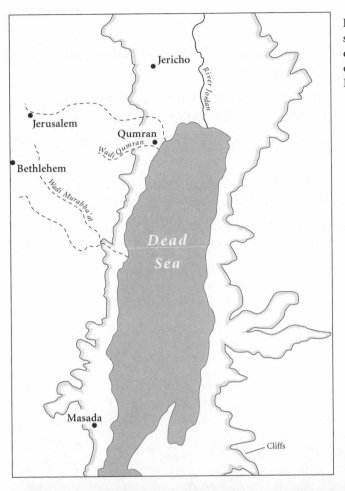

Fig. 1 *(left):* Map showing location of Qumran and other sites by the Dead Sea.

Jericho

River Jordan

Jerusalem

Qumran

Wadi Qumran

Bethlehem

Wadi Murabba'at

Dead Sea

Masada

Cliffs

Fig. 2 *(below):* View of Cave 4 at Qumran.

Fig. 3: Part of the Isaiah scroll from Cave 1.

Fig. 4: View of Qumran looking west, with the Dead Sea
and the mountains of Moab behind.

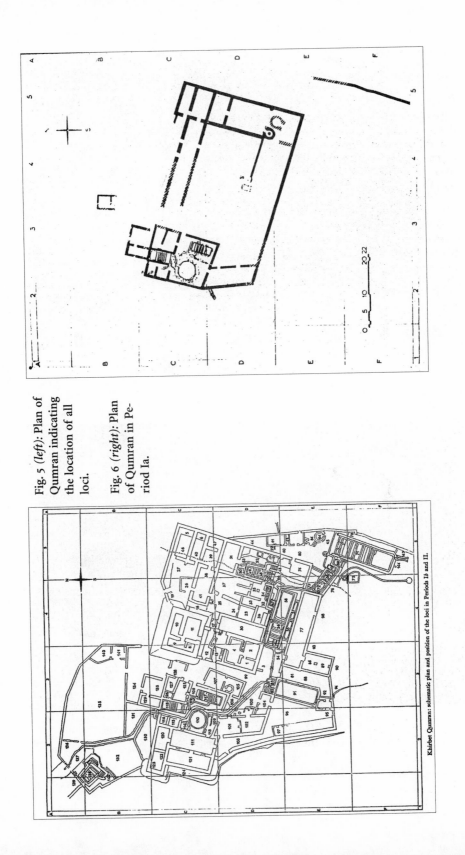

Fig. 5 (*left*): Plan of Qumran indicating the location of all loci.

Fig. 6 (*right*): Plan of Qumran in Period Ia.

Khirbet Qumran: schematic plan and position of the loci in Periods Ib and II.

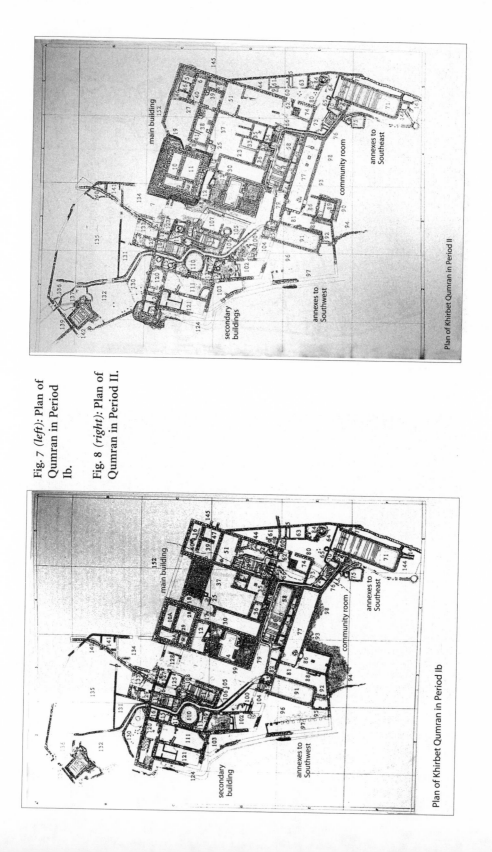

Fig. 7 *(left)*: Plan of Qumran in Period Ib.

Fig. 8 *(right)*: Plan of Qumran in Period II.

Fig. 9: View of Qumran looking south from the top of the tower.

Fig. 10: View of the northern and western sides of the tower.

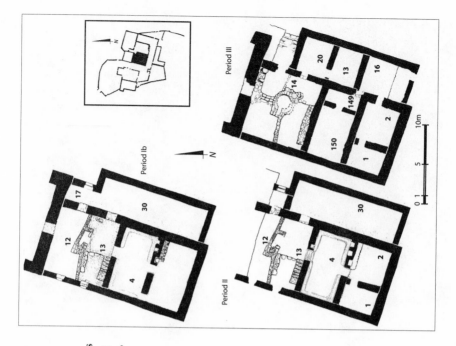

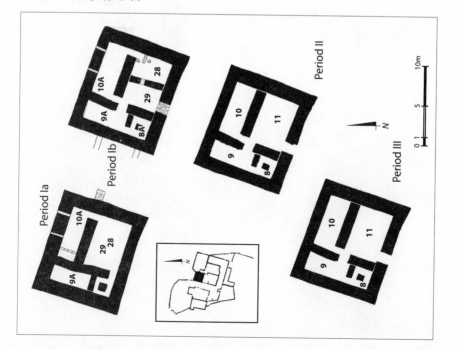

Fig. 11 (*left*): Plan of the tower.

Fig. 12 (*right*): Plan of the western rooms in the main building (including L1, L2, L4, L13, and L30).

Fig. 13 *(left):*
Plastered bench and
table from L30 (the
"scriptorium").

Fig. 14 *(below):*
The inkwells from
L30 and L31.

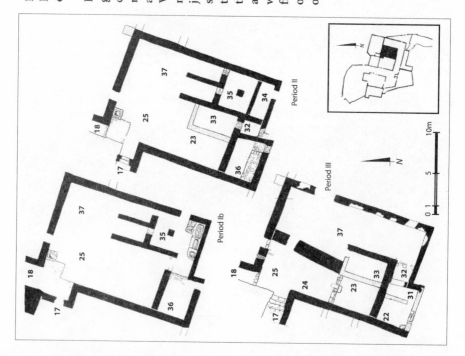

Fig. 15 (left):
Plan of the courtyard
of the main building.

Fig. 16 (right): Photo-
graph of L34 in the
courtyard of the
main building taken
at the time of de
Vaux's excavations;
notice the cylindrical
jar and the disc-
shaped lid lying on
the floor nearby. To
the right of the lid is
a chunk of a burnt
wooden ceiling beam,
from the destruction
of the site at the end
of Period II.

Fig. 17: The basins in L34 in the courtyard of the main building
as they appear today.

Fig. 18: The potters' kiln in L64 as it appears today.

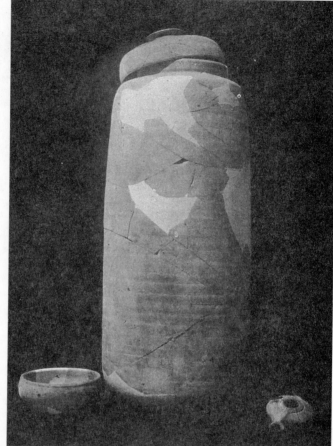

Fig. 19 *(right)*: A complete (restored) cylindrical jar and bowl-shaped lid from Qumran. At the lower right-hand side of the jar is an oil lamp of Hellenistic inspiration of the type characteristic of Qumran in Period Ib.

Fig. 20 *(below)*: An intact cylindrical jar with a bowl-shaped lid, as found by de Vaux embedded in the floor of L80. Notice the matching pierced ledge handles on the jar and bowl, which could be tied together.

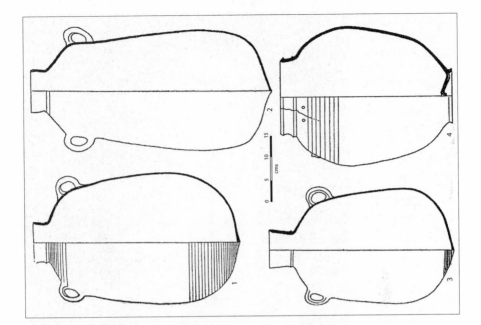

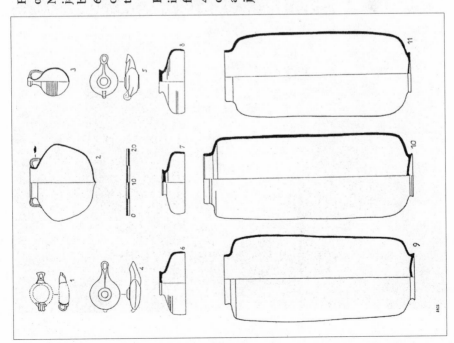

Fig. 21 (left): Drawings of pottery from Cave 1. Notice the cylindrical jars (numbers 9-11), the bowl-shaped lids (nos. 6-8), and the oil lamps of Hellenistic inspiration (nos. 4-5).

Fig. 22 (right): Drawings of storage jars from Ein Feshkha. No. 4 (lower right) is an ovoid jar; the others are bag-shaped storage jars.

Fig. 23 *(right):* Plan of the enclosure in the northwest corner of Qumran (including L130, L132, L135, and L138).

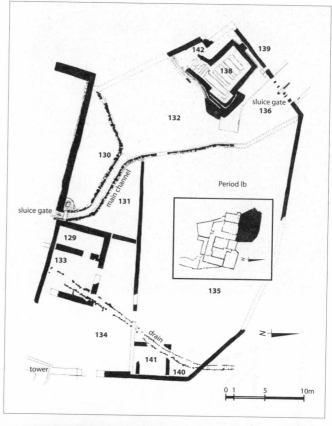

Fig. 24 *(below):* View of L130, showing the animal bone deposits at the time of de Vaux's excavations.

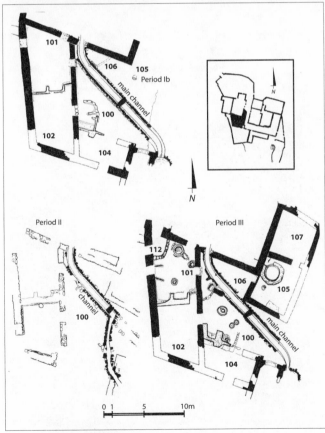

Fig. 25 *(above):* An animal bone deposit in L130 at the time of de Vaux's excavations.

Fig. 26 *(left):* Plan of the area with workshops in the southern part of the secondary building.

Fig. 27 *(above):*
Column bases in the
southern part of the
secondary building.

Fig. 28 *(right):*
View of the commu-
nal dining room in
L77, looking west.

Fig. 29: View of the pantry in L86.

Fig. 30: Broken dishes lying on the floor of the pantry in L86,
as they were found by de Vaux.

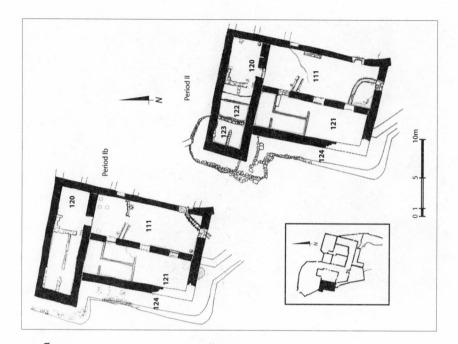

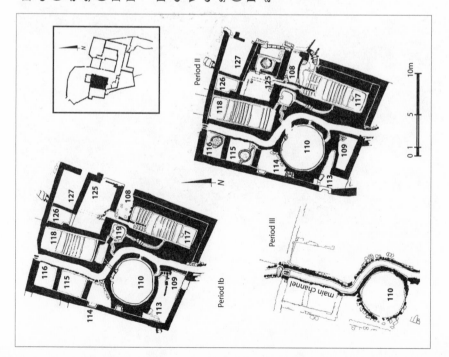

Fig. 31 (*left*): Plan of the round cistern (L110) and the area around it in the secondary building (including L113, L114, L117, and L118).

Fig. 32 (*right*): Plan of the rooms to the west of the round cistern (L110) in the secondary building (including L111, L120, L121, L122, and L123).

Fig. 33: View of the rooms to the northwest of the round cistern (L110)
in the secondary building, taken at the time of de Vaux's excavations.
L110 is in the foreground and L114 is to its left.

Fig. 34: View of the dishes lying on the floor of L114, as they were found by de Vaux.

Fig. 35: View of the area to the south of the round cistern (L110)
in the secondary building, taken at the time of de Vaux's excavations.
L110 is in the foreground, and the staircase in L113 is immediately
behind (above) it, in the center of the photograph.

Fig. 36: A wall-painting from an Etruscan tomb
showing banqueters reclining and dining

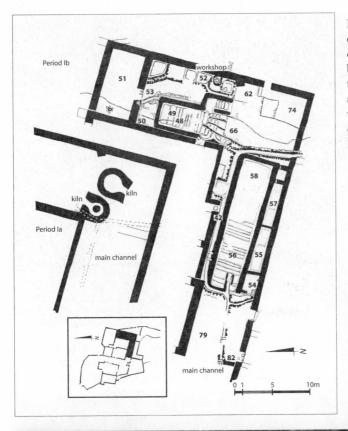

Fig. 37 *(left):* Plan of the southeast corner of the main building, including the toilet in L51 and the miqveh with earthquake damage in L48-L49.

Fig. 38 *(below):* View of the aqueduct, at the point where the channel is cut through the side of a cliff to Wadi Qumran behind.

Fig. 39: View of the miqveh in L48-L49. Notice the low, plastered partitions on the steps, and the earthquake damage which has caused the left-hand side of the steps to drop.

Fig. 40: The toilet in L51 at the time of de Vaux's excavations.

Fig. 41: The toilet in L51 at the time of de Vaux's excavations. Humbert and Chambon erroneously described the pit as a "receptacle jar." Instead, what appears to be a jar is actually the mud lining of the pit, into which the pipe is set.

Fig. 42: The Roman luxury latrine in the Scholastika Baths at Ephesus.

Fig. 43: The toilet in the House of Ahiel in the City of David, Jerusalem.

Fig. 44: A street at Pompeii; notice the high curbs and stepping stone.

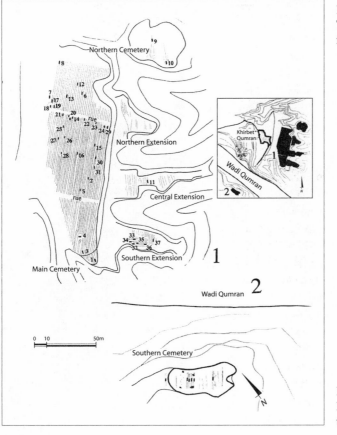

Fig. 45 *(above):*
The iron pick
from Cave 11.

Fig. 46 *(left):*
Plan of the ceme-
tery at Qumran.

Fig. 47 *(above):*
View of the area
of the cemetery
on the plateau
to the east of
the settlement,
looking west.

Tomb 18: Consolidation of skeleton

Tomb 18:
Skeleton after restoration

Tomb 18: Stones and bricks covering
the loculus

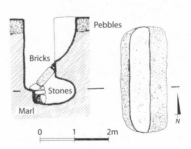

Pebbles

Bricks

Stones

Marl

0    1    2m

Section and outline of Tomb 18

Fig. 48 *(right):*
Tomb 18 at
the time of
de Vaux's
excavations.

Fig. 49: The hypocaust system showing the suspensura (the little columns that supported the floor) in the caldarium (steam room) of the large bathhouse at Masada. The furnace was located on the other side of the semi-circular opening in the wall.

Fig. 50: Molded and painted plaster (stucco) decorating a wall in the House of the Faun at Pompeii.

Fig. 51 *(above):* A wall painting in the Second Pompeian Style from a 1st-century-C.E. mansion in Jerusalem's Jewish Quarter.

Fig. 52: A mosaic floor from a 1st-century-C.E. mansion in Jerusalem's Jewish Quarter.

Fig. 53: A set of Eastern Sigillata A dishes from the "Herodian Residence" in Jerusalem's Jewish Quarter.

Fig. 54: Jerusalem painted or "pseudo-Nabatean" bowls from the 1st-century-C.E. mansions in Jerusalem's Jewish Quarter.

Fig. 55 *(right):*
Bronze mirrors
with wooden mir-
ror cases from the
Cave of Letters in
Naḥal Ḥever.

Fig. 56 *(below):*
Cosmetic items
from dwellings of
Jewish rebels at
Masada, including
a wooden comb
(lower right), a
bronze mirror case
(upper right), and
bronze eye-shadow
sticks (lower left).

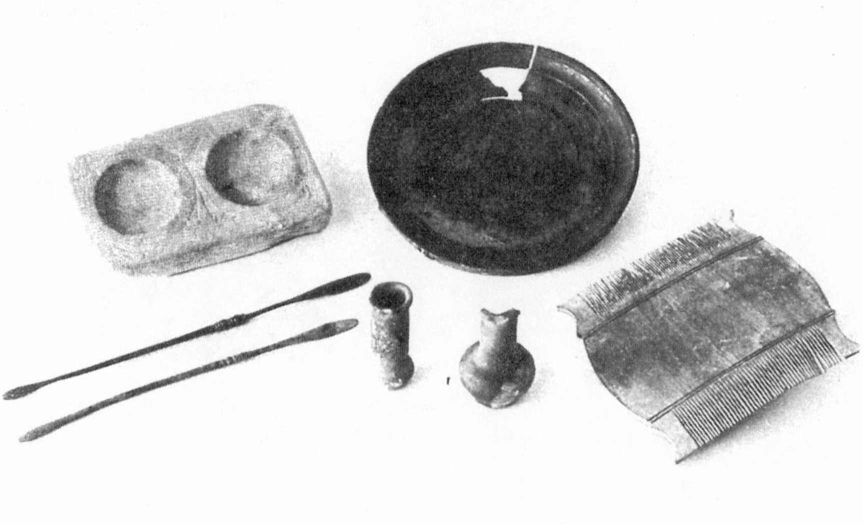

Fig. 57: A spindle whorl (upper left), wooden combs (center), and an iron cosmetic spoon (lower right) from the caves in Wadi Muraba'at.

Fig. 58:
Wool tunics with
colored stripes
(clavi) from the
Cave of Letters in
Naḥal Ḥever.

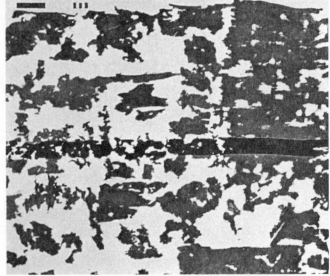

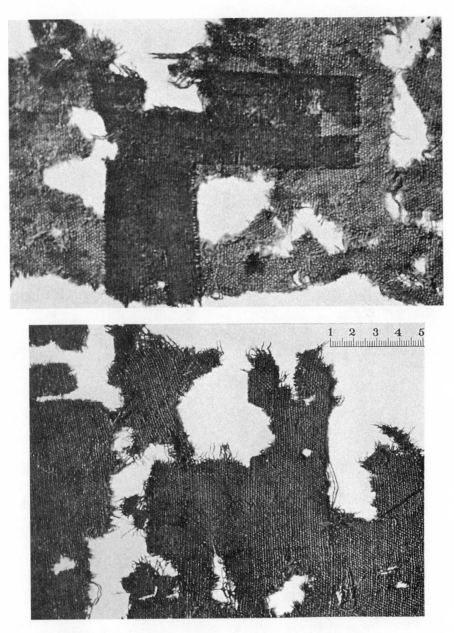

Fig. 59: Pieces of wool mantles with gamma-shaped designs
from the Cave of Letters in Naḥal Ḥever.

Fig. 60: A wall painting from the 3rd-century-c.e. synagogue at Dura Europos
in Syria, showing Moses and the burning bush. Notice that Moses wears
a tunic with colored stripes *(clavi)* and a mantle.

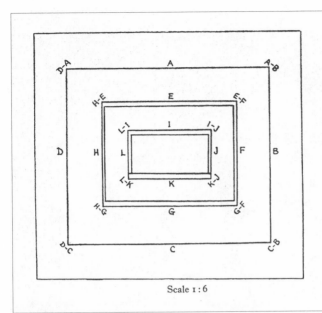

Scale 1 : 6

Fig. 61 *(left):* Drawing of a linen scroll wrapper with blue lines from Cave 1

Fig. 62 *(below):* Linen scroll wrappers with blue lines from Cave 1

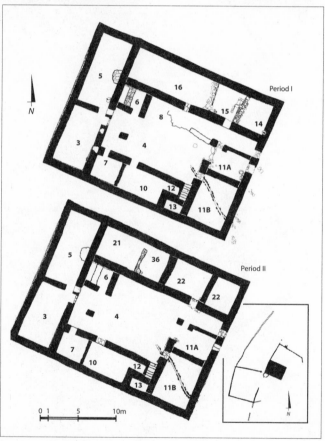

Fig. 63 *(above):* A piece of linen from the Cave of Letters in Naḥal Ḥever. The decorative woolen weft threads that had originally been woven in to create colored stripes *(clavi)* were removed from the web, creating self-stripes.

Fig. 64 *(right):* Plan of the main building at Ein Feshkha.

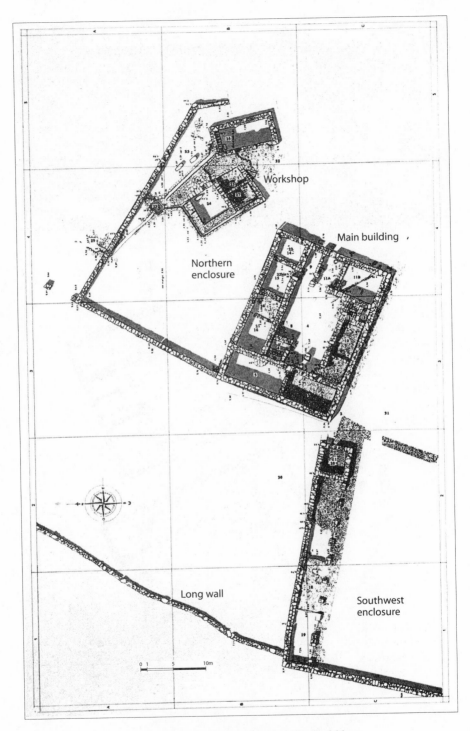

Fig. 65: Plan of the buildings at Ein Feshkha.

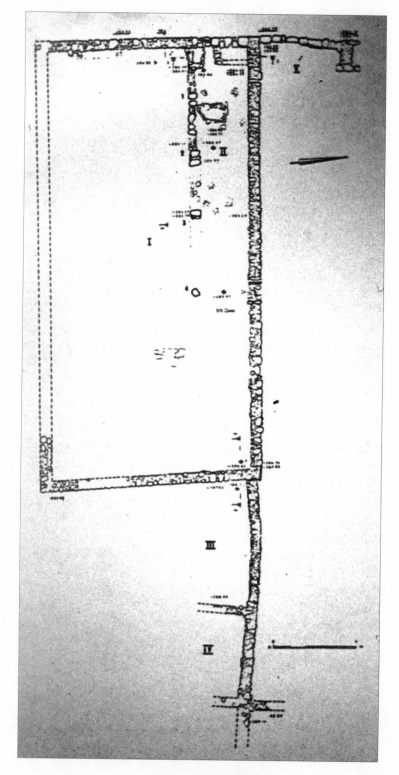

Fig. 66: Plan of Ein el-Ghuweir.

CHAPTER 1

# An Introduction to
# the Archaeology of Qumran

*At best, material culture is viewed as a rather uninteresting or
quaint by-product of the real meat of acted social relationships: the
props to the play. . . . But . . . when your wish is to understand people
who are dead, artifacts are all you have. They last.*

Qumran is one of the most famous and remarkable archaeological sites in the
world. It is famous because of its physical proximity to the caves in which the
Dead Sea Scrolls were discovered. It is remarkable because without that association it would probably never have attracted much attention. Every day
busloads of tourists are unloaded at the site. Many of them must be disap-
pointed, for after having heard of the Dead Sea Scrolls and having visited
Herod's visually stunning palaces at Masada earlier that day, they find themselves at a small, unimpressive ruin (see Fig. 9). The main attraction is Cave 4,
which is easily visible from the site (see Fig. 2) and which many visitors must
mistake for the cave in which the first scrolls were discovered (Cave 1). Cave 4
is a manmade cave cut into the marl terrace on which Qumran sits (see below), whereas Cave 1 is a natural cave in the limestone cliffs a little over 1 kilo-
meter (over half a mile) to the north, and is not visible or easily accessible
from the site.

Qumran was not a major tourist attraction before the late 1980s. When I
worked as a guide in the Dead Sea region in the late 1970s, Qumran was virtually deserted. The only visitors' facilities consisted of a crude shelter next to

the ruins (open on all sides, with wooden benches under a reed roof) and a lone vendor from Jericho who sold cold drinks from a portable cart. Today, a huge, air-conditioned tourist center (with extensive souvenir shop, restaurant, and snack concession) dominates the entrance to the site. The admission fees (collected by a friendly Israel Parks Authority employee in an air-conditioned booth) include the viewing of a short film about Qumran.

Qumran's popularity is largely the result of increased public awareness of the Dead Sea Scrolls. Much of this came about during the 1980s, when scandals surrounding delays due to alleged Vatican or scholarly conspiracies were widely publicized by the media. By the early 1990s, all of the Dead Sea Scrolls had been "freed" — that is, all of the scrolls, even those that were still unpublished, were made accessible to everyone. This pretty much put an end to the conspiracy theories surrounding the scrolls. At the same time, the controversies surrounding Qumran were just beginning.

Until the 1980s, the interpretation proposed by Roland de Vaux (who directed the excavations at Qumran in the 1950s) was widely accepted among scholars. According to this interpretation, the site of Qumran was inhabited by the same community that deposited the scrolls in the caves. These people were members of a Jewish sect that de Vaux and others identified with the Essenes mentioned in ancient historical sources. This consensus was shaken by a pair of Belgian archaeologists named Robert Donceel and Pauline Donceel-Voûte. The Donceels had been invited by Jean-Baptiste Humbert, who is now the staff archaeologist at the Dominican École Biblique et Archéologique Française (the French School of Biblical Studies and Archaeology in Jerusalem) to help prepare the material from de Vaux's excavations for publication. In a *Nova* television special about the Dead Sea Scrolls that was broadcast in 1991, the Donceels dropped a bombshell: in their opinion, Qumran was not a sectarian settlement as de Vaux believed, but a *villa rustica* — that is, a country villa! Although the Donceels left the project without completing their study of the material, they published several articles with their interpretation. A number of scholars have proposed other interpretations, including that Qumran was a fort, a manor house, or a commercial entrepot. Although none of these alternative theories has gained widespread acceptance, they have succeeded in calling into question the validity of de Vaux's interpretation.

One problem surrounding the archaeology of Qumran is that a full and final (scientific) report on de Vaux's excavations has never been published. Although he wrote several detailed preliminary reports (in French), and a general overview of the archaeology of Qumran (translated into English), de Vaux died in 1971 without having published all of the material from his excavations. In Israel, there is an unwritten but universally accepted custom that once a site is excavated, the material from that excavation (and sometimes even the site itself) "belongs" to the excavator. This means that the excavator has sole authority over the publication of and access to the material from the excavation. If the excavator dies without having published the material, it is "inherited" by the excavator's home institution. For example, when Yigael Yadin died in 1984, the unpublished material from his excavations was inherited by his home institution, the Hebrew University of Jerusalem. Together with the Israel Exploration Society, the unpublished material from Yadin's excavations at Hazor and Masada was divided among faculty members at the Hebrew University's Institute of Archaeology, who were put in charge of overseeing the publication process. As a result, I was invited to prepare the publication of the military equipment from Masada. This same procedure caused the delays in the publication of the Dead Sea Scrolls. In other words, instead of scholarly or Vatican conspiracies, the delays were caused by the fact that the scrolls belonged to the members of the original team that de Vaux had assembled. These scholars had the right to reassign the publication of their material (for example, to their students) and grant or deny access to it.

In 1991, universal access to the Dead Sea Scrolls was made possible because the Huntington Library in San Marino, California, which has copies of all of the scrolls on microfiche, decided to make them freely available. All of the scrolls that were still unpublished in 1991 have since been published. This is not the case with the material from de Vaux's excavations at Qumran. No "copies" exist of the archaeological artifacts from Qumran, most of which are now stored in the basement of Jerusalem's Rockefeller Museum. The unpublished records from de Vaux's excavations are also inaccessible. Without Humbert's permission, no one is allowed access to the unpublished artifacts or records from Qumran. In 1991, Humbert allowed me to look at the pottery from Qumran stored in the Rockefeller Museum, but I have had no further access to any of the material since then.

Although we still await a final excavation report, in 1994 Humbert and a Belgian archaeologist named Alain Chambon published a large volume described as the first in a series. This volume contains original photographs from the time of de Vaux's excavations, plans (line-drawings) of the excavated areas, and de Vaux's original field notes. The original edition, in French, has been translated into German, and Stephen Pfann is preparing a revised edition in English. Although this volume contains some previously unpublished information, there is still much that is unpublished and inaccessible. For example, although the artifacts that received registration numbers (which presumably represent the artifacts that were saved at the time of the excavation) are listed in this volume; they are not illustrated. Some of these objects

— especially the whole pottery vessels — are illustrated elsewhere in de Vaux's preliminary reports. But most of these artifacts are not illustrated or published elsewhere. This means that they are useless for scientific purposes, because it is impossible to identify pottery types without illustrations. In fact, the functions of some of the objects — such as the "clay balls" discussed in Chapter 9 — cannot be identified at all! The lack of a full and final scientific report also means that there is no published record of the whereabouts of some of these artifacts. For example, the Donceels reported that some of the coins from de Vaux's excavations have been lost. Have any other artifacts been lost? And how can we determine what was lost when we have no fully published record of what was discovered and saved? For example, in the case of the toilet at Qumran (see Chapter 6), I do not know whether de Vaux saved soil samples from the cesspit of the toilet. In addition, the pierced square stone block found in an adjacent room (which I believe could be the toilet seat) is nowhere illustrated, and I do not know its whereabouts. Finally, reports are circulating (by word of mouth) that the École has recruited scholars to work on the publication of the material from de Vaux's excavations. However, there has been no public announcement about the allocation of this material (that is, who is working on what), nor have a timetable or an advisory committtee (to oversee the publication) been set up, analogous to the process established for the Dead Sea Scrolls about a decade ago. In other words, the secrecy and delays in publication that created the Dead Sea Scrolls scandal still surround the material from de Vaux's excavations at Qumran.

Although my book represents the most recent survey of the archaeology of Qumran, it is not the definitive work on this subject. This is impossible without the full publication of the material from de Vaux's excavations. For this reason, most of the interpretations and conclusions presented in this book are tentative. However, I believe that although the eventual publication of all of the material from de Vaux's excavations might make it necessary to modify some details of these interpretations and will enrich our knowledge of the site, it will not substantially alter the current picture. This is because enough archaeological information has been published to give us a fairly accurate understanding of the site and its inhabitants.

## What Is Archaeology, and What Excavation Methods Do Archaeologists Use?

*The Oxford Companion to Archaeology* defines archaeology as "the study of the past as evident in the material remains available to us." In contrast, history is the study of the past based on information provided by written documents. In other words, although both archaeologists and historians study the past, they use different methods or sources to obtain their information. Archaeologists learn about the past through the study of the material remains left by humans, whereas historians study written records (texts). These sources of information often provide different (although not necessarily mutually exclusive or conflicting) pictures of the past. For example, since many texts were written by or for the ruling classes (elites) of ancient societies, they tend to reflect their concerns, interests, and viewpoints. In contrast, although archaeologists often uncover the palaces and citadels of the ruling classes, they also dig up houses and workshops which belonged to the poorer classes of ancient societies. Archaeological evidence can be used to complement or supplement the information provided by written records, and in cases where we have no written records (such as in prehistoric societies), it is our only source of information.

Some ancient sites were occupied for only one brief period or phase. However, many sites in Palestine were occupied over longer periods. At such multi-period sites, the buildings and debris from the successive phases of occupation accumulated, forming a series of levels one above the other like a layer-cake. In the case of many biblical sites in Israel, there can be 20 or more different occupation levels, forming an artificial mound called in Hebrew a *tel* (Arabic *tell*). The famous tels of Megiddo and Hazor provided the models for James A. Michener's 1965 novel, *The Source*. Archaeologists refer to these occupation levels as strata (singular, stratum) and to the sequence of levels as stratigraphy. At Qumran, we can distinguish at least three successive occupation levels (which de Vaux called periods) during the relatively brief existence of the sectarian settlement (1st century B.C.E.–1st century C.E.).

Although it is helpful to visualize the strata of ancient sites as a layer-cake, the reality is never that neat and simple. This is because the inhabitants frequently disturbed earlier levels when constructing the foundations of buildings or when digging pits. In the course of such activities, they cut into or through earlier strata, churning up earlier material (potsherds, coins, etc.) with the dirt and stones. This means that at multi-period sites, we always find earlier artifacts mixed in with the later material. For this reason, we use the latest artifacts to date the stratum we are excavating and disregard the earlier material (at least for dating purposes).

Imagine that we are standing inside a modern school building in Philadelphia that was built in 1972. When the school was built, a deep pit (trench) was dug into the ground for the foundations. At the time the floor was laid, it sealed the foundation trench and everything in it. If we dig under that floor today, we should find nothing later than 1972 in the fill. However, we would almost certainly find objects earlier than 1972 in that fill, such as old Coke bottles, coins dating to the 1950s and 1960s, and so on. Now let's suppose that the latest datable object we find under that floor is a penny minted in 1968. This coin would provide what archaeologists call a *terminus post quem* (Latin for "date after which") for the construction of the school. In other words, the coin would tell us that the school was constructed in 1968 or later, but not earlier. Now let's suppose that the school was destroyed by an earthquake in 1985, which caused the building to collapse, burying everything inside. The objects found on top of the floors would represent those items in use at the moment when the building collapsed. They would also provide us with a *terminus ante quem* (Latin for "date before which") for the construction of the school. In other words, if the latest objects found buried in the collapse were books printed in 1985, we would know that the school building must have been constructed on or before that date. One of the most famous examples of such a catastrophic destruction is the eruption of Mount Vesuvius in 79 C.E., which buried Pompeii and Herculaneum in volcanic ash and mud. Walking through the excavated streets of those towns today gives us a glimpse into what they looked like at the moment of their destruction (see Fig. 44).

During the course of excavation, archaeologists destroy the evidence they dig up. This is because once a shovel of dirt or a stone is removed from the ground it can never be put back in the same way. For this reason, archaeologists record the excavation process using every means possible. If you have ever visited an excavation, you might have noticed that archaeologists dig in squares measuring 5 × 5 or 10 × 10 m. The squares form a grid. The squares are separated by banks of earth about 1 m. wide called baulks (or balks). This system enables archaeologists to measure and record the exact location of every excavated object and feature (by feature, I mean something that is constructed as opposed to an artifact, which is a portable, manmade object). The recording is done by measuring levels (absolute heights within the excavated squares), keeping daily diaries, making drawings and taking photographs, and now with the aid of computers. Ideally, once a final excavation report is published, it should be possible for the reader to reconstruct the site as it looked before everything was dug up.

Archaeologists use various devices to keep track of the point of origin (provenance) of every excavated artifact and feature. One way to do this is to subdivide each square horizontally and vertically. One of the most common subdivisions used in excavations is a *locus* (plural *loci*). Locus means "spot" or "place" in Latin. In archaeology it can be used to define any excavated feature. For example, a locus can designate an oven, a pit, a room, or any part of a room. It is simply a device to help subdivide the area being excavated, to enable us to later pinpoint the exact spot where an artifact or feature was found. For example, let's say that we begin excavating a square on top of the modern ground surface. We would give the entire square one locus number (L1; L = Locus). About 10 centimeters below the ground surface, we notice that the soil is changing in color and composition from reddish brown to dark brown mixed with lots of stones. At this point, we would measure the absolute height (with the same kind of equipment used by surveyors) and change the locus number (from L1 to L2). Five centimeters below this, we begin to come upon a line of stones cutting diagonally across the square which looks like the top of a wall. We would again measure the absolute height and change the locus number, giving the areas on either side of the wall different locus numbers (L3 on one side and L4 on the other side). The pottery and other objects discovered during the course of excavation are saved and labeled according to their context.

This system of excavating and recording is the standard one used by archaeologists working in Israel today (with minor variations from excavation to excavation). Because this system has evolved over time, not all of the elements were used by earlier generations of archaeologists (just as this methodology will undoubtedly be refined by future archaeologists, especially as new technologies develop). For example, we will see that de Vaux used locus numbers at Qumran. However, he used the same locus number to designate a single room from the beginning to the end of the excavation, instead of changing the number as he dug through different levels or distinguished different features in the rooms. Although some scholars have recently criticized de Vaux's excavation techniques, it is important to remember that he was working according to the methods used in his time. For example, 10 years after de Vaux's excavations at Qumran, Yigael Yadin excavated at Masada using locus numbers in the same way to designate a single room for the duration of the excavation. At the same time (in the early 1960s), a University of Missouri expedition to the late Roman site of Jalame in Galilee did not use locus numbers at all (instead they used trench numbers). And like Qumran, we have few section drawings (drawings of the stratigraphy visible in the baulks) from the Masada and Jalame excavations.

## How Do Archaeologists Date the Remains They Dig Up?

When we excavate an ancient house, what objects or artifacts can we find that will tell us when it was built, occupied, and destroyed or abandoned? The type of object that provides an accurate date should fulfill one of two criteria: (1) it must be a very common find on archaeological excavations; or (2) it carries its own date. The main methods of dating used by archaeologists specializing in Roman Palestine include: (1) radiocarbon dating (sometimes called Carbon 14 or C14 dating); (2) coins; (3) inscriptions or other written materials found in excavations; (4) ancient historical sources; (5) pottery (ceramic) typology.

Before we discuss each of these dating methods, note that this list does not include human or animal bones, tools, or architectural styles. Although human and animal bones can provide much useful information (animal bones, for example, can tell us about the ancient environment and human skeletons can provide information about ancient populations), they cannot be dated unless enough collagen is preserved for the purposes of radiocarbon dating. As we will see, the skeletons from the cemetery at Qumran do not contain enough collagen to be radiocarbon dated (Chapter 8).

Tools are another matter. Stone tools used by prehistoric populations can be dated according to their type in a manner analogous to the way pottery is dated (see below). But once pottery appears in Palestine (ca. 5000 B.C.E.), it replaces stone tools as an accurate method of dating. And remember the criterion that the object must be a very common find on archaeological excavations? Well, tools made of bronze or iron are not common finds on archaeological excavations. This is because all metals were precious in antiquity, not just gold and silver, as it was costly to mine the ores out of the ground. When metal tools broke in antiquity, they were not discarded but were repaired or melted down to manufacture new objects. Nearly all of the Classical Greek statues of the 5th and 4th centuries B.C.E. were made of bronze. Most disappeared long ago because they were melted down and made into something else. All we have left today are later Roman copies in stone of the original Greek masterpieces and rare examples of bronze originals, most of which are recovered from ancient shipwrecks. In addition, because metal tools tend to be utilitarian they did not change much in shape over the centuries. For example, an ancient iron pick from Cave 11 at Qumran looks just like a modern one (see Fig. 45). For these reasons, metal tools are not useful for dating even when they are found in excavations.

What about architectural styles? Although archaeologists sometimes use distinctive architectural styles (or tomb types) as a means of dating, this can be done accurately only in rare instances. This is because once an architectural style was invented it could be copied or imitated by later generations. If you have ever seen the 30th Street Station in Philadelphia or any other modern building constructed in a Classical Greek style, you know what I mean. However, most of the remains archaeologists dig up are not that distinctive. The construction at Qumran, for example, is very simple, consisting mostly of uncut field stones and mudbrick.

Now let's discuss the dating methods listed above. Each method has its own advantages and disadvantages.

## 1. Radiocarbon (Carbon 14) Dating

*The Oxford Companion to Archaeology* defines radiocarbon dating as "an isotopic or nuclear decay method of inferring age for organic materials." This method works roughly as follows. Carbon 14 is a radioactive isotope of Carbon 12. All plants and living creatures contain Carbon 14 while they are alive. When a living thing dies, it begins to lose the Carbon 14 at a steady rate: approximately half of the Carbon 14 is lost every 5730 years (the "half-life" of radiocarbon). For example, if archaeologists find a piece of charcoal in an excavation, by measuring the amount of Carbon 14 in it a lab can determine roughly when the tree from which the charcoal came was chopped down. A type of radiocarbon dating called accelerator mass spectrometry (AMS) can be used for dating smaller samples of organic matter. Radiocarbon dating has the advantage of being the only "scientific" method listed here (in other words, the date is provided by a laboratory). However, it has the disadvantage that every date returned by the lab has a plus/minus range (this is a margin of statistical error). There is a 67 percent chance that the date provided by the lab falls within the plus/minus range. A date of 4000 plus/minus 100 would mean our tree was chopped down 4000 years ago, with a 67 percent chance that it was chopped down within a range of 100 years either way (the accuracy goes up if the range is doubled). Radiocarbon dates are conventionally published in the form of uncalibrated radiocarbon years Before Present (BP). Present is measured from 1950 C.E., which is approximately when radiocarbon dating was invented. Conversion of these dates to calendar years requires calibration because of past fluctuations in the level of Carbon 14 in the atmosphere. Calibration can increase the range of a radiocarbon date.

For these reasons, radiocarbon dating is most useful in cases where there are no other methods of dating, such as prehistoric sites in Europe or Native American sites in the United States. It is less useful at a site like Qumran where we have other, more accurate methods of dating available. On the other hand, radiocarbon dating has been used effectively on some of the scrolls and linens from the caves around Qumran. In this case, radiocarbon dating is useful because these objects do not have a stratigraphic context (that is, they come from caves instead of from a series of dated layers at an archaeological site). Radiocarbon dating confirmed the 2nd century B.C.E. to 1st century C.E. date that paleographers (specialists in ancient handwriting styles) had already suggested for the scrolls (a date consistent with the pottery types found with the scrolls in the caves).

Another disadvantage of radiocarbon dating is that it can be used only on organic materials, which are exactly the kind of materials that are rarely preserved in ancient sites. The arid conditions inside the caves around Qumran preserved the Dead Sea Scrolls, which are made of parchment (processed animal hide). In contrast, nearly all of the organic materials at Qumran (which would have included wooden furniture, rugs, woven mats and baskets, clothing, leather footware, and perhaps even scrolls) were consumed by the fire that destroyed the settlement. Although other laboratory-based methods of dating exist, I do not list them here because they have not been used at Qumran. These include dendrochronology or tree-ring dating and potassium-argon dating.

## 2. Coins

Coins have the advantage of carrying their own date. However, there are also disadvantages associated with coins. First, coinage was not invented in the Mediterranean world until about 600 B.C.E. This means they do not exist at Mediterranean sites that antedate the 6th century (or in other regions such as North America until much later). Second, coins in antiquity often remained in circulation for long periods — up to hundreds of years — after they were minted. Although this is especially true of the precious gold and silver coins, it can also be true of the lower value bronze coins. For this reason, finding a coin that was minted in 100 C.E. on the floor of a house can be misleading if the coin fell onto the floor 100 or 200 years later. It is best to use more than one coin when possible or coins plus other methods of dating to obtain an accurate date. Third, because coins were valuable, ancient peoples were careful not to lose them. This means it is possible to excavate a level at a site and not find any coins. Fourth, since most ancient coins are tiny pieces of bronze, they have often corroded to the point where the date can no longer be read. Although some of the coins that de Vaux found at Qumran were illegible, there were also many identifiable coins, including a hoard of silver sheqels (Tyrian tetradrachmas).

## 3. Inscriptions or Other Written Materials Found in Excavations

Although this type of object is an archaeological find because it comes from an excavation, it falls into the category of historical materials (written texts). Qumran is an unusual site because of the wealth of written materials, which include the scrolls found in the nearby caves and a small number of ostraca (inscribed potsherds) from the site. The scrolls from Qumran are an exceptional find which were preserved due to the arid conditions.

## 4. Relevant Ancient Historical Sources

These can be helpful for dating when they are available. For example, the Hebrew Bible is often used as a source of information by archaeologists excavating Iron Age sites in Palestine. In the case of Qumran, we are fortunate to have three valuable sources of information: Flavius Josephus, Philo Judaeus, and Pliny the Elder (see Chapter 3). For example, de Vaux found that Qumran was destroyed at some point during its existence by an earthquake. He was able to date this event to 31 B.C.E. because Josephus mentions that a strong earthquake affected the Jericho region during that year.

## 5. Pottery

This is the only type of object in this list that does not carry its own date. Have you ever wondered how an archaeologist can pick up a seemingly nondescript potsherd and tell you its date? Here's how we do it. Imagine that we are excavating a multi-period site with ancient occupation levels (strata) one above the other. In the lowest stratum, we find a certain type of bowl with red painted decoration. In the next stratum above (the middle level), we find a different type of bowl with rounded walls and a flat base. Above that, in the uppermost stratum, we find another type of bowl covered with a black glaze. We can now construct the following relative typology (that is, a relative sequence of types): the bowl with the red painted decoration is the earliest type; the bowl with the rounded walls and flat base is the middle type (in date); and the bowl with the black glaze is the latest type. In other words, we can construct a relative sequence of types in which one type is the earliest (relatively speaking), another is in the middle, and another is the latest. We determine the absolute date of these pottery types based on the dated objects found in association with them. For example, if we find coins minted by Augustus together with (in the same stratum as) the bowl with the red painted decoration, we can assume that this type of bowl dates to the 1st century. And if in the future we find that same type at the next site down the road, we will know its date.

Dating pottery in this way is a complex process that is done by specialists. This is because not only do pottery types change over time but they vary among geographical regions. For example, when I was working on my dissertation I found that the types characteristic of Jerusalem and Judea in the 4th to 7th centuries c.e. are completely different from those found in Galilee. In addition, certain types are better chronological indicators (that is, certain types can be more closely dated) than others. The best types for dating purposes are fine wares and oil lamps, since they tend to change in form and decoration fairly quickly. Fine wares are the dishes that were used for dining, that is, they are table wares: cups, plates, bowls. Fine wares and oil lamps are usually decorated, whereas utilitarian types such as storage jars and cooking pots tend to be plain and are more difficult to date precisely. We refer to undecorated utilitarian types as coarse wares. Because of their utilitarian nature, storage jars and cooking pots display little change in shape over long periods. For these reasons, pottery typologies must be constructed for different sites in different geographical regions and for every period and every vessel type. This has to be done on the basis of carefully excavated, multi-period sites which provide sequences of levels and associated pottery types.

Sometimes people wonder how ceramics specialists can tell different types apart. After all, couldn't the same types have been imitated in later periods (like architectural styles)? In fact, this is not true of pottery. The combination of shapes, clays, firing processes, and decorative techniques yielded a unique product. This means that even if a shape was precisely duplicated in a later period (and this rarely happened), the combination of different clays, firing processes, and decorative techniques yielded a visibly different product. For example, even a nonspecialist can tell the difference between modern imitations of Greek black-figured vases (such as those offered for sale to tourists in the shops in Athens's Plaka) and the originals displayed in museums.

Why do archaeologists go to so much trouble to date pottery? Why not rely on other methods of dating? The reason is simple: pottery is ubiquitous at archaeological sites. In antiquity everyone owned it. The rich people might have owned fine china while the poor people only had the cheap stuff from the local Kmart. But everyone owned it. And once that pot was fired in the kiln, it could break but you would have to work real hard to grind it up into dust. This means that an archaeologist might excavate a structure in which no organic materials were found (for radiocarbon dating), no coins were found, and there were no inscriptions or ancient historical sources to provide information. But if we find nothing else, we know we will find potsherds — and lots of them — at archaeological sites in Palestine. If we can date the pottery, we can date the levels we are excavating.

As an aside, I note that it is possible to date pottery using scientific techniques such as luminescence dating, but these are expensive and have been employed little if at all for the pottery of Roman Palestine. Other techniques such as petrography and neutron activation analysis are more commonly used in Israel to determine the source of the clay used to manufacture the pots.

## Why Is Qumran Controversial?

In an interview for the *Biblical Archaeology Review*, Hershel Shanks, the editor, asked me whether I think we would interpret Qumran as a sectarian settlement had the Dead Sea Scrolls not been found. I have two answers to that question: (1) No, we would probably not interpret Qumran as a sectarian settlement without the scrolls, although I doubt we would interpret it as a villa or fortress either. I think it would be an anomalous site because it has too many features that are unparalleled at other sites, including the animal bone deposits, the multiplicity of large ritual baths (miqva'ot), and the adjacent cemetery. (2) More importantly, why would we want to disregard the evidence of the scrolls (as advocates of the alternative interpretations have attempted to do)? Qumran provides a unique opportunity to use archaeological evidence combined with the information from ancient historical sources and scrolls to reconstruct and understand the life of a community. Why would we disregard the scrolls or use only part of the evidence instead of all of it — especially when (as we shall see) the scrolls and our ancient sources provide evidence that complements the archaeology? And, as we shall see, archaeology establishes the connection between the scrolls in the caves and the settlement at Qumran.

Masada provides a useful analogy. When Yigael Yadin excavated Masada in the 1960s, he might have identified the room with the benches in the casemate wall on the northwest side of the mountain as a synagogue on the basis of the archaeology alone. However, the mute stones would never have revealed the events that took place there, including Eleazar ben-Yair's speech followed by the mass suicide of the Jewish rebels. Whether or not that story is true, we know about it not from archaeology but from Josephus.

An example from Qumran is the area in the southeast corner of the site, which based on the presence of kilns and other remains can be identified as a potters' workshop. But the knowledge that this community manufactured its own pottery because of their concern with purity issues is based on information provided by the scrolls and ancient historical sources. In other words, archaeologists can often determine the date and function of the buildings and installations we dig up based on the artifacts and on comparisons with other sites. From certain types of archaeological remains such as burial customs and cultic installations we can make inferences about ancient people's belief systems. But there are some kinds of information that archaeology alone cannot provide.

Archaeology is not an exact science because it involves human behavior, both past and present. Present behavior includes the variable of interpretation. Excavation itself is an act of interpretation, since archaeologists must decide which site to excavate, which part of the site to excavate, and so on. Even when an entire site is excavated (and this occurs rarely, although de Vaux uncovered nearly all of the settlement at Qumran), the remains archaeologists dig up represent only a small part of what originally existed. Rarely are organic materials preserved, such as wooden furniture, carpets and rugs, ceilings and roofs made of wood or reeds, clothing, other objects made of organic materials (such as wooden dishes and utensils, mirror cases, jewelry boxes, combs, spindles, wood-frame looms, and woven baskets), and, of course, the humans and animals that inhabited the sites. Usually, the last or latest levels of occupation (those at the top) are better preserved than earlier levels below. This means that archaeologists must try to reconstruct a picture of the past based on very incomplete information. I like to compare it to putting together a puzzle when some of the pieces are missing and we don't know what the original picture looked like. This is what makes it possible for scholars to interpret the same evidence differently, as in the case of Qumran, which has been identified as a sectarian settlement, fortress, villa, manor house, or commercial entrepot based on the same evidence!

If this is the case, how is it possible to judge which interpretations are valid or reasonable? After all, only one interpretation can be correct. It is difficult for scholars who are not archaeologists (such as scroll specialists) and virtually impossible for others to judge the validity of different interpretations because this requires a certain level of expertise. For example, nonspecialists would have a difficult time evaluating the pottery evidence that I have cited in my discussions of Qumran, just as I do not have the expertise to independently evaluate many of the arguments concerning the scrolls. As a general rule, the interpretation that solves the most problems or accounts for the greatest percentage of the evidence is probably the correct one. Common sense is important in archaeological interpretation (remember the factor of human behavior?). As we shall see, all of the available evidence supports de Vaux's interpretation of Qumran as a sectarian settlement. Although the other interpretations could account for some of the evidence (for example, certain features of the settlement's design resemble contemporary villas), they leave much of it unsolved (for example, if Qumran was a villa, what is the connection between the scrolls and the inhabitants of the site?), or even create new problems (for example, if Qumran is a villa, why does it lack the rich interior decoration and fine pottery characteristic of contemporary villas in Judea?).

The alternative interpretations of Qumran have received much more publicity than the traditional interpretation. In my opinion, there are at least two reasons for this. First, scandal and controversy sell. For this reason, books and articles suggesting that Qumran was not a sectarian settlement and those which describe Vatican or scholarly conspiracies or claim that Jesus lived at Qumran have been highly publicized. This reflects the media-oriented and sensationalistic nature of our society. Second, we tend to side with the underdogs or minority cause. This feeds into a common perception of academics as being isolated and out of touch in their ivory towers.

In addition, we have developed a reluctance to be critical even when the criticism is constructive. Ironically, this is one outcome of the diversity of our society, in which we encourage and celebrate different backgrounds and views. For these reasons, in the minds of many people, different views and opinions should be given equal weight and any interpretation that challenges accepted scholarly consensus must be valid. Challenges to accepted scholarly consensus can be good because they force us to reexamine our assumptions (and sometimes cause us to change our interpretations). However, just because an interpretation happens to represent scholarly consensus does not mean it is wrong. The notion that all interpretations are equally valid is inherently flawed because Qumran could not have been a sectarian settlement *and* a villa *and* a manor house *and* a fort *and* a commercial entrepot! There can only be one correct interpretation, which is supported by a preponderance of evidence.

I find myself — an American Jewish woman — in the curious position of defending the interpretation proposed by de Vaux, who was a French Dominican priest! But this book is not about my personal beliefs and background or about de Vaux's. It is about the archaeological evidence. Obviously, de Vaux's interpretation of Qumran was influenced by his background (who isn't?). De Vaux's bias is evident in his use of monastic terms to describe some of the rooms and installations at Qumran (such as "refectory" and "scriptorium"). But the objections that have been raised by de Vaux's critics have obscured the fact that his interpretation of the site is basically correct.

In this book, I present more than just a description of the archaeology of Qumran based on de Vaux's interpretation. I present my understanding of Qumran, which combines all of the available (published) archaeological evidence and the information provided by the scrolls and our ancient historical sources. Although I believe that de Vaux was correct in identifying Qumran as a sectarian settlement, I disagree with him on some matters such as the dating of the occupation phases of the site. The following chapters are devoted to various aspects of the archaeology of Qumran. We begin with the story of the discovery of the scrolls and the history of exploration of Qumran.

## Bibliographical Notes

The quotation at the beginning of this chapter is from Sheena Crawford, "Reevaluating material culture: crawling towards a reconstruction of Minoan society," in *Minoan Society: Proceedings of the Cambridge Colloquium 1981*, ed. O. Krzyszkowska and L. Nixon (Bristol: Bristol Classical, 1983), 48-49.

Throughout this volume, unless otherwise indicated, all of the passages quoted from Josephus, Philo, and Pliny are from Geza Vermès and Martin D. Goodman, eds., *The Essenes According to the Classical Sources* (Sheffield: JSOT, 1989). Unfortunately, this useful reference is out-of-print. All passages quoted from the Dead Sea Scrolls are from Geza Vermès, *The Complete Dead Sea Scrolls in English* (New York: Penguin, 1997). This useful reference contains information on the Qumran community as well as English translations of the scrolls. All passages quoted from the Mishnah are from Jacob Neusner, *The Mishnah: A New Translation* (New Haven: Yale University Press, 1988).

I have listed all of the major references consulted in the bibliographical notes at the end of each chapter. Additional references to some of the subjects discussed in this volume can be found in the articles that I have published on Qumran, which are listed in the bibliographical notes to the relevant chapters.

The following are Roland de Vaux's preliminary reports on his excavations at Qumran and Ein Feshkha: "Fouille au Khirbet Qumrân: Rapport préliminaire," *Revue Biblique* 60 (1953): 83-106; "Fouilles au Khirbet Qumrân: Rapport préliminaire sur la deuxième campagne," *Revue Biblique* 61 (1954): 206-36; "Fouilles de Khirbet Qumrân: Rapport préliminaire sur les 3e, 4e, et 5e campagnes," *Revue Biblique* 63 (1956): 533-77; "Fouilles de Feshkha: Rapport préliminaire," *Revue Biblique* 66 (1959): 225-55. For the English version of his overview of the archaeology of Qumran, see de Vaux, *Archaeology and the*

*Dead Sea Scrolls,* rev. ed. (Oxford: Oxford University Press, 1973). The volume containing de Vaux's field notes and photographs from the time of the excavations was published by Jean-Baptiste Humbert and Alain Chambon, *Fouilles de Khirbet Qumrân et de Aïn Feshkha* 1 (Fribourg: Éditions universitaires, 1994).

For the pottery from the scroll caves around Qumran, see Roland de Vaux, "La grotte des manuscrits hébreux," *Revue Biblique* 56 (1949): 586-609; "La poterie," in *Discoveries in the Judaean Desert* 1: *Qumran Cave 1,* ed. Dominique Barthélemy and J. T. Milik (Oxford: Clarendon, 1955), 8-13; "Archéologie," in *Discoveries in the Judaean Desert* 3: *Les "Petites Grottes" de Qumrân,* ed. M. Baillet, Milik, and de Vaux (Oxford: Clarendon, 1962), 3-63; "Le matériel archéologique. La poterie," in *Discoveries in the Judaean Desert* 6: *Qumrân Grotte 4/2,* ed. de Vaux and Milik (Oxford: Clarendon, 1977), 15-20.

For the excavations at Ein el-Ghuweir, see Pesach Bar-Adon, "Another Settlement of the Judean Desert Sect at 'En el-Ghuweir on the Shores of the Dead Sea," *Bulletin of the American Schools of Oriental Research* 227 (1977): 1-25.

Radiocarbon dating was developed in 1946 by Willard F. Libby at the University of Chicago. For information on this and other methods of scientific dating and analysis, see *The Oxford Companion to Archaeology,* ed. Brian M. Fagan (New York: Oxford University Press, 1996). For radiocarbon dating of the Dead Sea Scrolls and the textiles from Cave 1 at Qumran see Grace M. Crowfoot, "The Linen Textiles," in Barthélemy and Milik, *Discoveries in the Judaean Desert* 1: *Qumran Cave I,* 27; G. Bonani, M. Broshi, I. Carmi, S. Ivy, J. Strugnell, and W. Wolfli, "Radiocarbon Dating of the Dead Sea Scrolls," *'Atiqot* 20 (1991): 26-32; A. J. Timothy Jull, Douglas J. Donahue, Magen Broshi, and Emanuel Tov, "Radiocarbon Dating of Scrolls and Linen Fragments from the Judean Desert," *Radiocarbon* 37 (1995): 11-19; Israel Carmi, "Radiocarbon Dating of the Dead Sea Scrolls," in *The Dead Sea Scrolls Fifty Years after Their Discovery. Proceedings of the Jerusalem Congress, July 20-25, 1997,* ed. Lawrence H. Schiffman, Emanuel Tov, and James C. VanderKam (Jerusalem: Israel Exploration Society, 2000), 881-88. For radiocarbon dating of charcoal from Qumran see Frederick E. Zeuner, "Notes on Qumrân," *Palestine Exploration Quarterly* 92 (1960): 27-36 (see 27-28); Joan Taylor and Thomas Higham, "Problems of Qumran's Chronology and the Radiocarbon Dating of Palm Log Samples in Locus 86," *Qumran Chronicle* 8/1-2 (1998): 83-95. As an aside, I note that an examination of the photographs from de Vaux's excavations reveals that the wood that was analyzed and discussed by Taylor and Higham lay on the Period II floor of L86, not on the Period Ib level as they suggested. For more on radiocarbon dating, and the unacceptable suggestion that all of the scrolls were deposited in the Qumran caves before 63

B.C.E., see Gregory L. Doudna, "Redating the Dead Sea Scrolls Found at Qumran: The Case for 63 BCE," *Qumran Chronicle* 8/4 (1999).

For the interpretation of Qumran as a *villa rustica,* see Pauline Donceel-Voûte, "Les ruines de Qumran reinterprétées," *Archeologia* 298 (1994): 24-35. Robert Donceel and Pauline Donceel-Voûte published a report on their work on the Qumran material: "The Archaeology of Khirbet Qumran," in *Methods of Investigation of the Dead Sea Scrolls and the Khirbet Qumran Site, Present Realities and Future Prospects,* ed. Michael O. Wise, Norman Golb, John J. Collins, and Dennis G. Pardee (New York: New York Academy of Sciences, 1994), 1-38. According to a variant of this interpretation, Qumran was a *villa rustica* before it was taken over by an Essene community; see Jean-Baptiste Humbert, "L'espace sacré a Qumrân," *Revue Biblique* 101 (1994): 161-214; "Qumrân, esséniens et architecture," in *Antikes Judentum und Frühes Christentum,* ed. Bernd Kollmann, Wolfgang Reinbold, and Annette Steudel (Berlin: Walter de Gruyter, 1999), 183-96. According to another view, Qumran was a manor house; see Yizhar Hirschfeld, "Early Roman Manor Houses in Judea and the Site of Khirbet Qumran," *Journal of Near Eastern Studies* 57 (1998): 161-89; "The Architectural Context of Qumran," in Schiffman, Tov, and VanderKam, *The Dead Sea Scrolls Fifty Years after Their Discovery,* 673-83. For Norman Golb's interpretation of Qumran as a fort and his views on the Dead Sea Scrolls see *Who Wrote the Dead Sea Scrolls?* (New York: Scribner, 1995); "Khirbet Qumran and the Manuscript Finds of the Judaean Wilderness," in Wise, Golb, Collins, and Pardee, *Methods of Investigation,* 51-72; "Who Hid the Dead Sea Scrolls?" *Biblical Archaeologist* 48 (1985): 68-82. For the suggestion that Qumran was a commercial entrepot, see Alan D. Crown and Lena Cansdale, "Qumran, Was It an Essene Settlement?" *Biblical Archaeology Review* 20/5 (1994): 24-35, 73-78; also see Cansdale, *Qumran and the Essenes* (Tübingen: J. C. B. Mohr, 1997), which contains a collection of sources on the Essenes and references to visits by early explorers to Qumran. For a response to the alternative theories, see Magen Broshi, "Was Qumran, Indeed, a Monastery? The Consensus and Its Challengers, an Archaeologist's View," in *Caves of Enlightenment: Proceedings of the American Schools of Oriental Research Dead Sea Scrolls Jubilee Symposium (1947-1997),* ed. James H. Charlesworth (North Richland Hills, TX: Bibal, 1998), 19-37. Also see Ernest-Marie Laperrousaz, "L'établissement de Qoumrân près de la Mer Morte: Forteresse ou Couvent?" *Eretz-Israel* 20 (1989): 118*-23*. For more on the villa interpretation, see Chapter 5.

CHAPTER 2

# The Discovery of the Dead Sea Scrolls
# and the Exploration of Qumran

*. . . they shall separate from the habitation of ungodly men and shall go into the wilderness to prepare the way of Him; as it is written, Prepare in the wilderness the way of . . . make straight in the desert a path for our God.*

Isaiah 40:3; 1QS 8.1-14

## Qumran's Setting

Qumran's setting overlooking the Dead Sea is dramatic, especially when the late afternoon sun turns the sea a dark blue color and the mountains on the other side of the sea (in modern Jordan) a deep orange (see Fig. 4). The Dead Sea is the lowest point on earth (about 400 m. or 1300 ft. below sea level) because it lies at the base of the Great Rift Valley (Afro-Syrian Rift) (see map in Fig. 1). If you have ever driven along the road that runs from Jerusalem to Jericho and Qumran, you might have felt your ears popping like in an airplane. The pressure is created by the steep descent from Jerusalem's mountainous location at about 800 m. (2400 ft.) above sea level, for a total drop of about 1200 m. (3700 ft.) down to the Dead Sea in just 30 minutes. The Great Rift Valley, which stretches from eastern Africa to southern Turkey, has been created by the parting of the Mediterranean and Arabian continental plates. Because this is an ongoing process, earthquakes occur frequently along the valley.

19

The Dead Sea is the saltiest body of water on earth, with a 30 percent salt content that is about 10 times higher than that of an ocean. The high concentration of salts is due to the fact that the sea lacks an outlet. In other words, the minerals washed into the sea by flash floods and the Jordan River remain there. This process is intensified by the high rate of evaporation caused by the intense heat (the mean monthly temperatures range from 55 to 90.5 degrees Fahrenheit), which creates a haze that hovers over the sea during the hot summer months. In addition, little water flows into the sea, both because of the low rainfall (only about 1 to 2 in. per year) and because most of the water from the Jordan River, which is the Dead Sea's main source, is now exploited by Israel and Jordan. Because of the high concentration of salt and other minerals, nothing aside from some tiny organisms can survive in the sea. The Romans called the Dead Sea the Asphalt Lake, referring to the lumps of bitumen which originate beneath the sea's floor and float to its surface, washing up along the shores.

Approximately 100 million years ago, Palestine and neighboring regions were covered by an ancestor of the Mediterranean Sea called the Tethys Sea. After this sea receded, the sediments that had accumulated on its floor hardened into layers of limestone, dolomite, and chalk. About 3 million years ago, the Great Rift Valley began to form, cutting through these layers of rock and creating the escarpment along the western side of the Dead Sea. The level of the Dead Sea has fluctuated over time; approximately 25 thousand years ago it was only about 180 m. below sea level. During this period, alluvial sediments accumulated at the bottom of the sea. When the level of the sea dropped these alluvial sediments were exposed along its sides. These sediments, which are called Lisan marls, consist of chalky white and clayey grey deposits that are so soft they can be scratched with a fingernail. Although they erode easily, they can still be seen around the Dead Sea including in the badlands at the foot of Masada. Many ancient sites in the Jordan Valley and along the Dead Sea, including Qumran, sit on terraces of Lisan marl. At Qumran, the soft white marl contrasts with the hard brown limestone and dolomite cliffs or escarpment behind the settlement. Some of the scroll caves (Caves 1Q, 2Q, 3Q, 6Q, 11Q) are natural caves in the limestone cliffs behind the site, whereas others (Caves 4Qa-b, 5Q, 7Q, 8Q, 9Q, 10Q) are manmade caves cut into the marl terrace. The southern end of the marl terrace ends with a steep, 200-ft. drop into Wadi Qumran, a river bed which flows into the Dead Sea.

The escarpment along the western shore of the Dead Sea and the Judean mountains behind (which rise to a height of 800-1000 m. or about 2400-3000 ft. above sea level) block rainfall and create a desert "in the shadow of rain." The cliffs are scored by deep river beds that flow into the Dead Sea. In Arabic a river bed is called a *wadi;* the Hebrew equivalent is *naḥal.* These river beds (including Wadi Qumran) are usually dry, with water flowing in them on rare occasions in the winter when heavy rains fall in a short period and the ground becomes saturated, resulting in flash floods.

There are no perennial sources of fresh water in the immediate vicinity of Qumran. The closest fresh-water springs are at the oasis of Jericho, about 9 mi. north of Qumran. These are fed by aquifers (underground water tables) in the limestone and dolomite layers in the hills to the west. When the Rift Valley formed, creating the escarpment, these water-bearing layers were exposed. Springs fed by water from similar aquifers are located at the Ein Gedi oasis. The word *ein* (sometimes spelled *ain* or *en*) means "spring (of water)" in Hebrew and Arabic. Water that rises up through cracks in the layers of rock along the sides and under the floor of the Dead Sea creates other springs. Because of their origin and proximity to the Dead Sea, these springs are brackish and some are hot and laden with sulfur (such as the hot sulfur springs on the shore at Ein Gedi and at Hammath Tiberias by the Sea of Galilee). Brackish springs with about 1 percent salt content are located along the shore of the Dead Sea at Ein Feshkha (Hebrew Einot Tzukim), Ein el-Ghuweir (Hebrew Ein Qaneh), and Ein et-Tureibeh (about 2 mi., 9 mi., and 12 mi. south of Qumran, respectively). Although fish live in these springs and the water can be used to raise plants that are tolerant of salt (such as date palms and spinach beets), it is only marginally potable. Edward Robinson and Eli Smith, two explorers who visited the region in 1838, described the springs at Ein Feshkha as follows: "The fountain boils up here near the shore, a very copious stream, or rather streams, of limpid water, beautiful to the eye, but brackish and having a slight taste of sulphuretted hydrogen." The bad-tasting water is described by another 19th-century explorer named De Saulcy (see below): ". . . the water of the spring is brackish, although, in the absence of better, it may be drank [*sic!*]. We are obliged to use it for our broth and coffee, unquestionably the worst I ever tasted; but as we have no choice, we must even make wry faces and content ourselves with what we cannot remedy." This explains why there were no major, multi-period settlements in antiquity (or even today) at Ein Feshkha, Ein el-Ghuweir, and Ein et-Tureibeh, in contrast to the sweet-water oases at Jericho and Ein Gedi.

In 1993, the Israeli archaeologist Yitzhak Magen discovered carbonized dates that are apparently associated with a date press at the southern edge of the settlement at Qumran. This suggests that the inhabitants of Qumran cultivated date palms by the springs at Ein Feshkha. It is likely they cultivated other crops as well, and they undoubtedly raised herds of sheep, goats, and cattle (see Chapter 10 for a possible tannery or datepress at Ein Feshkha and

Chapter 6 for animal bone deposits at Qumran). Some of the natural resources of the Dead Sea such as bitumen and salt could have been mined and traded. The inhabitants probably cultivated grain in the Buqeia, a valley close to the escarpment above Qumran which is dominated on the west by the Hasmonean-Herodian fortress of Hyrcania.

The steep and rugged cliffs along the shores of the Dead Sea create a natural barrier to traffic. The major routes down to the Dead Sea from the west have always followed the breaks in the escarpment at the northern and southern ends of the Dead Sea, following two major river beds: Nahal Prat (Wadi Qelt) to the north and Nahal Zohar to the south. Additional but secondary west-east roads were located along the western shore of the Dead Sea. These are called *ma'alot* (*ma'aleh* [singular] means "ascent" in Hebrew) because they consist of paths zigzagging up the cliffs. One example is the ancient road from Teqoa to Ein Gedi. Other paths ascend the cliffs behind Ein Feshkha (to Ras Feshkha) and Qumran (to the Buqeia). The existence of docks at a few points along the shores of the Dead Sea (for example, at Khirbet Mazin to the south of Qumran) and the depiction of boats on the Dead Sea in the Madaba Map (a mosaic map of the Holy Land dating to ca. 600 c.e.) indicate that boats were used on the Dead Sea in antiquity. An ancient graffito of a boat is etched into the plastered wall of the guardroom at the entrance to Herod's northern palace at Masada.

## Early Explorers

Qumran attracted little attention before the discovery of the Dead Sea Scrolls. In the winter of 1850-51, a Flemish explorer named Louis-Félicien Caignart de Saulcy led a small expedition to the Dead Sea. He described a series of ruins "called by the Arabs Kharbet-il-Yahoud, Kharbet-Feschkah, and Kharbet-Goumran (or Oumran), which form a continuous mass, extending without interruption over a space of more than six thousand yards." De Saulcy identified these sites collectively as the ruins of biblical Gomorrah. Kharbet il-Yahoud appears to denote the site at Ein Feshkha, while both Kharbet Feshkhah and Kharbet Goumran seem to refer to Qumran. The latter, according to de Saulcy, was "unquestionably the skeleton of a large city." Although much of de Saulcy's description is confused (the heaps of stones he identified as ruins are probably the graves in the cemetery), his reference to "the foundations of a tolerably extensive square enclosure" corresponds well with Qumran.

Shortly after de Saulcy's visit, the British explorer Henry B. Tristram failed to locate these ruins: "Nor were we more successful in discovering the remains of Gomorrah. We found at intervals many indistinct rows of unhewn stones, which, if at all the remains of human constructions, carry us back to a ruder period than the flints of our gravel beds. . . ." Tristram did note "traces of a square enclosure or ruin" at Ein Feshkha. In 1874, the French archaeologist Charles Clermont-Ganneau excavated one of the graves in the cemetery at Qumran. He described the site (which he called "Khurbet Kumran, pronounced *Gumran*") as insignificant ruins, "consisting of some dilapidated walls of low stones and a small *birkeh* [pool] with steps leading to it. . . . If there ever existed there a town properly so called, it must have been a very small one."

Clermont-Ganneau rejected de Saulcy's identification of the site with the biblical Gomorrah. He was more interested in the cemetery, in which he counted approximately 1000 graves covered by heaps of stones, with those on the main plateau arranged in regular rows divided by an east-west path. Clermont-Ganneau excavated one of the graves, which he described as follows: "After going down about a metre, our workmen came upon a layer of bricks of unbaked clay, measuring 15¾ inches by 8 inches by 4¾ inches, and resting on a sort of ledge formed in the soil itself. On removing these bricks we found in the graves proper that they covered the half decayed bones of the body that had been buried there. We managed to secure a fragment of a jaw with some teeth still adhering to it, which will perhaps enable us to arrive at some conclusions of an anthropological nature." Clermont-Ganneau noted that the head of the skeleton was towards the south, and the feet towards the north. His description of this grave is consistent with those later excavated by de Vaux.

Clermont-Ganneau was one of the best archaeologists working in Palestine in the late 19th century, and many of his observations are still valid today. He rejected the possibility that the burials at Qumran are Christian because they lack "some characteristic mark or emblem of a religious nature." On the other hand, because they resemble Muslim graves but are not oriented towards Mecca, Clermont-Ganneau suggested that they "belonged to some pagan Arab tribe of the period which the Musselmen call *Jahiliyeh*, that is to say before the time of Mohamet." Although he did not consider the possibility that the burials are Jewish, Clermont-Ganneau's reasoning was remarkably astute considering that he conducted his investigations at Qumran almost 75 years before the discovery of the Dead Sea Scrolls.

In November 1873, shortly before Clermont-Ganneau's expedition, Qumran was visited by Lieutenant Claude R. Conder and Charles Tyrwhitt-Drake, as part of their survey for the Palestine Exploration Fund. After

Tyrwhitt-Drake died of malaria during the course of the survey, he was re-placed by Horatio H. Kitchener. Condor and Tyrwhitt-Drake described the site (Khurbet Kumran) as follows: "The remains are very rough. On the west side is a wall, but on the south and east the slopes are very steep. At the north end of the wall are ruined buildings, now presenting nothing beyond heaps of rough stones. Outside the wall on the west is a small birkeh, rudely lined with stones, unhewn, the joints packed with smaller stones and roughly plastered. A flight of steps leads down the side." They noted the "immense number of graves occupying the plateau and the eastern slope . . . arranged close together in regular rows," which they estimated as numbering 700 or more.

Like Clermont-Ganneau, Conder and Tyrwhitt-Drake observed that the orientation of the burials indicates they could not be Muslim, and they too excavated one: "One was excavated and found to be 3 feet 5 inches deep, about 6 feet long by 2 feet 3 inches. The top of the shaft was covered with loose stones carefully arranged. At the bottom of the shaft is a narrow trough for the body, covered with sundried bricks 15 by 11 by 9 inches in dimensions. The bricks were supported by a ledge projecting on the sides of the grave. Re-mains of a skeleton with the head to the south were found, the bones much decayed."

In February 1914, a German explorer named Gustaf Dalman visited Qumran ("chirbet kumran"). Dalman was a theologian who served as the first director of the German Protestant Institute of Archaeology in Jerusalem. Like the explorers before him, Dalman described the heaps of stones (includ-ing part of a column base), and he noted the water channel (aqueduct) run-ning from Wadi Qumran to the site. Because of its location on a plateau over-looking the Dead Sea, Dalman concluded that Qumran must have been a fortress *(burg)*. Dalman's identification of Qumran as a fortress was repeated in print by the Israeli archaeologist Michael Avi-Yonah in 1936. However, after the discovery of the Dead Sea Scrolls and de Vaux's excavations, Avi-Yonah accepted the identification of Qumran as a sectarian settlement.

## The Identification of Qumran

Khirbet Qumran (or Kumran or Gumran) is the modern Arabic name of the site. It is first reported in de Saulcy's accounts. The site takes its name from the nearby riverbed (Wadi Qumran), although the name Qumran is of un-known origin. Perhaps it derives from the Arabic word *qmr*, which means "being white, moonlit." Similarly, Jericho's name comes from a Semitic word for the moon.

Contrary to de Saulcy and others, there is no evidence for a connection between Qumran and biblical Gomorrah. Instead, Qumran's ancient name was Secacah. Secacah is one of the six desert towns listed in Joshua 15:61-62: "Beth ha-'Arabah, Middin, and Secacah, and Nivshan, and Ir ha-Melah, and Ein Gedi: six towns, with their villages." The German scholar Martin Noth and others identified Qumran as Ir ha-Melah (the City of Salt). However, evidence from the Copper Scroll, which was found in Cave 3, indicates that Secacah is Qumran. The Copper Scroll (3Q15) is perhaps the most enigmatic scroll found in the caves near Qumran. It contains a list of hidden treasures (with fantastic amounts of gold and silver), inscribed on copper. There is no agreement about the date of this scroll (pre-70 C.E. or later?), the source of the treasure (perhaps the Jerusalem temple?), or even whether the treasure is real or imaginary.

Interestingly, Secacah is mentioned four times in the Copper Scroll (at the end of column 4 and in column 5), as a place where at least five treasures were hidden. The features described in connection with Secacah, which include a water conduit, a dam (?), and a tomb, are among those found at Qumran. In addition, Secacah is mentioned in the Copper Scroll after a reference to the Valley of Achor, which is the Buqeia. The book of Joshua (7:26) describes the Valley of Achor as the burial place of Achan, whose disobedience hampered the conquest of Ai. The references to Secacah in the book of Joshua and in the Copper Scroll indicate that it was inhabited during the Iron Age (Israelite period) and during the 1st century C.E. As we shall see, Qumran was occupied during both of these periods. Based on this evidence, Qumran can be identified as Secacah.

## The Discovery of the Dead Sea Scrolls

In 1896-97, two incomplete medieval (10th- and 12th-century) copies of the Damascus Document were discovered among documents that had been placed in a repository for old books and manuscripts (Hebrew *genizah*) in the Ben Ezra synagogue in Old Cairo, Egypt. Solomon Schechter published these manuscripts in 1910 in a volume entitled *Fragments of a Zadokite Work*. Fifty years later, fragments of the same work were discovered in the caves near Qumran (the copies from Cairo are designated CD, for "Cairo Damascus").

Accounts of the discovery and fate of the first scrolls from Qumran vary widely. Here I present one version of the story. The first scrolls were discovered by bedouins in the winter of 1946-47 in Cave 1, a little over half a mile to the north of Qumran. When they first entered the cave, the bedouins found a row of about 10 cylindrical jars. Eight of them were empty and a ninth was filled with dirt. However, one jar contained three scrolls, two of which were wrapped in linen. The bedouins later removed another four scrolls from this cave. Because they had been stored in jars, the scrolls from Cave 1 were well preserved and were complete or nearly complete. These seven scrolls are: one complete copy and another partial copy of the book of Isaiah (see Fig. 3); the Community Rule (= Manual of Discipline); the Pesher (Commentary on) Habakkuk (a book of one of the 12 minor prophets); the War Scroll; the Thanksgiving Hymns or Hymn Scroll (Hebrew *Hodayot*); and the Genesis Apocryphon. Since the scrolls were written on parchment (processed animal hide), the bedouins (who of course did not know what they were) sold them to a cobbler in Bethlehem named Kando (Khalil Iskander Shahin) who also happened to deal in antiquities. Because the scrolls appeared to be written in Syriac, and because Kando was a member of the Syrian Orthodox Church in Jerusalem, he was put in touch with Athanasius Yeshua Samuel, a metropolitan of that church. Kando sold one lot of four scrolls to Samuel for 24 British pounds (which at that time was equivalent to about $100). These four scrolls were the larger Isaiah scroll, the Community Rule, the Pesher Habakkuk, and the Genesis Apocryphon. Kando sold the second lot of three scrolls to Eleazar Lippa Sukenik, a biblical scholar and archaeologist at the Hebrew University of Jerusalem. Sukenik had heard about the scrolls and was anxious to acquire them. Because the first scrolls had turned up for sale on the antiquities market, no one at that time knew their exact find spot or date (that is, they had no archaeological context), and some scholars thought they might be modern forgeries! Sukenik was apparently the first to recognize that they were authentic ancient scrolls dating to about the time of Jesus, and he was the first to suggest a connection with the Essenes mentioned in ancient sources. He traveled to Bethlehem to purchase the three scrolls from Kando on November 29, 1947, the same day the United Nations passed the resolution allowing the creation of the State of Israel.

In the meantime, scholars based at the American School of Oriental Research (now the W. F. Albright Institute of Archaeological Research) in Jerusalem had seen the four scrolls belonging to Samuel and obtained his permission to publish them. John Trever, a fellow at the School who was a photographer as well as a scholar, photographed the four scrolls. Other scholars (including Millar Burrows, then director of the School, and William Brownlee) studied the photographs. By 1956 all seven scrolls from Cave 1 had been published (due to its state of decay, the Genesis Apocryphon could only be partially opened and read; it has recently been fully published). In 1948, Samuel took his four scrolls to Lebanon for safekeeping and then to the U.S., where he attempted to sell them. On June 1, 1954, he placed an ad in the *Wall Street Journal* offering to sell "The Four Dead Sea Scrolls." The ad was brought to the attention of Yigael Yadin, Sukenik's son, who happened to be in the United States at the time. Through middlemen, Yadin purchased the scrolls on behalf of the State of Israel for $250 thousand (and Samuel made a handsome return on his initial investment!). In this way, all seven scrolls from Cave 1 at Qumran came into the possession of the State of Israel. A special building called the Shrine of the Book was constructed on the grounds of the Israel Museum in Jerusalem to house and display these scrolls.

After the initial discovery of the scrolls, the bedouins, Syrians, and Kando (among others) visited Cave 1 and removed more manuscripts. However, the war that erupted in Palestine at the end of the British Mandate made it impossible for scholars to travel to the area. Finally, in January 1949, Cave 1 was located by Captain Akkash el-Zebn of the Arab Legion and a Belgian observer on the United Nations staff, Captain Phillipe Lippens. One month later (Febrary-March 1949), Roland de Vaux of the École Biblique in Jerusalem and G. Lankester Harding, who was the chief inspector of antiquities in Jordan, conducted excavations in the cave. Aside from pottery, pieces of linen cloth, and other artifacts, they found fragments of additional manuscripts, some of which belonged to the manuscripts that the bedouins had removed from the cave (thereby confirming that this was the cave from which those scrolls had been removed). De Vaux and Harding also surveyed Qumran and excavated two graves in the cemetery. However, they found no evidence for a connection with the scrolls from the caves and concluded that the site was a Roman fort dating to the 3rd or 4th century c.e.

Because of growing interest in the scrolls, Harding and de Vaux returned to Qumran two years later (November-December 1951) to conduct a first season of excavations. They excavated three rooms in the southwest corner (L1, L2, L4) and two in the northeast corner (L5, L6) of the main building and made a small sounding at the entrance to the site (L7) (see Fig. 12). Despite the limited scale of their excavations, de Vaux and Harding made a number of important observations. First, they noted that the poor quality of construction, with walls built of unhewn field stones or rubble and mud plaster, "in no way resembles that of a Roman fort which we first took it to be." Second, they noticed two or three phases during the existence of the settlement, indicated by the blocking of doorways and the raising of floor levels. Third, they found clear evidence that a great fire had destroyed the settlement, with pottery vessels lying on the floors. Fourth, de Vaux and Harding noticed that "sunk into the floor of one of the rooms was a jar identical with most of those found in the Scrolls cave [Cave 1]. . . . We thus, even in the small area so far excavated, have a direct connection with the Scrolls. . . ." In other words, they noticed that the pottery establishes a direct connection between the site of Qumran and the scrolls in the nearby caves. Lying on the floor next to the jar was a coin dated ca. 10 C.E. De Vaux and Harding noted that the same types of cooking pots and oil lamps found in Cave 1 were represented in the settlement. On this basis they were able to date these pottery types to the 1st century B.C.E. and 1st century C.E. instead of to the 2nd to 3rd centuries C.E. as they previously thought.

Harding described how radiocarbon dating of some of the linen from Cave 1 confirmed this chronology: "This is interesting confirmation of the accuracy of the date established by submitting some of the linen from the cave to what is known as the Carbon 14 test. In this test, the radio-active isotopes of carbon 14 contained in the material are measured and a date estimated on this basis." Notice that instead of using radiocarbon dating to confirm the date of the scrolls and the settlement at Qumran, the excavators confirmed the accuracy of this dating method, which was still a novelty when Harding published his article in 1952!

De Vaux and Harding's final observation was that Qumran was a "closed settlement," with little contact with the outside world. Harding concluded that "it would appear, then, that the people who lived at Khirbet Qumran deposited the scrolls in the cave [Cave 1], probably about A.D. 70. The situation fits in well with Pliny the Elder's account of the Essenes who had a settlement 'above Engeddi,' and the ruin itself, with its peculiar cemetery which is without parallel in other sites in Jordan, is clearly not an ordinary defensive or agricultural post." As we shall see, although later seasons of excavations and the discovery of more scrolls added information, the observations made by de Vaux and Harding in 1952 are still valid.

In the meantime, the bedouins continued and expanded their search for manuscripts (which they could sell for a profit) in the caves along the western shore of the Dead Sea. While de Vaux and Harding were excavating at Qumran in 1951, the bedouins found manuscripts dating to the time of the Second Jewish Revolt against the Romans (the Bar Kokhba Revolt; 132-135 C.E.) in caves in Wadi Murabba'at to the south of Qumran. After de Vaux and Harding rushed to Wadi Murabba'at to explore those caves, the bedouins returned to Qumran and discovered a second cave (Cave 2) containing scrolls. This prompted archaeologists from the American School of Oriental Research in Jerusalem to conduct a systematic survey of the caves and cavities in the rocky cliffs behind and around Qumran. During this expedition (March 10-29, 1952), the archaeologists discovered Cave 3, which yielded a number of manuscripts and the enigmatic Copper Scroll. However, the bedouins discovered the next and richest cave — Cave 4, which contained some 500 different scrolls! This was the first manmade cave in the marl terrace found to contain scrolls, and it is the one that visitors see from the site (see Fig. 2). It is curious that the archaeologists did not think of exploring this cave. Perhaps it did not occur to them to explore the caves in the marl terrace, or perhaps the entrance was blocked by collapse and was not easily visible.

Cave 4 actually consists of two separate and adjacent caves, 4a and 4b. Because the scrolls from the two caves were hopelessly mixed by the time the archaeologists learned of the discovery, they are referred to simply as coming from Cave 4. Access to Cave 4 is difficult because the marl terrace into which it is hewn has eroded. The scrolls in this cave had not been deposited in jars and had disintegrated into thousands of fragments. Whether the scrolls were left lying on the floor of the cave or were stored on wooden shelves is debated, as is whether this cave served as the community's library/archive or as a repository for scrolls on the eve of the destruction of the site. The recent scandals surrounding delays in publication of the Dead Sea Scrolls mostly concern the material from Cave 4. The delays were due to the fragmentary condition of these scrolls, which makes them difficult to read and study.

Eventually, 11 caves containing about 900 different (and mostly fragmentary) scrolls were discovered in the vicinity of Qumran. These caves are numbered 1-11. In addition, over 30 caves extending for a distance of 2 mi. to the north and south of the site contained the same pottery types as those found in the settlement at Qumran. Caves 5, 7-10 are located in the marl terrace. Caves 7-10 surround the terrace on which the settlement sits. Caves 6 and 11 are in the limestone cliffs behind Qumran. Cave 11, discovered by the bedouins in 1956, yielded a few scrolls that were nearly as complete as those from Cave 1. Altogether, the bedouins found five of the caves (1, 2, 4, 6, 11), including those with the richest and most important material, while the archaeologists discovered the other six caves (3, 5, 7-10). The finds of the 1951 season prompted de Vaux and Harding to undertake large-scale excavations at Qumran, which they conducted during four seasons from 1953-56. During the last season in 1956, de Vaux also conducted excavations at Ein Feshkha.

## Bibliographical Notes

An excellent overview of the archaeology of Qumran and the Dead Sea Scrolls (unfortunately out-of-print) is: Philip R. Davies, *Qumran* (Grand Rapids: Wm. B. Eerdmans, 1983).

For the geology of the Dead Sea region, see Larry G. Herr, "Dead Sea," in *Encyclopedia of the Dead Sea Scrolls,* ed. Lawrence H. Schiffman and James C. VanderKam (New York: Oxford University Press, 2000) 1:181-83. Magen Broshi has demonstrated that contrary to the claims of some scholars (especially advocates of the alternative theories), Qumran does not lie at a crossroads: "Was Qumran a Crossroads?" *Revue de Qumran* 19 (1999): 273-76. For the datepress at Qumran, see Broshi, "Qumran: Archaeology," in Schiffman and VanderKam, *Encyclopedia of the Dead Sea Scrolls,* 736. This installation was previously identified as a wine press; see Stephen Pfann, "The Wine Press (and *Miqveh*) at Kh. Qumran (loc. 75 and 69)," *Revue Biblique* 101 (1994): 212-14.

For an estimate that the graves in the Qumran cemetery number about 700 instead of 1100-1200, see Zdzisław J. Kapera and Jacek Konik, "How Many Tombs in Qumran?" *Qumran Chronicle* 9/1 (2000): 35-49.

For Edward Robinson and Eli Smith's visit to Ein Feshkha, see *Biblical Researches in Palestine, and the Adjacent Regions: Journal of Travels in the Year 1838,* 1 (Boston: Crocker and Brewster, 1856), 530-36. For Louis-Félicien Caignart de Saulcy's visit to Qumran, see *Narrative of a Journey Round the Dead Sea and in the Bible Lands, in 1850 and 1851,* 2 (London: Richard Bentley, 1854), 55-68. For Henry B. Tristram's visit, see *The Land of Israel: A Journal of Travels in Palestine* (London: Society for Promoting Christian Knowledge, 1866), 250-53. For Charles Clermont-Ganneau's visit to Qumran and his excavation of one of the graves, see *Archaeological Researches in Palestine During the Years 1873-1874,* 2 (London: Palestine Exploration Fund, 1896), 14-16. For Claude R. Condor and Charles Tyrwhitt-Drake's visit to Qumran, see Condor and Horatio H. Kitchener, *The Survey of Western Palestine,* 3: *Judea* (London: Palestine Exploration Fund, 1883), 210-11. For Gustaf Dalman's visit to Qumran, see *Palästinajahrbuch des Deutschen evangelischen Instituts für Altertumswissenschaft des heiligen Landes zu Jerusalem,* 10 (Berlin: Ernst Siegfried Mittler, 1914), 9-11. Before the discovery of the Dead Sea Scrolls and de Vaux's excavations, Avi-Yonah accepted Dalman's identification of Qumran as a fortress: see Michael Avi-Yonah, "Map of Roman Palestine," *Quarterly of the Department of Antiquities in Palestine* 5 (1936): 139-96 (Qumran is mentioned on p. 164). In his later publications he described Qumran (which he identified as Mezad Hasidim, or the Fort of the Pious Ones) as the "monastery" of the Dead Sea Sect: see Michael Avi-Yonah, *Gazetteer of Roman Palestine* (Qedem 5) (Jerusalem: Hebrew University, 1976) 80, s.v. "Mezad Hasidim." For an engaging account of the early exploration of Palestine, see Neil A. Silberman, *Digging for God and Country: Exploration, Archeology, and the Secret Struggle for the Holy Land, 1799-1917* (New York: Alfred A. Knopf, 1982).

The identification of Secacah with Qumran was first proposed by John Allegro; for recent discussions see Hanan Eshel, "The Identification of the City of Salt," *Israel Exploration Journal* 45 (1995): 37-40; Avi Ofer, "Qumran is Secaca," *Qadmoniot* 115 (1998): 65 (in Hebrew).

For the story of the discovery of the Dead Sea Scrolls with references, see James C. VanderKam, *The Dead Sea Scrolls Today* (Grand Rapids: Wm. B. Eerdmans, 1994). Also see Frank Moore Cross, "Reminiscences of the Early Days in the Discovery and Study of the Dead Sea Scrolls," in Schiffman, Tov, and VanderKam, *The Dead Sea Scrolls Fifty Years after Their Discovery*, 932-43.

For the first season of excavations at Qumran in 1951, see G. Lankester Harding, "Khirbet Qumrân and Wady Murabba'at: Fresh Light on the Dead Sea Scrolls and New Manuscript Discoveries in Jordan," *Palestine Exploration Quarterly* 84 (1952): 104-9. For a photograph of Cave 4 as it appeared in the 1920s, before the bedouins made a secondary opening to it, see Frank Moore Cross, *The Ancient Library of Qumran*, 3rd ed. (Minneapolis: Fortress, 1995), Figure 2.

# CHAPTER 3

# The Dead Sea Scrolls
# and the Community at Qumran

*A group claiming to constitute a holy community and comparing it-*
*self to the Temple would have to interpret in terms of its sectarian life*
*the Temple's chief characteristics, including purity rules, cult, and*
*priesthood.*

In this chapter, we consider the following questions: What are the Dead Sea
Scrolls? What is their connection with the community at Qumran? Can we
determine the identity of this community? The answers to most of these
questions are provided by the scrolls and ancient historical sources, not by archaeology. I include this discussion because the scrolls and our ancient historical sources provide information that aids in the interpretation of the archaeological remains. Because archaeology is the focus of this book, readers
interested in additional information on the scrolls and ancient historical
sources are advised to consult the bibliographical notes at the end of this
chapter.

## What Are the Dead Sea Scrolls?

Dead Sea Scrolls is a popular term designating those manuscripts or manuscript fragments found in the 11 caves near Qumran. Many scholars now prefer to refer to these manuscripts as "the Qumran scrolls" or "the library of

Qumran." Other ancient scrolls found in caves near the Dead Sea, such as the Bar Kokhba documents from Wadi Muraba'at, are not referred to as Dead Sea Scrolls. In this book, I use the terms Dead Sea Scrolls and Qumran scrolls to describe only those scrolls that were found in the caves by Qumran. Most of the Dead Sea Scrolls are made of parchment (processed animal hide). The rest (numbering about 100 texts, or 13 percent of the total) are of papyrus. The Copper Scroll is inscribed on sheets of bronze. The parchment scrolls were made by sewing together pieces of animal hide, probably reinforced with glue. Writing was usually done on one side of the sheet using a reed pen dipped in ink, similar to modern Jewish Torah scrolls (which preserve this Greco-Roman tradition). The Qumran caves yielded no books or codices, in which parchment or papyrus pages were covered with writing on both sides and bound together (a tradition that developed in the later Roman period and was adopted by the Christian church for the New Testament).

Most of the Dead Sea Scrolls are in Hebrew. About 20 percent are in Aramaic and a small number are in Greek. Most of the Hebrew and Aramaic scrolls are written in Aramaic script (letters), which is an early form of the Hebrew alphabet used today. In biblical times, the Hebrew language was written using a variant of the Phoenician alphabet. During the period of the Babylonian exile and Persian rule that followed the fall of the kingdom of Judah in 586 B.C.E., the Jews abandoned the Biblical Hebrew script and adopted a different but related script, the Aramaic alphabet. On a few later occasions the Jews revived the Biblical-Hebrew script (therefore called "Paleo-Hebrew"), for example, on coins minted during the First and Second Jewish Revolts against the Romans. Interestingly, this script was also used for some of the books of Moses and Job from Qumran or sometimes just for the name of God (YHWH), apparently as a sign of veneration for the authority of these ancient books and the Tetragrammaton.

The types of works represented at Qumran can be categorized or described in different ways, depending on one's point of view. For example, Devorah Dimant has suggested dividing the scrolls into three groups: (1) biblical manuscripts, (2) works containing terminology linked with the Qumran Community, and (3) works not containing such terminology. She has noted that Cave 4 yielded about three-quarters of the entire collection (from all 11 caves). In addition, each cave contained at least one copy of a work found in Cave 4. For the purposes of this discussion, I divide the scrolls into three main categories: biblical literature, sectarian works or compositions, and works that are neither biblical nor sectarian. The Dead Sea Scrolls include only a few fragmentary documentary records such as deeds to land or commercial transactions (e.g., 4Q342-358). There are no works of "profane" knowledge or historical works, including Jewish Greek works such as the Wisdom of Solomon. There are also no copies of the pro-Hasmonean work 1 Maccabees or the book of Judith. Contrary to claims made by a few scholars, no copies of the New Testament (or precursors to it) are represented among the Dead Sea Scrolls. Instead, the works represented include biblical texts, apocryphal and pseudepigraphical compositions, halakhic (legal) discussions, prayers and liturgical compositions, and sectarian works (see below). Because of this, we can describe this as an intentional collection of selected works. In other words, the scrolls represent a religious library. As Dimant has noted, "It is precisely this literary character which makes this collection a library, especially in light of the fact that in many cases the collection contains several copies of the same writing." The works represented in this library reflect a distinctively sectarian theological outlook (as well as a different calendar than the one used by other Jews at the time and different interpretations of *halakhah,* or Jewish law). In fact, there are no examples of any works that can be attributed to an opposing Jewish religious group. The presence of multiple copies of some works indicates that this library belonged to a community instead of to an individual. As Florentino García Martínez and Adam van der Woude have observed, "That to this group belong not only the clearly sectarian texts but all the texts of the library is shown by the fact that [manuscripts] coming from different caves, some of them biblical, some of them difficult to characterize, were copied by the same scribes who copied typically sectarian texts."

Why were these scrolls deposited in the caves around Qumran? The two most likely explanations (which are not mutually exclusive) are that some of the caves were used as the community's library or archive (for storing documents), and that some of the scrolls were placed in the caves for safekeeping on the eve of the Roman destruction of Qumran in 68 c.e. The first category of scrolls (biblical literature) includes the earliest extant copies of the Hebrew Bible. All 24 books of the Hebrew Bible are represented at Qumran (most are incomplete copies), with the exception of Esther (this is either an accident of preservation or this book was not present at all; Nehemiah is also not represented, but there is one copy of Ezra). Before 1947, the earliest copies of the Hebrew Bible we possessed dated to the 9th and 10th centuries c.e. The Dead Sea Scrolls, which were written (though not necessarily composed) between ca. 200 b.c.e. and 70 c.e., take us back much closer to the original date of composition of the Hebrew Bible. The books of the Hebrew Bible were composed and edited over the course of many centuries, with the end of this process dated from the 6th or 5th to 2nd centuries b.c.e.

The biblical scrolls from Qumran are important because they can be compared with the present form of the Hebrew Bible. The text of the Hebrew Bible used today is referred to as the Masoretic Text (from the Hebrew word *masorah,* which means "tradition"). However, in the pre-Christian centuries different versions of or variations on the text of the Hebrew Bible circulated (mostly with relatively minor differences). After the Masoretic Text became authoritative (ca. 100 C.E.), the other versions ceased to circulate and disappeared. The biblical scrolls from Qumran include not only early copies of the Masoretic Text (called "Proto-Masoretic"), but examples of other versions which disappeared or were preserved in the Samaritan Bible or in translations in Greek, Latin, and Syriac. A few fragments of the Septuagint, the 3rd-2nd century B.C.E. Greek translation of the Hebrew Bible, are also represented at Qumran. This Greek translation originally provided the basis for the Christian Old Testament (but eventually only for the Roman Catholic Old Testament).

Although nowadays we use different translations of the Hebrew Bible or Old Testament, we could hardly conceive of having more than one version of the text. The Dead Sea Scrolls indicate that there was no such standardization in the pre-Christian centuries. There was also no established biblical canon, which means there was no set list of books that was considered authoritative. The number of copies of different books represented at Qumran gives us an idea of those which were considered authoritative or used most extensively by the sectarians. Books represented in eight or more copies include the Pentateuch (Five Books of Moses), Isaiah, the Twelve Prophets, Psalms, and Daniel. James VanderKam has observed that "perhaps it is not strange that the three books that appear on the largest number of copies at Qumran are also the three [Deuteronomy, Isaiah, Psalms] that are quoted most frequently in the New Testament."

Another type of biblical scroll represented at Qumran is Targums, which are ancient translations or paraphrases of the Hebrew Bible into Aramaic. Aramaic was the language spoken by the Jews of Palestine in the first centuries B.C.E. and C.E. Because many of them no longer understood Hebrew, after the scriptural passage was read during a service it was translated orally into Aramaic. Eventually these translations were written down. Targums of two biblical books — Leviticus and Job — are represented at Qumran.

The second category of scrolls from Qumran consists of sectarian literature such as the Damascus Document (CD plus fragments from the Qumran caves), the Community Rule (Manual of Discipline) (1QS), the War Scroll (1QM/4QM), and 4QMMT *(Miqsat Ma'aseh HaTorah).* There are also commentaries (Hebrew *pesher;* plural *pesharim*) on biblical books, such as the Pesher Habakkuk from Cave 1. Unlike his modern counterparts, the Qumran exegete (commentator) assumed that the prophecies mentioned in the Bible were directed specifically to his own time, and that the correct interpretation had been revealed to the Teacher of Righteousness (see below). We can also include in this category poetic works such as the Thanksgiving Hymns (Hebrew *Hodayot*). The sectarian literature provides information on the beliefs and practices of the sect that used (and in some cases composed) these scrolls and deposited them in the caves at Qumran. They tell us that this group separated from the rest of the Jews in Judea around the middle of the 2nd century B.C.E. or even earlier over differences in the interpretation and practice of Jewish law. In general, this sect was stricter in its interpretation of Jewish law than other Jews.

The third category of scrolls from Qumran are works that are neither biblical (in the sense that they did not become part of the Hebrew Bible) nor sectarian (that is, they are not sectarian compositions, although they were used by the sect). Examples of such works include Apocrypha and Pseudepigrapha. Apocrypha is a Greek term that literally means "hidden books." This term denotes those books that were included in the Catholic Old Testament (also called Deuterocanonicals), but not in the Hebrew Bible (= Protestant Old Testament). The Apocrypha from Qumran include Tobit and Sirach (= Ecclesiasticus). Pseudepigrapha are Jewish religious books of the first centuries B.C.E. and C.E. that are not included either in the Hebrew Bible or Catholic Old Testament. The term Pseudepigrapha (Greek for "false writings") derives from the fact that sometimes the authors used fake names (pseudonyms), usually those of biblical figures, to give their work greater authority (a practice that VanderKam characterizes as a sort of reverse plagiarism!). Pseudepigrapha from Qumran include the books of Enoch and Jubilees. The Temple Scroll (11QTS) also falls into this category because it is probably not a sectarian composition, although the Qumran community apparently considered it authoritative.

The sect was founded and led by priests who called themselves the sons of Zadok (the high priest in the time of David and Solomon), and it had a strong priestly orientation. Many of the disagreements about Jewish law concerned the cult (sacrifices) in the Jerusalem temple, including the sect's preference for a solar instead of lunar calendar. This means that their holidays and festivals would have fallen on different dates than those observed by other Jews. During the second quarter of the 2nd century B.C.E., the Zadokites lost their monopoly over the office of high priest in the Jerusalem temple. Soon afterwards, with the establishment of the Hasmonean dynasty (as a result of the Maccabean Revolt), the Hasmonean kings took on the role of high priests. These events not only contributed to the formation of this sect but caused its members to do the most radical thing a Jew could do at that time: they rejected the cult in the Jerusalem temple. Jews atoned for their sins by offering sacrifices in the Jerusalem temple (whereas Christians accept Jesus as the sacrifice). This sect believed that because the sacrificial cult in the Jerusalem temple was not being conducted properly, it would not bring salvation or atonement. Instead, according to the Community Rule (9.4-5), "they shall atone for guilty rebellion and for sins of unfaithfulness, that they may obtain loving-kindness for the Land without the flesh of holocausts and the fat of sacrifice. And prayer rightly shall be as an acceptable fragrance of righteousness, and perfection of way as a delectable free-will offering."

The founder or refounder of the sect was the Teacher of Righteousness. The members believed that God had revealed to the Teacher of Righteousness the secrets of biblical prophecies. Like most of the other historical figures mentioned in the scrolls, the Teacher's identity is hidden behind a nickname; others include the Wicked Priest, the Spouter of Lies, the Lion of Wrath, and the Kittim. Scholars try to identify these nicknamed figures with known historical personalities. For example, scholars agree that the Kittim are the Romans. The term Wicked Priest refers to a high priest, since the name is a transparent play on words: *haKohen haRasha* (the Wicked Priest) for *haKohen haRosh* (the high priest). However, there is no consensus regarding the identity of most of the nicknamed individuals or the dates they lived. For example, it has been suggested that the Wicked Priest is either Jonathan or Simon, brothers of Judah Maccabee. The Teacher of Righteousness might not even be mentioned in contemporary historical sources, in which case we cannot establish his identity. Contrary to the claims of a few scholars, these nicknamed figures cannot be identified with Jesus and his associates (such as John the Baptist and James the Just) because the scrolls that mention these figures were composed or written (or refer to events that occurred) before their time.

Those who wished to join the sect were required to undergo a rigorous process of initiation that lasted two to three years. Once admitted, they gave up at least some of their personal property and possessions to the sect. The sect was organized in a strict hierarchy led by priests. Some members were married and lived in towns and villages around Palestine (as we learn from the Damascus Document), including in Jerusalem. Others lived in isolation in the desert under more severe conditions. The settlement at Qumran was one such desert community; we do not know whether there were others.

The community at Qumran (called the *yahad*, which means "the unity") modeled itself after the historical Israel. It was divided into priests and Levites on the one hand and Israelites on the other. We also do not know if the community at Qumran included married members from other parts of the country who perhaps joined the group for limited periods or on certain occasions. Because of their concern with ritual purity and because the Community Rule (Manual of Discipline), which includes the sect's penal code, does not include legislation dealing with marriage, women, and children (in contrast to the Damascus Document, Rule of the Congregation, War Scroll, and Temple Scroll, for example), many scholars believe that the group at Qumran was celibate. Ancient historical sources also seem to indicate that the community at Qumran was composed of adult, celibate men (see below). As we shall see, although it is not unambiguous, the archaeological evidence supports this point of view (see Chapter 8).

The sectarian scrolls indicate the members believed that the end of days (*eschaton*) was at hand. In other words, this was an apocalyptic group awaiting the eschaton. Frank Moore Cross has described the sect as "priestly apocalyptists." They viewed their community as a substitute temple and believed that they would soon reinstitute the cult in the Jerusalem temple according to their interpretation of halakhah. The sect therefore applied the temple purity laws to the lives of its members. In other words, the sectarians conducted their lives as if the community were a virtual temple. For this reason, they observed the same strict regulations governing purity (including immersion and purity of food, drink, and dishes) as were required for the temple cult. There is no definite evidence that this sect conducted animal sacrifices at Qumran, although they probably considered at least some of their communal meals to be a substitute or preparation for the sacrifices (see Chapter 6). Living at Qumran, the sect imitated the ancient Mosaic 40-year exodus in the desert, in anticipation of the dawning kingdom of God and the arrival of two messiahs (a secular messiah "of Israel" descended from David, and a priestly messiah "of Aaron"). They believed that this messianic era would be ushered in by a 40-year-long war (notice the symbolic number 40 again) between the forces of good ("Sons of Light") and the forces of evil ("Sons of Darkness"), as described in the War Scroll. They identified themselves as the Sons of Light, and everyone else — not only the Kittim (Romans) but other Jews as well — as the Sons of Darkness. This sect believed that everything including their victory in this war was preordained by God.

## Were the Inhabitants of Qumran Essenes?

Many scholars identify the community at Qumran as Essenes. However, nowhere in the Dead Sea Scrolls is the term Essene mentioned (but see below). The Essenes are also not directly alluded to in the New Testament or in Talmudic literature. Instead, our information about the Essenes comes from the writings of several Greek and Latin authors. The most important of these are Flavius Josephus, Philo Judaeus, and Pliny the Elder. In addition, a passage in Hippolytus's *Refutatio omnium haeresium (Refutation of All Heresies)* reproduces much of the information provided by Josephus and seems to have drawn on the same source.

Flavius Josephus (ca. 38 to after 93 c.e.) was a Jew from a priestly family in Jerusalem. His Hebrew name was Yosef ben Mattitiyahu (Joseph son of Mattathias). When the First Jewish Revolt against the Romans began in 66 c.e., Josephus was appointed commander of the Jewish forces in Galilee. He surrendered to the Romans in 67 c.e. and, after the revolt, settled in Rome. There Josephus wrote books about the history of the Jewish people. His surviving works include *Jewish War* (which tells the story of the First Jewish Revolt, including the famous mass suicide at Masada) and *Jewish Antiquities* (a history of the Jewish people beginning with creation). In *War* 2.119-61, Josephus provides a long and detailed description of the Essenes, with shorter passages about them in *Antiquities.* To help his Roman (non-Jewish) audience understand the lifestyle and beliefs of the Essenes and other Jews and to make the Jews more sympathetic to his non-Jewish readers, Josephus sometimes couched his explanations in Greco-Roman terms. For example, his passage on the Essenes begins: "Indeed, there exist among the Jews three schools of philosophy: the Pharisees belong to the first, the Sadducees to the second, and to the third belong men who have a reputation for cultivating a particularly saintly life, called Essenes" (*War* 2.119). Notice the way Josephus describes groups in contemporary Judean society as schools of philosophy! He devoted the longest description to the Essenes, who were the smallest and most marginal of these three groups. Why? One reason is that Josephus, like Philo and Pliny, admired the Essenes for their ascetic lifestyle, which was considered virtuous. Another reason is that, like other ancient historians (going back to Herodotus), Josephus tended to focus on the different and exotic because he was writing to entertain his audience. The Romans read history books for fun, not for objective history in the modern sense. For example, Josephus devoted an entire paragraph to the toilet habits of the Essenes because they were different from everyone else's (see Chapter 6). In contrast, we have no such description of the toilet habits of the Romans from any Roman writers, because there was no need to describe something that was ordinary and familiar to everyone and was therefore taken for granted.

Josephus's testimony about the Essenes is especially valuable because in his autobiography he claimed to have had personal acquaintance with them: "At about the age of sixteen I wished to get experience of the schools of thought to be found among us. There are three of these — Pharisees the first, Sadducees the second, Essenes the third . . ." (*Life* 10). As we shall see, the points of correspondence between the information Josephus provides and the archaeological evidence suggest that much of his description of the Essenes in *War* focused on the community at Qumran.

Our second main source for the Essenes is Philo (ca. 30 B.C.E.–45 C.E.), a Jewish philosopher who lived in Alexandria in Egypt. Philo was a great admirer of Jewish sects with an ascetic lifestyle, including the Essenes and another group called the Therapeutae that lived in Egypt. Much of his information on the Essenes is in works called *Every Good Man Is Free* (75-91) and the *Hypothetica*. Although some of Philo's information corresponds with that provided by Josephus, it is less specific. It is not clear whether Philo ever visited Judea or had firsthand knowledge of the Essenes.

Our third main source for the Essenes is Pliny the Elder (Gaius Plinius Secundus, 23/24-79 C.E.). Pliny was a renowned Roman geographer and naturalist who perished during the eruption of Mount Vesuvius in 79 C.E. He had no firsthand knowledge of the Essenes and his description is limited to a single paragraph in a work that he wrote in about 77 C.E. (*Natural History* 5.73). However, this passage contains information about the location of the settlement of the Essenes that is not provided by the other authors:

> To the west [of the Dead Sea] the Essenes have put the necessary distance between themselves and the insalubrious shore. They are a people unique of its kind and admirable beyond all others in the whole world, without women and renouncing love entirely, without money, and having for company only the palm trees. Owing to the throng of newcomers, this people is daily re-born in equal number; indeed, those whom, wearied by the fluctuations of fortune, life leads to adopt their customs, stream in in great numbers. Thus, unbelievable though this may seem, for thousands of centuries a race has existed which is eternal yet into which no one is born: so fruitful for them is the repentance which others feel for their past lives! Below the Essenes was the town of Engada [Ein Gedi], which yielded only to Jerusalem in fertility and palm-groves but is today become another ash-heap. From there, one comes to the fortress of Masada, situated on a rock, and itself near the Lake of Asphalt [Dead Sea].

This passage reveals that Pliny, like the other writers, admired the Essenes because of their ascetic lifestyle (which includes giving up sexual relations and money) and focused on them because they were different and exotic. He referred to them in Roman terms as a *gens* ("tribe") who recruited new members instead of reproducing.

The most controversial point about this passage is that Pliny described the Essenes as living among the palm trees on the western shore of the Dead Sea, above Ein Gedi. A few scholars have claimed that because Pliny placed Ein Gedi "below" (Latin *infra*) the settlement of the Essenes, the settlement should be sought in the hills above and to the west of Ein Gedi (instead of at Qumran, which is north of Ein Gedi). On this basis, Yizhar Hirschfeld has identified a site he excavated in the hills overlooking the oasis at Ein Gedi as the Essene settlement described by Pliny. However, Hirschfeld's site appears to consist of agricultural installations such as storage cells and irrigation pools and not a settlement of the Second Temple period. Moreover, Menahem Stern and other scholars have shown that Pliny's description of the Dead Sea appears to progress from north to south, beginning with the Jordan River to the settlement of the Essenes to Ein Gedi and then to Masada. This means that Ein Gedi lay downstream from or south of the settlement of the Essenes. Because this corresponds with Qumran's location, many scholars identify Qumran as the Essene settlement mentioned by Pliny (a suggestion first made by Sukenik). On the other hand, Pliny's passage is somewhat confused, probably because he drew his information from another source (or sources) and did not have firsthand knowledge of the region. For example, Pliny mentioned that Jerusalem and Ein Gedi are lying in ruins. This was indeed the case when he wrote in 77 C.E., seven years after fall of Jerusalem and the destruction of the Second Temple. But as we have seen, Qumran was destroyed during the revolt (in 68 C.E.), which means that by the time Pliny composed this work it too was lying in ruins. But he described the settlement of the Essenes in the present tense, that is, as if it still existed when he wrote the work. In addition, Pliny confused Jerusalem with Jericho when he described Ein Gedi as second only to Jerusalem in the fertility of its land and in its groves of palm trees.

Despite the problems with Pliny's passage, most scholars identify Qumran with the Essene settlement he described. As we shall see, the archaeological evidence supports this identification. But if the inhabitants of Qumran were Essenes, why does this term not appear in the Dead Sea Scrolls? Perhaps (as in the case of other historical figures and groups mentioned in the scrolls), this sect hid its identity behind nicknames (such as the Sons of Light) or did not refer to themselves at all. It is also possible that the term

Essene appears in the scrolls but in a different form. If this is the case, it is a result of the different languages used in the scrolls (Hebrew and Aramaic) and by Josephus (Greek), Philo (Greek), and Pliny (Latin). In other words, the sectarian scrolls might contain a Hebrew or Aramaic equivalent for the Greek and Latin term Essene *(Essenoi, Esseni, or Essaioi)*. For example, scholars have suggested that a word such as *hasid* ("pious one"), *'osei* ("doers," an abbreviated form of "the doers of the Torah"), or *'asayya* ("healers") represents the Semitic equivalent of the Greek and Latin term Essene.

Even among scholars who agree that Qumran was a sectarian settlement, there is no consensus regarding the identification of this group with the Essenes mentioned in our ancient sources. Scholars who reject this identification note that Josephus is presenting a grossly oversimplified picture of Judean society by describing only three groups (Sadducees, Pharisees, and Essenes). The Sadducees represented the aristocratic upper class of Judean society in the 1st century B.C.E. and 1st century C.E. Although most of them were priests or members of priestly families, they were willing to accommodate Roman rule and adopted some aspects of Greek and Roman culture (in other words, they were Hellenized). The Sadducees derived their name from Zadok, the high priest of the First Jewish Temple at the time of Solomon (ca. 960 B.C.E.). The descendants of Zadok served as high priests through the First Temple and Second Temple periods, until the Hasmonean kings usurped control of this office. The community at Qumran was apparently founded and led by priests who called themselves the sons of Zadok. Because of this, the community at Qumran shared some common points of view with the Sadducees, especially in their strict approach to the interpretation of Jewish law. However, they also differed on significant points, such as the doctrine of predestination and their attitude towards Hellenization.

The Pharisees derived their name from the Hebrew term *perushim*, which means "separate." They belonged mostly to the middle and lower classes of Judean society in the 1st century B.C.E. and 1st century C.E. The Pharisees opposed the adoption of Greek and Roman customs (Hellenization) by Jews. They were scrupulous in their observance of Jewish law and supplemented the Written Law (Pentateuch) with the Oral Law. The Oral Law represents the interpretations of the Written Law that were passed down orally from successive generations of teachers to their disciples. In contrast, the Sadducees seem to have rejected the authority of much of the Oral Law. Unlike the Pharisees, the Sadducees also rejected the idea of the immortality of the soul and denied the notion of divine interference in human affairs. On the other hand, the Essenes believed in predestination. After the destruction of the Second Temple in 70 C.E., the rabbinic class developed out of Pharisaism.

Judean society in the late Second Temple period was undoubtedly much more complex than the picture Josephus presents. Because of this, some scholars argue that the community at Qumran represents not the Essenes but a different Jewish group that is not described in our sources and had similar beliefs and practices. They point to contradictions within and between the sectarian scrolls and the ancient sources. For example, the Damascus Document describes sectarians who were married and had children, whereas the Community Rule (Manual of Discipline) contains no legislation for women and children (see Chapter 8). Similarly, Josephus devotes most of his description of the Essenes to a group consisting of adult celibate men, but at the end mentions "another order of Essenes" who marry and have children (*War* 2.160-61). So perhaps when Josephus described the Essenes, he grouped different Jewish ascetic sects under the same rubric. In fact, various ancient sources (such as Josephus and the New Testament) mention other groups in Judean society at this time, including the Zealots, Sicarii, and Boethusians. For these reasons, the identification of the community at Qumran depends largely on one's interpretation of the scrolls and the historical sources. In my opinion, the points of correspondence between the archaeological evidence and the information provided by the scrolls and our ancient sources indicate that the community at Qumran should be identified as Essenes.

## What Is the Connection between the Community at Qumran and the Dead Sea Scrolls?

The last question I wish to consider here is whether it is possible to establish a connection between the inhabitants of Qumran and the scrolls. This connection is problematic because no scrolls were discovered in the settlement at Qumran. Instead, all of the scrolls come from the caves surrounding the site. The absence of scrolls from Qumran is precisely what has made it possible for some scholars to suggest that there is no connection between the site and the caves, and that Qumran was therefore not a sectarian settlement but a different kind of site (villa, manor house, fort, or commercial entrepot). These scholars claim that the people who lived at the site were not the same ones who used the scrolls and deposited them in the caves.

However, the reasoning behind this argument is flawed, for archaeology establishes a connection between the settlement at Qumran and the scrolls in the caves. The best evidence is provided by the pottery, for the same ceramic types were discovered in the settlement and in the scroll caves. If we disassociate the scrolls from the settlement, we must assume that in the 1st century

B.C.E. and 1st century C.E. a different group from the one living in the settlement deposited the scrolls in the caves. This is hardly likely given the proximity of some of the scroll caves to the settlement. For example, Cave 4 (with its collection of 500 different manuscripts!) is less than 500 m. from the site, and Caves 7, 8, and 9 are hewn into the southern edge of the marl terrace on which the settlement sits. The fact that the pottery found in the settlement and in the scroll caves includes types that are virtually unique to Qumran provides the best evidence for this connection. These types include the so-called "scroll jars," which are tall, cylindrical jars with wide mouths that were covered with bowl-shaped lids. Not only were these jars found in the settlement and inside the scroll caves, but some of the scrolls from Cave 1 were reportedly deposited in a jar of this type. On the other hand, cylindrical jars are hardly attested outside of Qumran and the caves (see Chapter 5).

The pottery thus establishes a connection between the inhabitants of Qumran and the scrolls from the nearby caves. If this is the case, why were no scrolls or scroll fragments discovered at Qumran? The reason is simple: the sectarian settlement at Qumran was destroyed twice by fire during the course of its existence, first in ca. 9/8 B.C.E. and again in 68 C.E. (see Chapter 4). If there were any scrolls in the settlement (and given the proximity of the scroll caves and the discovery of three inkwells at the site, it is likely there were), they would have been burned in these fires. This explains why de Vaux found almost no organic materials in his excavations. Few traces of organic materials remained from the earlier destruction (ca. 9/8 B.C.E.), aside from a thin layer of ash (from the burnt roofs) that blanketed the site. The burnt mat in the "scriptorium" (L30), a wooden plaque from the "pantry" (L86), a piece of cut wood from L92, a palm mat from L124, and a few chunks of charred roof beams found on some of the floors were about all that survived the Roman destruction in 68 C.E. (see Fig. 16). In contrast, the dry conditions inside the caves preserved not only the scrolls but other organic materials such as wooden combs and linen textiles (see Chapter 9).

For these reasons, the absence of scrolls from the settlement at Qumran does not prove that there were none. Similarly, although no examples are preserved, no one doubts that Torah scrolls were stored in ancient Palestinian synagogues (and over 100 of these buildings are known). However, because of the accident of preservation or the manner in which these synagogues were destroyed, no ancient Torah scrolls have survived (with the exception of the synagogue at Ein Gedi, where burned manuscripts that are probably Torah scrolls were discovered lying on the floor).

## Bibliographical Notes

The quotation at the beginning of this chapter is from Jacob Neusner, *The Idea of Purity in Ancient Judaism* (Leiden: E. J. Brill, 1973), 33.

For introductions to the Dead Sea Scrolls, I recommend the following: James C. VanderKam, *The Dead Sea Scrolls Today;* Lawrence H. Schiffman, *Reclaiming the Dead Sea Scrolls* (Philadelphia: Jewish Publication Society, 1994); Frank Moore Cross, *The Ancient Library of Qumran;* Hershel Shanks, ed., *Understanding the Dead Sea Scrolls* (New York: Random House, 1992); Hartmut Stegemann, *The Library of Qumran* (Grand Rapids: Wm. B. Eerdmans, 1998).

For observations on the composition of the Dead Sea Scrolls, see Devorah Dimant, "The Library of Qumran: Its Content and Character," in Schiffman, Tov, and VanderKam, *The Dead Sea Scrolls Fifty Years after Their Discovery,* 170-76; Devorah Dimant, "The Qumran Manuscripts: Contents and Significance," in *Time to Prepare the Way in the Wilderness,* ed. Dimant and Lawrence H. Schiffman (Leiden: E. J. Brill, 1995), 23-58; Florentino García Martínez and Adam S. van der Woude, "A 'Groningen' Hypothesis of Qumran Origins and Early History," *Revue de Qumran* 14 (1990): 521-41.

For a discussion of the Qumran community within the framework of other ascetic groups, see Steven D. Fraade, "Ascetical Aspects of Ancient Judaism," in *Jewish Spirituality,* 1: *From the Bible through the Middle Ages,* ed. Arthur Green (New York: Crossroad, 1986), 253-88. For the structure of the sectarian community, see Nathan Jastram, "Hierarchy at Qumran," in *Legal Texts and Legal Issues. Proceedings of the Second Meeting of the International Organization for Qumran Studies, Cambridge 1995,* ed. Moshe Bernstein, Florentino García Martínez, and John Kampen (Leiden: E. J. Brill, 1997), 349-76.

For information on Josephus, Philo, and Pliny (as well as other ancient sources on the Essenes), see Geza Vermès and Martin D. Goodman, eds., *The Essenes According to the Classical Sources* (Sheffield: JSOT, 1989). For Martin Goodman's view that the community at Qumran does not represent the Essenes described by our ancient sources, see "A Note on the Qumran Sectarians, the Essenes and Josephus," *Journal of Jewish Studies* 46 (1995): 161-66.

For Pliny's use of *infra hos,* see Menahem Stern, *Greek and Latin Authors on Jews and Judaism* (Jerusalem: Israel Academy of Sciences and Humanities, 1976) 1:480-81; also see Ernest-Marie Laperrousaz, "'Infra Hos Engadda': Notes a propos d'un article récent," *Revue Biblique* 69 (1962): 369-80; Christoph Burchard, "Pline et les Esséniens: A propos d'un article récent," *Revue Biblique* 69 (1962): 533-69. For references to Hirschfeld's publications on Qumran, see the bibliographical notes to Chapter 1. For the site that Hirsch-

feld excavated above Ein Gedi, see Yizhar Hirschfeld, "A Settlement of Hermits above 'En Gedi," *Tel Aviv* 27 (2000): 103-55. For a different interpretation
of Hirschfeld's site, see David Amit and Jodi Magness, "Not a Settlement of
Hermits or Essenes: A Response to Y. Hirschfeld, A Settlement of Hermits
above 'En Gedi," *Tel Aviv* 27 (2000): 273-85. For the burnt Torah scrolls from
the Ein Gedi synagogue (with bibliographical references), see Dan Barag,
"En-Gedi," in *The New Encyclopedia of Archaeological Excavations in the Holy
Land*, ed. Ephraim Stern (New York: Simon and Schuster, 1993) 2:409.

# CHAPTER 4

# The Buildings and Occupation Phases of Qumran

## A Description of Qumran and Its Chronology according to de Vaux

De Vaux divided the sectarian settlement at Qumran into three phases, which he termed "Period Ia," "Period Ib," and "Period II." A late Iron Age settlement preceded these periods, and they were followed by a brief phase of Roman occupation referred to by de Vaux as Period III. The "periods" were defined on the basis of stratigraphic and architectural evidence (in other words, they were based on discernable changes in the occupation levels and architecture). In approximate terms, de Vaux dated Period Ia to the third quarter of the 2nd century B.C.E. (roughly 130-100 B.C.E.), Period Ib from about 100 B.C.E. to 31 B.C.E., and Period II from 4-1 B.C.E. to 68 C.E. Here I present a brief description of the remains from each of these periods. We first follow de Vaux's chronology, and afterwards we shall review my revised chronology for the occupation phases. In later chapters we will examine many of the issues raised here in greater detail (such as the animal bone deposits, the water system, and the cemetery). In this discussion, I present some of the remains associated with the destruction of the site at the end of Period II under Period Ib. I have done this in cases where the features remained the same during both periods (for example, evidence for the wooden door in L4, which was burned in the destruction at the end of Period II, is described under Period Ib, since this room would have had a wooden door in Period Ib).

In all of the occupation periods, the buildings were constructed of rough (uncut) field stones held together by mud mortar. Some of the walls, especially the partition walls inside the buildings, were made of mud brick. They were poorly preserved, having collapsed or reverted to mud over the course of the last 2000 years. The corners and areas around the windows and doors (thresholds, sills, lintels, posts) were constructed of cut stones to provide structural reinforcement. The interior walls of at least some of the rooms were covered with plain mud plaster, and the floors were usually of packed earth (and in a few cases were plastered or cobbled). Jars sunk into the floors of rooms were used for storage, mostly of food items such as grain. There is evidence for windows and built-in cupboards in some of the walls. A number of rooms in the settlement had a second-story level. The roofs were flat and were made of relatively short wooden beams (obtained locally from desert trees such as date palms and acacia) overlaid by layers of reeds, palm branches, and mud. When the settlement was destroyed by the Romans in 68 C.E., the wooden beams and thatch burned and the roofs collapsed onto the floors of the rooms. In a number of places, de Vaux found chunks of burnt mud from the roofs in which the reed impressions were still visible. The wooden doors also burned, as indicated by clusters of iron nails found lying on the floors next to some of the doorways. A burnt mat was found covering part of the floor in the "scriptorium" (L30; see below). The flat roofs created open terraces which could have been used for various purposes. The channels and pools of the elaborate hydraulic system were dug into the marl terrace and were covered with thick coats of plaster to prevent the water from seeping into the ground. Because the latest main occupation phase (Period II) is best preserved, it is often difficult to determine the plans and functions of rooms during the earlier phases (Periods Ia and Ib).

The description of the archaeological remains presented in this chapter lays the necessary groundwork for the discussions in the following chapters. Readers are encouraged to consult the relevant plans of the site and locate on the plans the locus numbers that are mentioned in the text. This will make it easier to follow the discussion (for a plan of the site showing all loci, see Fig. 5).

## Iron Age

The site of Qumran was first inhabited during the late Iron Age (8th-7th centuries B.C.E.). De Vaux found that the foundations of some of the walls, which lay at a lower level than the others, were embedded in a layer of ash containing numerous sherds of late Iron Age date. Other finds from this phase included a jar handle stamped with the paleo-Hebrew inscription *lamelekh* ("[belonging] to the king"). De Vaux reconstructed the Iron Age settlement as a rectangular building with a row of rooms along the east side of an open courtyard. An enclosure attached to the west side of the building contained a large round cistern (L110) that was filled by surface runoff. This cistern remained in use until the destruction of the sectarian settlement at the end of Period II (though in later phases it was fed by water channels connected to an aqueduct). The long wall running southwards from the southeast corner of the settlement to Wadi Qumran, which encloses the esplanade to the south of the site, belongs to this phase and remained in use until the end of Period II. De Vaux noted similarities between the layout of this settlement and Israelite strongholds in the Buqeia and Negev. He suggested that the destruction of this settlement occurred at the time of the fall of the kingdom of Judah (ca. 586 B.C.E.).

## *Period Ia* (see Fig. 6)

The site of Qumran had been abandoned for several hundred years when it was occupied by a new population that established the sectarian settlement. According to de Vaux, this first occupation phase was modest in size and short-lived. Parts of the ruined Iron Age building were rebuilt and reoccupied. The round Iron Age cistern was cleared, and a new channel and decantation basin (L119) were built to supply it and two new rectangular pools (L117-L118) that were dug nearby. Surface runoff was collected from the area to the south by a small channel that fed L117. A room or enclosure (L101-L102) was built in this area. Rooms were constructed around the Iron Age cistern (L115, L116, L125, L126, L127) and to the north (L129, L133, L140, L141). De Vaux had difficulty distinguishing the remains of Period Ia in the eastern half of the settlement. Some of the walls in the area of the central courtyard were reused and the south wall of L34-L36 (on the south side of the courtyard) was constructed at this time. De Vaux attributed to this phase two side-by-side potters' kilns (L66) in the southeastern corner of this part of the site. They were covered by the steps leading down to a pool constructed during the next phase.

De Vaux had difficulty dating Period Ia because no coins were associated with this phase, and because the few potsherds he recovered were identical in type with those of the next phase. The fact that the end of Period Ia was not marked by a destruction makes it difficult to identify pottery associated with this phase. Because coins of Alexander Jannaeus (103-76 B.C.E.) were plentiful in the next phase (Period Ib), de Vaux assumed that Period Ia must have begun before that time. He therefore dated Period Ia to the reign of John

Hyrcanus I (135-104 B.C.E.). Only one coin of John Hyrcanus and one of Judah Aristobulus (104-103 B.C.E.) were recovered in the excavations at Qumran.

## Period Ib (see Fig. 7)

According to de Vaux, the sectarian settlement at Qumran acquired its definitive form when it expanded greatly in size during the reign of Alexander Jannaeus. In addition to the large number of coins of this king, six silver and five bronze Seleucid coins dating to the years around 130 B.C.E. were found in Period Ib contexts. The main entrance to the settlement was through a gate in an enclosure wall (south of L141) to the north of a square, two-story high tower (L9-L11) (see Fig. 10). Two more entrances to the site were located by the small stepped pool to the northwest (L138), and by L84 in the area of the potters' workshop on the eastern side of the settlement. The tower is preserved to the beginning of the second-story level. Its ground-floor rooms were used for storage (the ground-floor locus numbers in the tower are differentiated from the second-story rooms by the letter "A," for example L10A) (see Fig. 11). A staircase consisting of wooden steps winding around a square pillar occupied the southwest corner of the tower (L8; for another example of a spiral staircase see L35 below). This kind of staircase is mentioned in some of the Dead Sea Scrolls. For example, the houses in a new Jerusalem at the end of days were supposed to have spiral staircases to the second floor: "And a pillar is inside the staircase around which the stairs ri[se]" (5Q15 2.4; the New Jerusalem texts). Even the ideal temple described in the Temple Scroll was envisaged as having this kind of staircase: "You [shall make] a staircase north of the Temple, a square house.... (There shall be) a square column in its middle, in the center; its width four cubits on each side around which the stairs wind" (11QT$^a$ 30.4-6). Staircases could also be built alongside a wall, turning a 180-degree angle at a landing midway up (examples are found in L13 and L113, as we shall see).

The location of the tower in the middle of the north side of the settlement indicates that it served as a watch tower. This is because, like today, most people approaching Qumran in antiquity would have come from the direction of Jerusalem and Jericho to the north. There was no entrance to the tower at the ground level. Instead, it was accessed at the second-story level by climbing the staircase in L13 to the south. This staircase consisted of a flight of stone steps attached to the south wall of L13. The steps rose towards the west wall of the room, where there was a landing. From there the steps turned 180 degrees and continued up along the north wall of the room, supported by the partition separating L13 from L12. At the top of the steps, a wooden gangway or bridge leading north provided access to the tower at the second-story level. The staircase also provided access to the second-story rooms above L1, L2, and L30 (see below). Because the tower could only be entered at the second-story level, the staircase in its southwest corner provided access to the rooms at the ground-floor level. De Vaux noted that the isolation of the tower reflects the inhabitants' concern for security. It was separated from the rest of the settlement by two open spaces on the east (L18) and south (L12, L17), each of which were closed at the end by doors.

The tower guarded the main point of entry into the settlement. Those entering by way of the gate to the north of the tower or the gate by the stepped pool to the northwest (L138) proceeded south through another gate (L128) at the western foot of the tower. This gave access to a passage or corridor that divided the site into two main parts: an eastern sector dominated by the tower in the northwest corner (de Vaux called this sector the "main building"), and a western sector centered around the round Iron Age cistern (L110) (referred to by de Vaux as the "secondary building"). The eastern sector (main building) incorporated the remains of the Iron Age building and measured ca. 30 × 37 m. It consisted of rooms grouped around a central, open-air courtyard (L25, L37). The large room on the north side of the courtyard (L38-L41) was a kitchen in Period II, but its function in Period Ib is unknown. A doorway opened from this room into what de Vaux thought was an enclosed but unroofed courtyard to the north (L19, L27, on the east side of the tower). Other rooms were located on the east side of this conjectured courtyard (L40, L46).

During the first season (1951), de Vaux and Harding excavated a group of three rooms (L1, L2, L4) in the southeast corner of the main building (see Fig. 12). These were entered through corridors L12 and L13 to the south of the tower. The fact that the cobblestone floor in L1 and L2 continued beneath the wall and doorway that divided them indicates they were originally one room (L1). Cupboards were built into both sides of the wall separating these rooms (L1-L2 and L4). A low (20-cm. high) plastered bench encircling the interior of L4 suggests that it was used as an assembly room. Iron nails lying on the packed chalk floor of this room belonged to the wooden door in the north wall. Based on their placement and dimensions, de Vaux concluded that the door had been constructed of four wooden planks and was about 2.25 m. high. A small basin or niche built into the wall to the east of this doorway could be fed by a channel from the outer (north) side of the wall. De Vaux suggested that this was a receptacle through which members in closed sessions in the room could be served food or water without being disturbed. In addition to providing access to the tower, the staircase in L13 (mentioned above) led to a roof terrace above L4 and to the second-story rooms above L1, L2, and L30. According to de Vaux, during this phase L30 (the "scriptorium") had a large open bay window on its north side and could have been used as an assembly hall. A burned palm trunk found in the debris that filled L4 would have been placed in a posthole that was still visible in the middle of the plastered floor of the room. It supported the ceiling beams of the roof terrace above.

A group of small basins in the southeast corner of the central courtyard of the main building (L34) was emptied by a system of channels to the east (see Figs. 15-17). An intact cylindrical jar with a Hebrew name crudely painted in red on the shoulder was set into one of the basins. The jar's unusual double rim and the red paint coating its interior suggest that this was an installation for dyeing wool. To the east of the central courtyard and separated from it by a wall, a toilet was found (L51; see Chapter 6) (see Fig. 37). This room opened onto two adjacent stepped pools (L49, L50). The steps of L49 (designated L48) covered the potters' kilns of Period Ia (L66). De Vaux identified the area next to these pools (L52), which contained a stone basin and a large sump, as a "washing-place." A group of bronze and iron tools was stored nearby (L53, on the north side of L52; the tools are listed in Humbert and Chambon's volume under L52).

The long wall that abutted the outside of L51 continued south to Wadi Qumran and enclosed the esplanade. The triangular space between this long wall and the southeast corner of the main building was occupied by small storage rooms or workshops separated from each other by thin mud-brick partitions (L44, L45, L59-L61). A bronze jug and pottery vessels including two cylindrical jars were piled in L45, L59, and L61. The walls of L61 were of unbaked mud brick covered with mud plaster. A deep cupboard was built into the west wall. Three jars were embedded in the floor of L61, and two cylindrical plastered pits or silos were sunk into the floor against the south wall. A cylindrical jar embedded in the southwest corner of the room rested on a cylinder of unbaked earth that resembled a silo. A potters' workshop (L64 and L84) and a large stepped pool (L71) were located immediately to the south.

The potters' workshop included a shallow plastered basin fed by the main water channel in which the clay was washed (L75), a pit where the clay was left to mature (L70), a mixing-trough adjoining this pit, and a stone-lined pit for a potters' wheel just to the north (L65). Two circular kilns were located to the north of these installations just inside the long wall (L64, which is the larger of the two kilns, and L84) (see Fig. 18). Steps descending to the space between the kilns provided the potters with access to the furnace. This space was filled with ash and potsherds. An iron hook found on the steps was apparently used to stir the fire. The interior of each kiln was divided into an upper and lower chamber by a shelf pierced with flues. The hot air from a furnace in the lower chamber rose through the flues and fired the pots placed on the shelf. De Vaux noted that the openings of the two kilns faced each other, enabling the potters to take advantage of the prevailing north-south winds along the Dead Sea.

The largest room in the settlement (L77; measuring 22 m. long × 4.50 m. wide) is located to the south of the main building and functioned as an assembly hall (see Fig. 28). A circular paved area that de Vaux identified as a speaker's platform was found at the western end of the room. The adjacent pantry (L86 in Period Ib; divided into L86, L87, L89 in Period II) containing a store of over 1000 dishes indicates that L77 was also used as a communal dining room (see Figs. 29, 30). The walls and floor of L77 were plastered. During Period Ib, its floor sloped gently down from the western end to a doorway in the southeast wall, and from there rose slightly to the eastern end of the room. A water channel that opened through the doorway in the northwest wall (from L54) made it possible to wash the floor, with the water draining through the doorway in the southeast wall (to L98).

The rooms in the western sector (secondary building), which centered around the Iron Age cistern, included storerooms, industrial installations, and workshops. An open-air courtyard to the west of the round cistern (L111) gave access on the north and west to two rooms (L120 and L121) that were subdivided by thin partition walls and were apparently used for storage (see Fig. 32). L111 had a doorway opening south to L103, one in its north wall (leading into L120), and one in its west wall (leading into L121). The doorway in the west wall was flanked by two more doorways, in which cupboards were installed — the southern one facing into L121 and the northern one facing into L111. L123, a room at the northwest end of L120, and the exterior (west) wall of L121 were reinforced with stone revetment (buttressing) because of their position at the edge of the ravine. A hoard of silver Tyrian tetradrachmas was discovered buried beneath the floor of L120. L115 and L116 (constructed in Period Ia), which adjoined the channel feeding the round cistern, had a plastered floor and seems to have been used for some industry requiring water. L125 was also used as a workshop, and L126 was a storeroom. The functions of L100 (an open-air space adjoining the water channel to the south of the round cistern), L101 (opening to the north towards the round cistern), L102, and L104 during this phase are unknown (see Fig. 26). However, a large stone mortar found in association with the Period Ib floor in L105 suggests that some of these rooms were used for food preparation, like in Period II (perhaps only in the post–31 B.C.E. phase of Period Ib; see below). De Vaux identified a long, narrow lean-to overlooking the ravine at the southwest edge of the site (L97) as a stable for pack animals.

The hydraulic system was greatly expanded in Period Ib. De Vaux described this elaborate water system as the most striking feature of Qumran. It remained in use with some modifications until the destruction of the sectarian settlement at the end of Period II. The water was brought by an aqueduct from Wadi Qumran, which flows into the Dead Sea at the foot of the southern end of the marl terrace on which the settlement sits. Wadi Qumran is a relatively small, dry river bed, with a waterfall just a few hundred yards behind and to the southwest of the site. The inhabitants dammed the pool at the foot of this waterfall. On rare occasions when flash floods filled the riverbed, the water would have risen behind the dam. From there it flowed into a channel (aqueduct) along the north bank of the wadi for a distance of some 750 yds. to the site. For much of its length, the channel is cut into limestone or marl. Its sides and bottom were coated with thick layers of plaster and it was covered with stone slabs. At one point the channel is cut as a square tunnel (about 3 ft. high and 2 ft. wide) through a rocky cliff (see Fig. 38). The channel is still visible for most of its length and can be followed by modern visitors to the waterfall by crawling on hands and knees through the tunnel along the way. Although visitors are understandably impressed by this feat of engineering, much grander hydraulic systems which were constructed using similar principles can be seen in the contemporary Hasmonean and Herodian desert palaces (such as Masada and Hyrcania).

Branches of the Qumran aqueduct wound through the settlement and supplied all of the pools, which could have been filled by a single flash flood. Decantation basins placed in front of each pool or group of pools served as settling tanks, catching the silt carried by the flood waters before it entered the pools. The aqueduct entered the settlement at its northwest corner, where there was a sluice-gate to break the rapid flow of the flood waters (L137). From here the water spread out into a broad, shallow decantation basin (L132, L137) adjoined by a small stepped pool (L138) (see Fig. 23). The pool was accessed by an open doorway near the point where the aqueduct entered the decantation basin, and probably also by means of a wooden bridge from the open courtyard to the east (L135). From the decantation basin the water flowed south through a channel, filling in succession the round Iron Age cistern (L110) and the two rectangular stepped pools nearby (L117 and L118, which were constructed in Period Ia) (see Fig. 31). Because the ground level had risen, the walls of the round cistern were raised and a decantation basin was installed to serve L117 and L118 (L119 *bis;* de Vaux sometimes used *bis* to indicate a subdivision of a locus). The decantation basin would have been covered with wooden planks, creating a bridge for foot traffic. Some of the overflow from these pools was carried off by a drainage channel that ran to the north and under the walls of L125, L127, L129, L133, L134, L140, and L141 (de Vaux therefore assigned all of these loci to Period Ia, except for L134, which is not mentioned anywhere in association with Period Ia).

From the area of the round cistern, the main channel turned southeast and opened into another decantation basin (L83). The water flowed out from the west side of this basin into a large rectangular pool (L85, L91) and from the east side of the basin into the continuation of the channel. The channel then filled a large, stepped pool (L56, L58) between the main building and the dining hall/assembly room (L77) and continued along the northern side of this pool, crossing decantation basin L67 (two more small, narrow pools [L55, L57] lay along the southern side of L56, L58). When it reached the eastern end of this pool (L56, L58), the channel branched off in two directions. One branch supplied the stepped pools to the northeast (L49, L50; L48 designates the steps of pool L49). Another branch continued southward, through a breach in the southeast corner of the main building (an Iron Age wall) and into a small stepped pool (L68). From here the channel flowed through a basin serving the potters' workshop (L75; see above) into a final decantation basin (L69), before entering a large stepped pool at the southeast corner of the site (L71). The overflow was carried by gutters southwards onto the esplanade from the two large pools at the southeast and southwest corners of the settlement (L71 and L91).

As an aside, I note that in *Revue Biblique* 61 (1954): 211, de Vaux stated that L71 was constructed in Period II, after the earthquake of 31 B.C.E., when the channel that had filled L48-L49 was diverted to fill L71. But he did not mention this anywhere else, and L71 appears in the plans of Periods Ib and II in Humbert and Chambon's volume. I suspect that L71 was constructed after the earthquake, that is, in the post–31 B.C.E. phase of Period Ib (a phase that de Vaux did not recognize; see below).

The sectarian settlement is characterized by the absence of private dwellings. Instead, many of the rooms appear to have been used as workshops (such as the potters' workshop) or for communal purposes (such as the dining room/assembly hall). Exactly where the community lived is debated. Some of the second-story rooms might have been used as sleeping quarters, but many of the inhabitants apparently occupied huts or tents around the site, as well as some of the caves (see below). In the open spaces between and around the buildings, sheep, goat, and cow bones were found carefully deposited under potsherds or inside pots (see Chapter 6).

According to de Vaux, the end of Period Ib was marked by an earthquake and a fire. The evidence for earthquake destruction was found throughout the settlement but is perhaps clearest in the case of one of the pools (L48-L49), where the steps and floor had split and the eastern half had dropped about 50 cm. (see Fig. 39). This crack continues through the small pool just to the north and can be traced for some distance through L40 to the north and L72 to the south. In the pantry, the wooden shelves with the stacks of dishes (L86) collapsed onto the floor (see Fig. 30). Earthquake damage was also evident in the tower, where the lintel and ceiling of one of the rooms at the ground level (L10A) had collapsed. The northwest corner of the secondary building was damaged, as indicated by another earthquake crack running diagonally from southwest to northeast through L111, L115, L118, and L126. The western edge of the large decantation basin (L132) slid into the ravine below. This evidence indicates that the site was occupied when the earthquake occurred. Presumably any human or animal victims were removed and buried when the settlement was cleared and reoccupied after the earthquake. De Vaux noted that three of the tombs he excavated in the cemetery contained secondary burials of four individuals, who he speculated were earthquake victims.

The testimony of Flavius Josephus (*War* 1.370-80; *Ant.* 15.121-47) enabled de Vaux to date the earthquake to 31 B.C.E. In addition to the earthquake damage, a layer of ash that had blown across the site when the wood and reed roofs burned indicates there had been a fire. De Vaux concluded that the earthquake and fire were simultaneous, because it was the simplest solution, but admitted that there was no evidence to confirm this. Fires often accompanied earthquakes in antiquity, because the tremors overturned lighted oil lamps. He used the numismatic evidence to support his interpretation: only 10 identifiable coins of Herod were found, all of which came from mixed contexts of Period II, where they were associated with later coins. De Vaux noted that the Herodian coins were not dated, and cited a then-recent study assigning such coins to the period after 30 B.C.E. More recently, it has been suggested that Herod's undated bronze coins were minted after 37 B.C.E.

## Period II (see Fig. 8)

According to de Vaux, the buildings damaged by the earthquake and fire were not repaired immediately. Because the water system ceased to be maintained, the site was flooded and silt accumulated to a depth of 75 cm. This silt overflowed the large decantation basin at the northwest corner of the site (L132) and spread into L130 up to the northern wall of the secondary building, growing progressively thinner towards the east. The sediment overlay the layer of ash from the fire, indicating that the period of abandonment was subsequent to the fire (and leading de Vaux to suppose that the two events — earthquake and fire — were related).

Following this period of abandonment, the site was cleared and reoccupied by the same community that had left it, as indicated by the fact that the general plan remained the same and many of the buildings seem to have been used for the same purposes as before. Most of the rooms were cleared out and debris was dumped over the slopes of a ravine to the north of the site (where it was discovered in Trench A). Debris was also thrown outside the walls of the buildings, in heaps against the north and west walls of the secondary building (north of L120 and in L124), and in L130 in the main building. This process cleared out the objects that would have helped us to identify the function of these rooms during Period Ib. Some of the damaged structures in the settlement were strengthened, while others were left filled with collapse and abandoned. The store of more than 1000 dishes in the pantry (L86), which had fallen and broken in the earthquake, was left lying on the floor at the back of the room. This area (now designated L89) was sealed off by a low stone wall that incorporated the square pillar (pier) in the center of the room. A narrow area in front of it was enclosed by poor partition walls (L87) and the floor adjacent to the doorway leading into L77 was plastered (L86). The eastern and southern walls of L89 were buttressed on the exterior by a stone revetment. The northwest corner of the secondary building, which had begun to slide into the ravine, was buttressed, as were the inner faces of the east walls of the rooms at the northeast corner of the site (L6, L47).

The tower on the northern side of the site was reinforced by the addition of a sloping stone rampart (or "glacis") around the outside of its walls. On the northern and western sides (facing outside the settlement and along the entrance passage), the rampart is 4 m. high, but it is lower and thinner on the other two sides (facing in towards the settlement). The rampart blocked two narrow windows or light slits at the ground-floor level of the tower's north side (in L10A), and obstructed the open passages around the tower in L12, L17, and L18. Because of this, the doorway between L17 and L25 (the central courtyard of the main building) was narrowed. The ground-story room inside the tower with the collapsed ceiling (L10A) was abandoned, and the door connecting it with the next room (L28) was blocked. As an aside, I note that in Humbert and Chambon's volume, L28 is illustrated only in Periods Ia and Ib; it is replaced in Period II by L11. However, a coin of the Procurators under Nero is listed from L28, which means that this locus must have existed in Period II. Perhaps L28 represents the ground-floor level in Period II, and L11 is the second-story level. In Period Ib, the locus might be L28-L29 (instead of L28).

De Vaux relied on the numismatic evidence to date the beginning of Period II. Since only 10 identifiable coins of Herod the Great were found, all from mixed contexts, he assigned them to Period II. He reasoned that these coins could have continued in circulation after Herod's death. De Vaux therefore dated the beginning of Period II to the time of Herod's son and successor, Herod Archelaus, who ruled Judea, Idumaea, and Samaria from 4 B.C.E. to 6 C.E. He based this on several considerations. First, 16 coins of Archelaus were recovered, after which point the numismatic sequence of Period II continues without interruption to the First Jewish Revolt. Second, one of Archelaus's coins was found among the debris from the buildings. This debris was dumped by the returning inhabitants when they cleared and reoccupied the site at the beginning of Period II. The fact that the other coins in this deposit all date to Period Ib and do not include any coins of Herod the Great suggests that the reoccupation of the site was undertaken during Archelaus's reign. Finally, there is the evidence provided by a hoard of 561 silver coins from L120 (a room on the north side of the secondary building), which had been placed in three pots and buried under the floor. Most of these are Tyrian tetradrachmas (sheqels) from the period after 126 B.C.E., with the most recent coin in the hoard dating to 9/8 B.C.E. (and several earlier pieces countermarked in the same year). As de Vaux noted, this provides a *terminus post quem* of 9/8 B.C.E. for the burial of the hoard. Because in de Vaux's time there was thought to be a lacuna in the issues of Tyrian tetradrachmas from 9/8 B.C.E. to 1 B.C.E./1 C.E. (a gap which has since been filled), he dated the beginning of Period II to some time between 4 and 1 B.C.E. — that is, to early in the reign of Herod Archelaus. In other words, the presence of coins of Herod Archelaus provided de Vaux with a *terminus post quem* of 4 B.C.E., while the absence of Tyrian tetradrachmas of post–1 B.C.E. date in the hoard suggested a *terminus ante quem* for the beginning of Period II.

Aside from the strengthening or abandonment of the structures mentioned above, de Vaux noted that some minor modifications and changes were made to the rooms and the water system when the site was reoccupied in Period II. L1 in the southwest corner of the main building was divided into two rooms (L1, L2). A cylindrical jar covered by a limestone slab was sunk up to its rim in the floor in the northwest corner of L2. Two bronze coins lay nearby and two more were found in the earth that covered it. Three additional bronze coins were discovered on the floor of the room. Three are coins of Mattathias Antigonus (the identifications of two are tentative), and the others are coins of Herod Agrippa I or the Procurators. A similar discovery was made in L13, the corridor with the staircase through which L4 was entered. A niche in the north wall contained an oven with a chimney that was apparently constructed at the end of Period II. It covered a group of three cylindrical jars, one of which had a broken base when it was installed. The oven and chimney postdated the installation of the jars and had no connection to them. Four bronze coins were found in the fill of the first jar, and there were three more coins inside the third jar. All of them are of Agrippa I and the Procurators.

A storeroom divided into three compartments was constructed in the northeast corner of the main building (L46), opening onto an enclosed courtyard (L27) that had a doorway by the northeast corner of the tower (L19). A new room was established in the central courtyard of the main building (L33). The large room on the north side of this courtyard (L38, L41) was used as a kitchen, as indicated by the ovens and hearths found in it. Two small jars which had their tops cut off were embedded up to their shoulders in the floor of L23, an open space on the southwest side of the central courtyard. A cooking pot containing animal bones was found in the southeast corner of this locus. The small basins on the south side of the courtyard (L34) were abandoned and covered over, and a staircase (L35) leading to a second-story level above L77 was installed in the southeast corner of the courtyard (see Fig. 15 and Chapter 6). The "washing place" to the east (L52) apparently continued to function, using water drawn from a channel nearby. However, the pools that had been split by the earthquake (L48, L49, L50) and the toilet to the north (L51) went out of use. This area seems to have become an open-air courtyard in Period II. Further to the southeast, the potters' workshop continued in use (L64, L84) with no significant modifications.

In the secondary building, the eastern wall of open-air courtyard L111 was doubled in thickness and it was now roofed over (see Fig. 32). A semicircular partition in the southwest corner of the room was filled with ash. The door in the south wall (leading to L103) and the two cupboards in its west wall were blocked. A couple of jars were embedded in the floor. The room to the north of L111 was divided by walls into two (L120 and L122-L123). A staircase installed in L113 (five stone steps of which were preserved) led to a dining room above these loci (see Fig. 31 and Chapter 6; in my opinion, the changes noted here to L111 and L113 occurred after the earthquake of 31 B.C.E.). Workshops were installed in many of the rooms in this sector in Period II. Two rooms (L105, L107) were added to the east side of the main building, in the middle of the passage that divided the site. One room contained a large baking oven (L105), inside which were fragments belonging to about 15 restorable pottery vessels (mostly plates and bowls) and a bronze bowl. A smaller oven was located to the south of the large one. Another oven was installed in the northeast corner of L109, next to the round Iron Age cistern. Silos with earthen walls were installed in L115 and L116.

A little to the north, a large furnace associated with a plastered platform was uncovered in L125. The presence of a drainage channel in the platform suggests that water was utilized for the industry in this room. A room to the south of the round Iron Age cistern contained a large mud-brick furnace that had been exposed to intense heat, with a smaller furnace next to it (L101) (see Fig. 26). A wooden cylinder covered with plaster of unknown use was set up on the pavement nearby. A mill for grinding grain was discovered a little farther to the south (L100). It contained a circular platform with a trough carved into its upper surface, on top of a stone pavement. The millstones that had been set on the platform were found nearby (L102, L104), where they were dumped during Period III.

After the earthquake, the roof of the dining room/assembly hall (L77) had to be rebuilt. Three square pillar (pier) bases were erected in a row on top of the Period Ib floor at the eastern end of the room, ending with a pilaster (square pillar) base abutting the east wall. The bases were made of mud brick covered with plaster. Wooden posts placed on these bases supported the ceiling beams. The door opening onto the southern esplanade was blocked and the water channel leading through the north doorway of the room was diverted. Because of this and because the floor was now leveled (with a step at its eastern end), the room could no longer be washed in the same way as before. The dining room was now moved to the second-story level of L77 (see Chapter 6).

The bay window on the north side of L30 (the "scriptorium") was blocked in Period II. A thick burnt mat was spread over the 2 m. of floor at the southern end of the room at the ground-floor level. The room was filled with the debris of the collapsed second-story level, which yielded the remains of a long, narrow, mud-brick table covered with plaster (about 16 ft. long and 16 in. wide and 20 in. high, narrowing at the base to a width of 7 in.). Fragments belonging to two smaller tables were also recovered. A low mud-brick bench covered with plaster was attached to the eastern wall of the room (see Fig. 13). The debris from this room also included the remains of a plastered platform or low table with a raised border and two cup-shaped depressions (which was placed against the north wall of the room) and two inkwells (one of pottery and the other of bronze). Another ceramic inkwell was found in an adjacent locus (L31) (see Fig. 14). One of the inkwells from L30 still contained the remains of dried ink.

De Vaux's interpretation of this room as a "scriptorium" (writing room) has been challenged because there is no evidence that scribes at this time wrote at a table while seated on a bench (instead they squatted or sat with the material on their laps). One alternative proposal (favored especially by advocates of the villa theory) is that this room was a triclinium (dining room) in which the diners reclined on the benches, as was customary in the Greco-Roman world (see Fig. 36). However, since the benches are only 40 cm. wide, they are too narrow for reclining. In addition, inkwells are not common finds on archaeological excavations in Israel. For example, Nahman Avigad mentioned finding only two inkwells (both ceramic) in the Herodian-period houses he excavated in Jerusalem's Jewish Quarter. The discovery of three inkwells at Qumran suggests that some sort of writing activity took place in this room (L30), even if we do not understand exactly how the furniture was used.

The water system was also modified during Period II. The large decantation basin at the northwest corner of the site (L132) had silted up and was now used for depositing animal bones (see Chapter 6). It was replaced by a small basin by the sluice-gate (L137). A new channel was constructed from this basin along the eastern wall of the old basin (L132). The large pool to the south of the main building was divided into two (L56, L58).

A cemetery containing about 1100 graves is located 50 m. to the east of the site (see Figs. 46, 47). The tombs, which are arranged in neat rows along the top of the plateau, are marked by heaps of stones on the surface. All but one are oriented from north to south. Other tombs located at the edges of the cemetery or on low hills to the north, east, and south do not have the same regular alignment and orientation. The bodies were placed in a loculus or niche at the bottom of a rectangular cavity dug into the marl of the plateau (see Fig. 48). According to de Vaux, of the 43 graves he excavated, those in the main sector all contained adult male burials, whereas those in the extensions included women and children (see Chapter 8).

The Period II settlement suffered a violent destruction by fire, which de Vaux attributed to the Roman army at the time of the First Jewish Revolt. Except for the tower, which was protected by the rampart, the damage was evident throughout the settlement. The area to the south of the tower (L12, L13, L17) and the rooms in the main and secondary buildings were filled with the collapse of the walls and roofs to a depth of 1.10 to 1.50 m. Iron arrowheads found in the debris indicate that fighting occurred and that this destruction was caused by hostile human agents. These arrowheads, which have three barbed wingtips (to stick in the flesh) and a long tang that was inserted into a wooden shaft, represent the characteristic Roman type of arrowhead in the 1st century C.E.

De Vaux used the numismatic evidence and Josephus's testimony to pinpoint the date of the destruction to 68 C.E. Ninety-four coins of the First Revolt (all of bronze) were associated with Period II. Most of them come from two groups: a hoard of 39 coins that had been deposited in a cloth bag in

L103, and 33 coins that were found in a decantation basin (L83, mixed with other coins and debris that was dumped at the beginning of Period III). The latest coins date to Year Three of the revolt, 68/69 C.E. Since Josephus mentions that Vespasian occupied Jericho in June 68 C.E., de Vaux concluded that the Romans must have destroyed Qumran at that time. This marks the end of the sectarian settlement at Qumran.

## Period III

Following the destruction in 68 C.E., Qumran seems to have been occupied by a small garrison of Roman soldiers who were probably members of the Tenth Legion. They inhabited only part of the main building, including the ground-story rooms of the tower which were still accessible. The soldiers dumped the debris that they cleared from these rooms to the north of the main building and in the cisterns to the south. The debris formed heaps in the northwest corner and against the east face of pool L58, covered the bottom of L56, filled the decantation basin L83, and blocked the steps (L85) leading into pool L91. The debris dumped in L83 included the 33 coins of the First Revolt mentioned above. The soldiers leveled the collapse that filled the rooms to the south of the tower and occupied L4, L13, and L30 (each of which was subdivided into smaller rooms). A large circular oven was installed in L14, a new locus above L13. The wall enclosing the northern side of the site (to the west of the tower) was doubled in width. A small room (L26) was constructed above the ashy destruction layer in courtyard L27 (inside the enclosure wall to the west of the tower). A mud-brick wall divided L36 on the south side of the central court-yard of the main building into two small rooms (L31, L22) which were entered from the outside (south). A jar embedded in the west wall of L22 contained poultry bones. A large wall erected in the middle of the central courtyard marked the eastern limit of the settlement in this phase. A poorly constructed wall with a large doorway (L43) marked the southern boundary of the settlement. In the areas to the south and east of the main building, the old potters' workshop (L84) was used to store lime, and two rooms were built above the stepped pool in L68 and in L72. An oven was installed against the north wall of L77.

The soldiers renovated a small part of the water system, using only one large cistern to the southeast which had suffered little damage (L71). This was filled by a new, poorly constructed channel that was connected with the old channel in the area of L100 (to the south of the round Iron Age cistern). This new channel was built along the south wall of L77 and over pool L91. To support the crossing of the channel, pool L91 was filled in with debris from the building and with earth from pits dug in the rooms nearby (L102, L104). The earth fill also came from a defensive ditch that was dug from the entrance to L91 towards the north, parallel with the western side of the main building. The settlement did not extend beyond this ditch, except for using the mill in L100. The numismatic evidence and historical considerations led de Vaux to suggest that this phase came to an end around the same time as Masada fell, in 73 or 74 C.E.

There also seems to have been some activity or small-scale occupation at Qumran at the time of the Second Jewish Revolt (Bar Kokhba Revolt; 132-135 C.E.). The main evidence consists of 10 coins found in a bowl buried under the floor of a room in the ground story of the tower (L29). A few late Roman and Byzantine coins recovered in the excavations were dropped by visitors or passers-by during the course of the centuries that followed. As an aside, I wonder whether a few potsherds described by de Vaux as "Islamic" instead represent Nabatean cream ware (a type of light-colored pottery that is frequently confused with a similar-looking early Islamic ware).

## A Revised Chronology for Qumran

As we have seen, de Vaux distinguished three main periods of occupation in the sectarian settlement at Qumran, which he dated as follows: Period Ia, from ca. 130 to 100 B.C.E.; Period Ib, from ca. 100 B.C.E. to 31 B.C.E.; and Period II, from ca. 4-1 B.C.E. to 68 C.E. I have proposed a different chronology from de Vaux's for Periods Ia and Ib.

### Period Ia

In my opinion, there is no clear or convincing evidence for de Vaux's Period Ia. De Vaux found no coins associated with Period Ia, and there were only a few potsherds which he could not distinguish in type from those of Period Ib. It is difficult to identify evidence for Period Ia because nearly all of the pottery that de Vaux published (and perhaps saved?) consists of whole (intact or restored) vessels, as opposed to potsherds. These whole vessels come from the destruction levels that mark the end of each occupation phase, when they were smashed and left lying on the floors and buried in the collapse. This means that this pottery dates to the end of each occupation phase. For this reason, it is difficult to determine exactly when the first sectarian occupation phase (de Vaux's Period Ia) began. And because Period Ia (assuming it existed) did not end in a destruction but was marked instead by the expansion of the settlement, there are no assemblages of whole vessels associated with it. However, the fact that none of the pottery that de Vaux published from Qumran has to antedate the 1st century B.C.E. (only one storage jar he illustrated could be dated earlier) suggests to me that most of the architectural remains attributed to Period Ia belong to Period Ib (see below).

On the other hand, in a few places de Vaux distinguished architectural remains which he believed postdated the Iron Age but were covered by Period Ib structures. For example, two potters' kilns (L66) in the southeastern part of the settlement were covered by a stepped pool that was destroyed by the earthquake of 31 B.C.E. (L48-L49). The south wall of L34-L36, on the south side of the central courtyard in the main building, was discovered below the walls of L32 and L30. Also during this phase, a channel that supplied the round Israelite cistern (L110) with surface runoff was constructed under L115 and L116. De Vaux attributed these two rooms (L115 and L116) to Period Ia because their west wall was built up against the Iron Age wall of L114. Two more rectangular stepped pools (L117-L118) were constructed in this area during this phase. De Vaux also attributed to Period Ia two rooms to the north of pool L118 (L129, L133), as well as two rooms or enclosures further to the north (L140-L141), the walls of which were cut by a drainage channel of Period Ib.

As an aside, I note that in all of de Vaux's publications (the preliminary reports in the *Revue Biblique* and his book, *Archaeology and the Dead Sea Scrolls*), the establishment of the tower is associated with Period Ib. However, in Humbert and Chambon's volume, the tower appears on the plans of Period Ia. We must await the publication of future volumes in this series to understand why Humbert and Chambon assigned the initial construction of the tower to Period Ia.

As we shall see, de Vaux's Period Ib should be subdivided into a pre-31 and a post-31 B.C.E. phase. Most if not all of the architectural remains he attributed to Period Ia might belong to the pre-31 B.C.E. phase of Period Ib, while his Period Ib certainly includes both pre-31 B.C.E. and post-31 B.C.E. remains. Perhaps some of the Period Ia remains should be assigned to the Iron Age, such as the kilns in L66, which represent a type of circular kiln with a central pillar that is attested in Palestine from the Bronze Age on. In the notes published by Humbert and Chambon, de Vaux tentatively assigned these kilns to the Iron Age. Only the final publication of all of the material from Qumran, including the pottery, coins, and stratigraphy, will make it possible to reconstruct and date these phases accurately.

If de Vaux's Period Ia exists, the currently available evidence suggests that it should be dated to the early 1st century B.C.E. instead of to ca. 130-100 B.C.E. De Vaux placed the beginning of Period Ib no later than the reign of Alexander Jannaeus because he found 143 coins of that king. However, these only provide a *terminus post quem* for the beginning of the settlement, and, in fact, the coins of Alexander Jannaeus are known to have remained in circulation at least until the time of Herod the Great. This and the apparent absence of 2nd-century pottery types suggest that the sectarian settlement was established later than de Vaux thought. Based on the abundant finds and significant architecture associated with the first phase of Period Ib, which was destroyed in the earthquake of 31 B.C.E. (see below), it is reasonable to date the initial establishment of the sectarian settlement to the first half of the 1st century B.C.E. (that is, some time between 100-50 B.C.E.).

I suspect that de Vaux pushed the foundation date of the settlement somewhat earlier than the evidence warrants, not only because of the coins, but because the Damascus Document suggests that the sect's beginnings date to 390 years after the Babylonian destruction of Jerusalem and the First Jewish Temple (Solomon's temple) in 586 B.C.E.:

> For when they were unfaithful and forsook Him, He hid His face from Israel and His sanctuary and delivered them up to the sword. But remembering the Covenant of the forefathers, He left a remnant to Israel and did not deliver it up to be destroyed. And in the age of wrath, three hundred and ninety years after He had given them into the hand of King Nebuchadnezzar of Babylon, He visited them, and He caused a plant root to spring from Israel and Aaron to inherit His Land and to prosper on the good things of His earth. And they perceived their iniquity and recognized that they were guilty men, yet for twenty years they were like blind men groping for the way. And God observed their deeds, that they sought Him with a whole heart, and He raised for them a Teacher of Righteousness to guide them in the way of His heart. (CD 1.3-11)

If the 20 years that passed before the appearance of the Teacher of Righteousness are added to the figure of 390 years, we arrive at a date ca. 175 B.C.E. If we add another 40 years for the period between the death of the Teacher and the dawn of the messianic era, we reach a total of 450 years after 586 B.C.E. — in other words, ca. 135 B.C.E. — which coincides with de Vaux's date for the establishment of the sectarian settlement at Qumran. Because many of the numbers mentioned in the above passage are symbolic or theological (for example, the number 40 clearly has biblical allusions, and 20 is half of 40), this reckoning cannot be taken too literally. Nevertheless, this chronology corresponds roughly with the period when this sect seems to have formed — that is, around the mid-2nd century B.C.E. On the other hand, there is at present no good evidence for dating the establishment of the sectarian settlement at Qumran earlier than ca. 100 B.C.E.

Humbert has suggested that during Period Ia, Qumran was a nonsectarian, agricultural settlement *(villa rustica)* and that this occupation phase continued until the site was destroyed in 57 B.C.E. (by the Roman general/governor Gabinius) or in 31 B.C.E. (not by the earthquake, but during Herod's establishment of control over Jericho and the Dead Sea region). Could Qumran originally have been an agricultural settlement (or a fortress or other kind of nonsectarian settlement) that was later occupied by sectarians? I do not believe that the archaeological evidence supports such a possibility. This is because the presence of miqva'ot (ritual baths), the pantry containing more than 1000 dishes (L86), and possible evidence for animal bone deposits outside the buildings in pre-31 B.C.E. contexts indicate that the settlement was sectarian from the beginning (see Chapter 5).

## Period Ib

According to de Vaux, Qumran lay in ruins and was unoccupied for about 30 years after the earthquake of 31 B.C.E. This period of abandonment ended when the site was reoccupied between 4 and 1 B.C.E. by the same community that had inhabited it 30 years earlier. Most scholars have accepted de Vaux's chronology, though many have grappled with the problems raised by the 30-year gap in occupation. For example, it does not make sense that an earthquake would have caused the community to abandon the site for 30 years. One might expect political turmoil or unstable social conditions to cause an abandonment, but not an earthquake. In fact, scholars have wondered why the community at Qumran (assuming they were Essenes) would have felt it necessary to abandon the site, since Josephus indicates that Herod the Great held the Essenes in high regard. Also, how is it that after such a long period the site was reoccupied by the same population with the buildings being put to the same use? And where did the community go for 30 years?

Because of these problems, some scholars have suggested that the earthquake and fire were not simultaneous. They have proposed that the settlement was burned during the turbulent period of the Parthian invasion and the reign of Mattathias Antigonus (the last Hasmonean king; 40-37 B.C.E.) and then abandoned. The site would have been ruined and empty when the earthquake struck in 31 B.C.E. De Vaux argued convincingly against this suggestion, which again fails to account for the whereabouts of this community during such a long gap in occupation.

I believe that a reconsideration of the archaeological evidence and especially the coins provides a solution to these problems. As I mentioned above, only 10 identifiable coins of Herod the Great were found at Qumran, all undated bronze issues from mixed levels. Because of their small number and mixed contexts, de Vaux associated these coins with the Period II settlement, claiming that they remained in circulation after Herod's death. In fact, Herod seems to have minted relatively few coins, and as we have seen, the coins of Alexander Jannaeus remained in circulation through Herod's reign. In addition, other coins dating to Herod's time were found at Qumran. They are among the silver coins found in the hoard from L120, most of which are Tyrian tetradrachmas dating from 126 to 9/8 B.C.E. More important, however, is the context of this hoard, which de Vaux described as follows: "These three pots [containing the coins] were buried *beneath* the level of Period II and *above* that of Period Ib" (my emphasis). De Vaux associated the hoard with the reoccupation of the site at the beginning of Period II, which means that the inhabitants buried the coins when they reoccupied the site between 4-1 B.C.E. However, de Vaux's description of the context makes it clear that the hoard could equally be associated with Period Ib, and common sense suggests this is the case. Hoards are often buried in times of trouble and can remain buried if the owner fails to return and retrieve the valuables. It is reasonable to assume that the hoard at Qumran was buried because of some impending danger or threat, and remained buried because the site was subsequently abandoned for some time. For whatever reason, the hoard was never retrieved even after the site was reoccupied.

The assignment of the hoard to Period Ib suggests a different chronological sequence for the settlement at Qumran. The site was not abandoned after the earthquake of 31 B.C.E. The inhabitants immediately repaired or strengthened many of the damaged buildings but did not bother to clear those beyond repair. So, for example, the badly damaged pools in L48-L50 were abandoned, and the pottery store in the pantry (L86) was left buried beneath the collapse. The settlement of Period Ib then continued without apparent interruption until 9/8 B.C.E. or some time thereafter. The coin hoard provides a *terminus post quem* of 9/8 B.C.E. for the abandonment of the site. The fact that the hoard was buried, combined with the presence of a layer of ash, suggests that the fire which destroyed the settlement should be attributed to human agents instead of to natural causes. In other words, in 9/8 B.C.E. or some time thereafter, Qumran suffered a deliberate, violent destruction. Such a destruction better accounts for the abandonment of the site by the inhabitants. However, it was not the prolonged abandonment postulated by de Vaux. Instead, the site was abandoned in 9/8 B.C.E. or some time thereafter and reoccupied early in the reign of Herod Archelaus in 4 B.C.E. or shortly afterwards. On the basis of the presently available evidence, it is impossible to narrow the range any further. The fact that the water system fell into disrepair and silt covered the site (carried by the flash flood waters through the aqueduct) indicates that the abandonment lasted for at least one winter season. The site was abandoned for a period of one winter season to several years, within a range from 9/8 B.C.E. to some time early in the reign of Herod Archelaus. Since it is impossible to pinpoint the date, the causes leading to the destruction of the site must remain unknown, though it is tempting to associate them with the revolts and turmoil which erupted in Judea upon the death of Herod the Great in 4 B.C.E.

A short period of abandonment better accounts for the fact that the site was reoccupied and put to the same use as before by the same community. It also solves the problem of accounting for the whereabouts of this community for 30 years. When the inhabitants returned to the site, they cleared away the silt and destruction debris and dumped them in various places outside the settlement. As I mentioned, de Vaux used a coin of Herod Archelaus from one of these dumps as evidence for dating the reoccupation of the site to the beginning of that king's reign, which was in 4 B.C.E. He suggested that this coin was lost during the work of clearance. My revised chronological sequence means that de Vaux's Period Ib should be subdivided into a pre-31 and post-31 B.C.E. phase. De Vaux's description of the hoard's context suggests that its burial should be associated with the post-31 B.C.E. phase of Period Ib, a phase that he did not recognize (the coins were buried "beneath the level of Period II and above that of Period Ib"). This revised sequence also means that some if not all of the remains de Vaux associated with Period Ia might belong to the pre-earthquake phase of Period Ib. The following diagram compares my revised chronology with that of de Vaux:

|  | de Vaux | Magness |
|---|---|---|
| Period Ia | ca. 130-100 B.C.E. | does not exist |
| Period Ib | ca. 100-31 B.C.E. | Pre-earthquake phase: from between 100-50 B.C.E. to 31 B.C.E. Post-earthquake phase: from 31 B.C.E. to 9/8 B.C.E. or some time thereafter (4 B.C.E.?) |
| Period II | 4-1 B.C.E. to 68 C.E. | 4-1 B.C.E. to 68 C.E. |
| Period III | 68 C.E. to 73 or 74 C.E. | same |

A few nicely cut architectural elements that were reused in Period III and II contexts were found in various places around the site: one column drum (a drum is part of the column shaft) in L6 (Period II or III); two column drums and one column base in L14 (Period III); a stone from a pier and a voussoir (a stone belonging to an arch or vault) in L19 (Period III); two column drums, several voussoirs, and a console (the springing stone of an arch) built into the base of the wall between L23 and 33 (in the central courtyard of the main building) (Period III); one column drum in L24 (Period III); a frieze fragment found just south of L34; a cornice block in L42 (Period III); one column drum and two large, nicely cut stone blocks at the bottom of pool L49 (Period II or the post-31 B.C.E. phase of Period Ib?); one column drum in pool L56 (Period III); two column bases in L100; one column drum and a base in L102 (Period III?); and one column drum in L120 (Period III?) (see Fig. 27).

De Vaux suggested that some of these elements originated in a colonnade that stood on a stylobate (a low wall on which columns were placed) between L35 and L49 (see Chapter 6). Whether or not this is the case, all of these elements seem to have originated in structures that were destroyed by the earthquake of 31 B.C.E. (that is, they either originated in Period Ia, if it existed, or more likely, in the pre-31 B.C.E. phase of Period Ib). This is suggested by the following considerations. First, de Vaux attributed the construction of a wall covering the stylobate to the period following the earthquake (his Period II). Second, three of the architectural pieces were found in L49, which went out of use after the earthquake. Because these elements were distributed throughout the site and their original location is unknown, it is impossible to determine whether they belonged to one or more structures. The fact that they include four column bases indicates that at least four columns originally stood in one or more locations around the site.

## Where Did the Inhabitants of Qumran Live?

The question of where the inhabitants of Qumran lived is related to the interpretation of the site. For example, if Qumran was a villa or fort, the inhabitants would have lived inside the settlement. However, even those who accept de Vaux's interpretation of Qumran as a sectarian settlement do not agree on the location of the living quarters. Some scholars, including Humbert and Joseph Patrich, are convinced that the entire sectarian population resided inside the settlement. Because only a few rooms had second-story floors that could have been used as sleeping quarters, the population would have been small, with estimates ranging from 10-15 to 50-70 inhabitants. According to Patrich, if members of the community had lived in tents, huts, or caves outside the site, we should find a network of constructed paths connecting them with the settlement. He has also argued that the caves are not suitable for the purposes of dwelling and that convincing evidence for the remains of huts and tents outside the site has not been found.

Other scholars believe that at least some members of the community lived in tents and huts around the site and in some of the caves. For example, Magen Broshi and Hanan Eshel claim to have discovered the remains of tent encampments outside the settlement. They have noted that the presence of certain types of domestic pottery vessels (cooking pots, cups, plates, and bowls used for dining, storage jars, and oil lamps) inside some of the caves indicates that they served as dwellings, even if this occupation was seasonal or temporary in nature. Additional evidence of habitation comes from Cave 8, in which a *mezuzah* (a manuscript of biblical verses that is affixed to the doorpost of a Jewish home) was found; from Cave 10, which had a reed mat on the floor; and from Cave 17 (located just to the south of Cave 1, and not a scroll cave), which contained five wooden poles (two with forked ends). De Vaux believed that these poles belonged to a tent or hut that had been brought to the cave for safekeeping. Only the manmade caves cut into the marl terrace have yielded evidence for regular habitation. This is because they are much cooler and better ventilated than the natural caves and crevices in the hard limestone cliffs behind the site. Broshi and Eshel have excavated additional habitation caves (without scrolls) cut into the marl terrace to the north of Qumran, which were previously undetected because their soft marl walls and ceilings had collapsed. According to Broshi, the community at Qumran did not exceed 150-200 members. This is based on his estimate that the dining room (L77) could not hold more than 120-150 diners, keeping in mind that only full members were allowed to participate in the communal meals. This number accords better than lower estimates with the presence of over 1000 dining dishes in the pantry (L86).

In my opinion, few if any of the members of the community lived (that is, slept) inside the settlement. The rooms in the settlement seem to have been used mostly if not entirely for communal purposes: communal dining rooms and assembly rooms, kitchens, workshops, and industrial installations. On the other hand, the presence of certain domestic types of pottery indicates to me that some of the caves were inhabited, because no one carries cooking pots, dining dishes, and storage jars to a cave unless they are living there! Other members of the community must have lived in tents and huts around the site. Some of this habitation could have been seasonal — that is, perhaps some of the members lived at Qumran on a temporary basis.

I believe that De Vaux's observation regarding the nature of the settlement at Qumran is still accurate: "Khirbet Qumrân is not a village or a group of houses; it is the establishment of a community. We must be still more precise: this establishment was not designed as a community residence but rather for the carrying on of certain communal activities. The number of rooms which could have served as dwellings is restricted as compared with the sites designed for group activities to be pursued."

## Bibliographical Notes

For reports on de Vaux's excavations, see the bibliographical notes to Chapter 1. The jar with the red dipinto is illustrated in de Vaux's preliminary report in *Revue Biblique* 61 (1954); also see Ze'ev Safrai and Hanan Eshel, "Economic Life," in Schiffman and VanderKam, *Encyclopedia of the Dead Sea Scrolls* 1:231. The red dipinto consists of the name "Yoḥanan Haṭla," apparently the name of one of the members of the community.

For a description of Qumran's water system, see Zwi Ilan and David Amit, "Die Wasserleitung nach Qumran," in *Wasser im Heiligen Land: Biblische Zeugnisse und archaologische Forschungen,* ed. Wiel Dierx and Gunther Garbrecht (Mainz: Philip von Zabern, 2001), 159-64.

For the suggestion that L30 was a dining room (triclinium) instead of a "scriptorium," see Pauline Donceel-Voûte, "'Coenaculum' — La salle a l'étage du *Locus* 30 à Khirbet Qumrân sur la Mer Morte," in *Res Orientales IV (Banquets d'Orient)* (1992): 61-84. Earlier scholars suggested that L30 was a dining room; see de Vaux, *Archaeology and the Dead Sea Scrolls,* 29, n. 1. Ronny Reich has demonstrated that the benches from L30 are too narrow to have served as dining couches; "A Note on the Function of Room 30 (the 'Scriptorium') at Khirbet Qumrân," *Journal of Jewish Studies* 46 (1995): 157-60. For a discussion of the "scriptorium" in L30 see Katharine Greenleaf Pedley, "The Library at Qumran," *Revue de Qumran* 2 (1959-1960): 21-41; Bruce M. Metzger, "The Furniture in the Scriptorium at Qumran," *Revue de Qumran* 1 (1958-59): 509-15. For the inkwells from Qumran and other sites, see Stephen Goranson, "Qumran: A Hub of Scribal Activity?" *Biblical Archaeology Review* 20/5 (1994): 36-39; for the inkwells from the Jewish Quarter see Nahman Avigad, *Discovering Jerusalem* (Nashville: Thomas Nelson, 1983), 127.

For my redating of the end of Period Ib at Qumran, see Jodi Magness, "The Chronology of the Settlement at Qumran in the Herodian Period," *Dead Sea Discoveries* 2 (1995): 58-65 (with bibliography; some additional references are provided here). Ernest-Marie Laperrousaz correctly noted that the archaeological evidence points to a date ca. 100 B.C.E. for the establishment of the sectarian settlement at Qumran; see "Brèves remarques archéologiques concernant la chronologie des occupations esséniennes de Qoumrân," *Revue de Qumran* 12 (1986): 199-212; also see Philip R. Davies, "How Not to Do Archaeology: The Story of Qumran," *Biblical Archaeologist* 51 (1988): 203-7. For the suggestion that Qumran was not abandoned after the earthquake of 31 B.C.E., see David Flusser, "Qumran and the Famine during the Reign of Herod," *Israel Museum Journal* 6 (1987): 7-16. For Laperrousaz's views on the archaeology of Qumran, see *Qoumrân: L'Établissement essénien des bords de la Mer Morte: histoire et archéologie du site* (Paris: A. & J. Picard, 1976). For examples of the passage from CD 1.3-11 quoted here (describing the sect's beginnings) found in Cave 4 at Qumran, see Joseph M. Baumgarten, *Qumran Cave 4 XIII, The Damascus Document*. Discoveries in the Judaean Desert 18 (Oxford: Clarendon, 1996), 35 (4Q266), 120 (4Q268).

For the view that all of the members of the community lived inside the settlement at Qumran, see Joseph Patrich, "Did Extra-Mural Dwelling Quarters Exist at Qumran?" in Schiffman, Tov, and VanderKam, *The Dead Sea Scrolls Fifty Years After Their Discovery*, 720-27. For the results of explorations conducted by Patrich in the caves near Qumran, see Patrich, "Khirbet Qumrân in Light of New Archaeological Explorations in the Qumran Caves," in Wise, Golb, Collins, and Pardee, *Methods of Investigation*, 73-95. In one cave Patrich discovered a juglet that might have contained balsam oil; "A Juglet Containing Balsam Oil (?) From a Cave Near Qumran," *Israel Exploration Journal* 39 (1989): 43-59. Zohar Amar has suggested that a red substance found by Vendyl Jones in a cave near Qumran (and identified by Jones as a component of the incense burned in the Jerusalem temple) represents ancient Hebrew *borit*, a lye that was produced at Qumran and used for cleansing purposes: Amar, "The Ash and the Red Material from Qumran," *Dead Sea Discoveries* 5 (1998): 1-15. For residential caves in the marl terrace to the north of Qumran, see Magen Broshi and Hanan Eshel, "Residential Caves at Qumran," *Dead Sea Discoveries* 6 (1999): 328-48. Broshi and Eshel believe that the community at Qumran lived in tents and huts around the site and in some of the surrounding caves; Broshi and Eshel, "How and Where Did the Qumranites Live?" in *The Provo International Conference on the Dead Sea Scrolls: Technological Innovations, New Texts, and Reformulated Issues*, ed. Donald W. Parry and Eugene Ulrich (Leiden: E. J. Brill, 1999), 266-73. According to Broshi's estimates, the community at Qumran numbered no more than 150-200 members; see Broshi, "The Archaeology of Qumran — A Reconsideration?" in *The Dead Sea Scrolls: Forty Years of Research*, ed. Devorah Dimant and Uriel Rappaport (Leiden: E. J. Brill, 1992), 103-15 (see 113-14). The quote from the end of the chapter is from de Vaux, *Archaeology and the Dead Sea Scrolls*, 10.

# CHAPTER 5

# What Do Pottery and Architecture Tell Us about Qumran?

## The Pottery from Qumran

In this chapter and those that follow, we shall examine various aspects of the archaeology of Qumran and especially the peculiar features of the site: the toilet, a hoard of silver coins, the animal bone deposits, the water pools, and the cemetery. We begin this chapter by considering the pottery from Qumran, the most common and mundane of archaeological finds. The local pottery of Roman Palestine is often overlooked by archaeologists (or, at best, is dealt with as a by-product of the excavations), who prefer to focus their attention on monumental architecture, decorated mosaics, and inscriptions. This is perhaps understandable, given the plain appearance of the locally produced pottery in contrast with the masterpieces produced by the ancient Greek black- and red-figure vase painters. However, a careful study of the pottery from any archaeological site yields valuable information that is not provided by other kinds of remains. This is certainly true of the pottery from Qumran. In the second part of this chapter, we shall compare the architecture and pottery of Qumran with those of contemporary Judean palaces and villas. These comparisons support the interpretation of Qumran as a sectarian settlement.

Although the final report on de Vaux's excavations has not yet appeared, he published examples of most of the ceramic types represented at Qumran. These include cups, bowls, plates, kraters, cooking pots, jars, jugs, juglets, flasks, lids, and oil lamps. The pottery from the caves is identical with that from the site except that it is more limited in repertoire. The types of vessels found at Qumran reflect the activities carried out there. The inhabitants drank out of the cups and ate from the plates and bowls. Kraters (deep bowls) were used for the mixing of wine and for serving food. Cooking pots were used for the preparation of food. Jugs, juglets, and flasks served as containers or servers for water, oil, and other liquids. Jars were used for the storage of goods such as grain, wine, and oil. Oil lamps illuminated the interiors of rooms and caves. The vessels from Qumran are made of smooth, well-levigated clay (that is, clay that was cleaned of pebbles and other large inclusions). They have relatively thin, hard-fired walls that sometimes produce a metallic sound when flicked with a finger. The cooking pots are made of a brittle, thin, brick-red colored clay that is typical of cooking vessels in Roman Palestine. Otherwise, most of the vessels from Qumran are made of a pink, light red, or gray clay, often with a whitish slip covering the exterior (a slip is a thin solution of clay mixed with water that was applied to the vessel before firing). The presence of a potters' workshop at Qumran indicates that at least some of the vessels were manufactured at the site.

The clay from which some of the Qumran vessels were manufactured has been subjected to neutron activation analysis (NAA) with surprising results. Some of the vessels are made of Jerusalem clay, while the others are made of a non-Jerusalem clay that is presumed to be local to Qumran (although there is no chemical evidence that the latter is indeed local to Qumran). Vessels made of the non-Jerusalem (presumably Qumran) clay include a cup and a bowl from the pottery annex (L86) next to the dining room in L77. Vessels made of Jerusalem clay include the ceramic inkwell from L30 (the "scriptorium"), the double-mouthed jar inscribed with a Hebrew name from L34 (the basins in the central courtyard of the main building), and cylindrical jars and lids from the caves.

Although about half of the vessels analyzed were of Jerusalem clay and the other half were of non-Jerusalem clay, the four cylindrical jars and three lids that were tested belong to the former group. In my opinion, the most reasonable explanation for these results is that the clay was brought from Jerusalem and used to manufacture the vessels at Qumran. This makes sense not only because no cylindrical jars have ever been found in Jerusalem, but because the cost of transporting finished vessels overland to Qumran (on pack animals) would have been prohibitively expensive. In contrast, transport on boats has always been less expensive and more efficient. In addition, vessels transported overland could have easily cracked or been broken before reaching their destination. This is especially true of large vessels such as jars. In antiquity, foodstuffs (such as oil, wine, and grain) were usually transported overland in skins and baskets and then emptied into jars for permanent storage at their final destination.

Ceramic vessels transported overland to Qumran would also have been in danger of incurring impurity along the way. Magen Broshi has noted that the presence of a potters' workshop throughout the existence of the sectarian settlement reflects the community's concern with purity. In other words, the inhabitants of Qumran manufactured much of their own pottery to ensure its purity. Similar concerns are expressed in the Mishnah tractate *Ḥagigah* (3:5), which states that the purity of clay vessels manufactured and brought to Jerusalem from areas beyond Modiin cannot be trusted: "From Modiin and inwards [toward Jerusalem, people] are deemed trustworthy in regard to the status of clay utensils. From Modiin and outwards, they are not deemed trustworthy. How so? A potter who sells pots — [if] there came within the border of Modiin [toward Jerusalem] that potter, those pots, and those purchasers — he is deemed trustworthy. [If] he went beyond the limit, he is not deemed trustworthy." Perhaps the Qumran community preferred Jerusalem clay because it was of higher quality. Frederick Zeuner's analyses indicated that sediments washed into the pools at Qumran and the Lisan marls found nearby would have been unsuitable for the manufacture of pottery. Neutron activation analysis has also indicated that the ceramic vessels from Qumran and Ein el-Ghuweir are made of unrelated clays (see Chapter 10).

Although much of the pottery found at Qumran was probably manufactured at the site, many of the vessel shapes resemble those found at contemporary Judean sites such as Herodium and Jerusalem. However, the vessels from Qumran differ in their fabric (clay) and surface treatment. For example, contemporary pottery from Jerusalem tends to be made of a light orange, light brown, or orange brown fabric. This is undoubtedly the result of different clay beds and firing processes than those used at Qumran. In addition, although some of the vessels from Jerusalem are covered with the kind of whitish slip that is common at Qumran, many have a drippy red, brown, or red brown paint or slip that is rare at Qumran.

The ceramic corpus (body of pottery) from Qumran displays a number of peculiarities, both in terms of the types that are present and the types that are absent. A number of types found at contemporary sites in Judea are rare or unattested at Qumran. Most conspicuous by their apparent absence from Qumran are imports. There are no published examples of Western Terra Sigillata, amphoras, or Roman mold-made oil lamps. Western Terra Sigillata is a fine, red-slipped tableware that was produced in Italy and Gaul (ancient France) in the 1st century C.E. *Terra sigillata*, which means "stamped clay" in Latin, takes its name from the potter's stamps sometimes found on the base of the vessel. Amphoras are large jars with pointed bases that were used for transporting wine, oil, grain, and fish sauce by ship around the Mediterranean. Roman mold-made oil lamps of the 1st century have a round body that often bore figured decoration in relief on the discus (the top of the lamp). Because many of the Jewish inhabitants of Judea were offended by the figured images, they preferred to use undecorated, locally-made oil lamps.

Although they are not found in abundance, examples of Western Terra Sigillata, imported amphoras, and Roman mold-made oil lamps are attested at Herod's palaces at Herodian Jericho and Herodium, and in Jerusalem (including the site of Herod's palace in the modern Armenian Quarter, the Herodian-period Jewish villas in the Upper City or Western Hill [the modern Jewish Quarter], and the City of David). Amphoras containing Italian wine and imported fish sauce *(garum)* have even been discovered in Herod's palaces atop Masada.

According to Jewish law, the contents of imported amphoras (usually wine or oil) were considered impure (for purity and impurity in Judaism, see Chapter 7). Donald Ariel has noted that the number of stamped handles belonging to imported wine amphoras found in the City of David drops dramatically after about 150 B.C.E. Since this corresponds with the establishment of Hasmonean rule, Ariel has suggested this phenomenon might be due to the development of purity laws and their adoption among Jerusalem's population. On the other hand, the discovery of a group of Italian wine amphoras in one of the Herodian-period villas in Jerusalem's Jewish Quarter prompted Nahman Avigad (the excavator) to remark that "It would seem that there have always been more and less observant Jews." Amphoras have also been found at the site of Qasr el-Yahud (Khirbet Mazin), a Hasmonean anchorage to the south of Qumran, located at the point where the Kidron Valley empties into the Dead Sea (see map in Fig. 1).

Even more striking than the lack of imports is the apparent absence of Eastern Sigillata A (ESA) from the corpus at Qumran. Eastern Sigillata A is a fine, red-slipped table ware produced at sites in the eastern Mediterranean in the 1st century B.C.E. and 1st century C.E. It is much more common than Western Terra Sigillata at sites in Palestine. Examples are published from Herodian Jericho, Herodium, and Masada. Complete sets of Eastern Sigillata A dishes including plates, bowls, and jugs have been discovered in the Herodian houses in the Jewish Quarter (see Fig. 53). No examples of Eastern Sigillata A are published from Qumran, although Humbert reports that a few fragments were recovered. On the other hand, at least one group of bowls from Qumran appears to have been inspired by Eastern Sigillata A. These bowls are relatively broad and shallow and have strongly carinated (angular) walls. At the point of carination there is a sharp ridge, above which the wall rises vertically to the rim. The base is usually a disc. They are made of the local Qumran pink, light red, or gray ware, sometimes with a whitish slip. At Qumran all of the bowls of this type come from Period II contexts. They are clearly related in form to a type of Eastern Sigillata A that is dated from ca. 50-70 C.E. This means that the inhabitants (or at least the potters) at Qumran were not isolated from contemporary ceramic trends in Palestine and the eastern Mediterranean. However, they apparently preferred to manufacture and use their own versions of these types.

A type of local (Judean) fine ware that appears to be unattested at Qumran is "pseudo-Nabatean" ware (also called "Jerusalem painted bowls"; one example is published from Ein Feshkha, and Joseph Patrich mentions that two were found in Cave [FQ] 37). These are delicate, thin-walled bowls decorated on the interior with red, brown, or black painted floral designs (see Fig. 54). Scientific analyses have indicated that Jerusalem was the center for the production of this ware. Most of these bowls have been found at sites in Judea, including in Jerusalem's Jewish and Armenian Quarters, Herodian Jericho, Herodium, and Masada in contexts dating mainly to the 1st century C.E. Painted decoration is common on other types of 1st–century C.E. vessels from Jerusalem. The red or brown paint was usually applied unevenly with drips running over the rim or base. Sometimes it is found over a whitish slip that covers the entire vessel. The paint occurs on open forms (such as plates, cups, and bowls) and closed forms (such as jugs and juglets). It is also found on a number of vessels from Herodium, but seems to be much less common at Jericho. Drippy red or brown paint is also very rare at Qumran. Only one unguentarium (a small bottle used for perfume, scented oil, or other precious liquids) published by de Vaux has red slip or paint over the rim, and I saw one cookingware jug with splashes of red paint on the shoulder in storage at the Rockefeller Museum. A sherd described as Nabatean (presumably from a painted Nabatean bowl — that is, a kind of bowl with eggshell thin walls and red painted decoration) is mentioned in de Vaux's notes for L126 but it is not illustrated. An unguentarium with painted black lines and a fragment of a painted Nabatean bowl are published from Ein Feshkha.

The recent publication of pottery from contemporary sites along the Dead Sea, including Upper Herodium and Machaerus, but especially Ein ez-Zara and Ein Boqeq, places the Qumran corpus in a different light. Ein ez-Zara (ancient Callirrhoe) is the site of thermal springs on the eastern shore of the Dead Sea (in modern Jordan). A 1st-century C.E. villa uncovered at Ein ez-Zara is clearly inspired by the design of Herod's palaces, and the presence of stone vessels indicates that at least some of the inhabitants were Jewish (for more on this villa, see below). Ein Boqeq is a small oasis on the southwestern shore of the Dead Sea (south of Masada). The excavators identified a 1st–century C.E.

building at this site as an *officina,* due to the large number of industrial installations and workshops it contained. Interestingly, the only fine wares found at Ein
ez-Zara consist of two small fragments of painted Nabatean bowls and two
fragments of Eastern Sigillata. Only two Eastern Sigillata D bowls were found in
association with the 1st–century c.e. occupation at Ein Boqeq. The rest of the
fine pottery recovered consists of Nabatean wares (mostly painted Nabatean
bowls, but including one red-slipped piece). This evidence indicates that, although imports such as amphoras and Eastern Sigillata A are represented at the
palaces of Jericho, Herodium, and Machaerus, they are rare at other sites in the
Dead Sea region. I believe this represents a regional phenomenon: due to the
high cost of overland transport, only residents of the local palaces could afford
to purchase fine dining dishes or amphoras containing expensive wine and
other luxury foodstuffs.

Andrea Berlin has noted that, whereas fine, red-slipped table wares
(Eastern Sigillata A) are found at Jewish sites in Galilee in the 1st century
b.c.e., they disappear there during the 1st century c.e. She credits this to a deliberate rejection of Roman control and influence by the Jews of Galilee, an
expression of solidarity with the traditional, unadorned Jewish lifestyle over
against that of their Latinized Phoenician neighbors (who produced this pottery) and "the wealthy, display-oriented, Jewish aristocracy of Jerusalem." In
contrast, evidence that some wealthy Jews of the northern coastal region
adopted the customs of the Jerusalem aristocracy is provided by an early Roman farmhouse called Horvat ʿAqav at Ramat Hanadiv (near Caesarea). The
presence of a miqveh (ritual bath) at this farmhouse indicates that the occupants were Jewish. The pottery they used includes Eastern Sigillata A, Eastern
Terra Sigillata II (a type of Cypriot Sigillata), and Roman mold-made oil
lamps with a decorated discus (including one with a griffin).

Altough I agree with Berlin's observation, the evidence from the villa at
Ein ez-Zara suggests that, in contrast to the situation in Galilee, the absence
of Eastern Sigillata A from sites in the Dead Sea region is due largely to economic and regional factors (that is, the high cost of overland transport from
coastal ports and from Phoenicia). In the Dead Sea region, Eastern Sigillata A
seems to be restricted almost entirely to palatial sites. In addition, whereas
Eastern Sigillata A is found in Jewish towns in Galilee in 1st-century b.c.e.
contexts but disappears during the 1st century c.e., it appears to be rare or
unattested in Judea before the time of Herod the Great. For example, Rachel
Bar-Nathan has noted that imported pottery including Eastern Sigillata A is
either rare or unattested in the Hasmonean palaces at Jericho, appearing instead during the reign of Herod. In other words, beginning in the time of
Herod the consumption of imported wine and other goods and the acquisi-

tion of fine, red-slipped table ware became markers of status among the ruling elite. These products were used by Herod and his associates and were adopted by the uppermost classes of Jerusalem society, including priestly families. Although the inhabitants of the villa at Ein ez-Zara adopted and imitated this lifestyle (as indicated by the design of the villa and its finely molded stucco decoration), the high cost of overland transport put the acquisition of imported wine and fine, red-slipped pottery beyond their reach. It is possible that the absence of imported pottery (including Eastern Sigillata A) at Qumran reflects a deliberate rejection of these products by the inhabitants. However, even if the community at Qumran had wanted to acquire these products, it is doubtful they could have afforded them.

Oil lamps also provide evidence for regionalism in pottery types. During Period II, the inhabitants of Qumran used a type of wheel-made oil lamp (sometimes called "Herodian oil lamps") that has a circular body and a short, splayed nozzle. These oil lamps are characteristic of Judea in the 1st century c.e. Examples were found in some of the scroll caves. However, another type of oil lamp is found at Qumran and in the caves during the post-31 b.c.e. phase of Period Ib (that is, during Herod's reign). These lamps have a large circular body and a narrow, elongated nozzle (see Figs. 19, 21). In shape they resemble contemporary Hellenistic oil lamps (called "delphiniform lamps") but differ in having a plain, wheel-made body (instead of a decorated mold-made body). They also do not have the gray slip found on the Hellenistic oil lamps. Lamps of the same type as those from Qumran are published from Herodian Jericho and Masada, where they also seem to occur in contexts dating to the time of Herod the Great. These lamps therefore represent a regional type, although so far they have a very limited distribution. A similar lamp was found in the "Herodian Residence" in Jerusalem's Jewish Quarter (a house that was occupied during Herod's reign), though it differs from the Qumran examples in being mold-made and slipped.

## The "Scroll Jars"

There is perhaps no more distinctive object associated with Qumran than the cylindrical jars that reportedly contained the first scrolls discovered in Cave 1 (and which are therefore sometimes called "scroll jars") (see Figs. 19, 21). According to one account of the initial discovery, when the bedouins first entered Cave 1, they discovered a row of these jars covered with bowl-shaped lids. Most of the jars were empty, but one contained three scrolls, two of which were wrapped in linen. Two of the intact jars removed from the cave by the bedouins were purchased by Sukenik for the Hebrew University of Jerusalem. In February and March 1949, Harding and de Vaux conducted excavations in Cave 1. In addition to fragments of scrolls and linen, they recovered sherds representing at least 50 different cylindrical jars and the bowl-shaped lids that covered them. Two years later, Harding and de Vaux conducted the first season of excavations at Qumran. Sunk into the floor of one of the rooms (L2) they found an intact but empty cylindrical jar covered with a limestone slab. On the floor beside it was a coin of the Roman Procurators dated ca. 10 C.E. The excavators noted that the jar was identical with those found in Cave 1, and concluded, "We thus, even in the small area so far excavated, have a direct connection with the Scrolls."

The later seasons of excavations at the site and in the caves yielded many more examples of cylindrical jars. Some of the jars at the site were sunk into the floors and were covered with round stone slabs or plaques, like the one from L2. According to de Vaux, cylindrical jars were found in Period Ib and Period II contexts at Qumran. However, most of the published examples come from Period II contexts. Although cylindrical jars are represented in the post–31 B.C.E. phase of Period Ib (that is, between 31 and ca. 9/8 B.C.E.), no examples are published from contexts that clearly antedate 31 B.C.E. A similar observation has been made by Rachel Bar-Nathan, who wrote an M.A. thesis on the pottery from Ehud Netzer's excavations in the Hasmonean and Herodian palaces at Jericho. Cylindrical jars first appear there in contexts dating to the reign of Herod the Great. The cylindrical jars from Jericho are categorized by Bar-Nathan as her Types 2b and 2c.

The chronology of the cylindrical jars (and their distribution outside Qumran) depends on how the type is defined. In his first report on Cave 1, de Vaux described these jars as follows: "Regarding the jars, the most constant type is a cylindrical vase that is about 60 cm. tall and only about 25 to 28 cm. in diameter. The base, very flattened, is carried on a thin disc and is slightly concave. There are no handles. The shoulder is well marked, sometimes sharply carinated, but it is always narrow, as all of the jars have a very large mouth, with a very low and plain vertical neck" (my translation from the French). Some of the cylindrical jars have four small horizontal ledge handles on the shoulder. These jars were covered with bowl-shaped lids, which de Vaux noted were designed to serve not as bowls but as lids for the cylindrical jars (see Fig. 20).

Not all of the jars described by de Vaux as cylindrical correspond with the above description. One variant differs in having a wider, bag-shaped body, sometimes with an everted (outturned) rim and/or two large, vertical ring handles on the sloping shoulder (see Fig. 22). De Vaux sometimes referred to these as "ovoid jars" or "large jars." Unlike the cylindrical jars, ovoid jars are attested in pre-31 B.C.E. contexts (as indicated by the presence of examples in L10A in the tower and the pantry in L86, both of which were destroyed in the earthquake of 31). In fact, de Vaux noted that ovoid jars are characteristic of Period Ib. This accords with Bar-Nathan's dating of this variant (her Type 2a) at Jericho to the Hasmonean (ca. 100-31 B.C.E.) and Herodian periods.

Cylindrical and ovoid jars are common at Qumran and in the nearby caves, but are rare or unattested at other sites in the region. The largest number of examples outside Qumran published to date comes from Herodian Jericho, though even there they do not seem to be common. Both the ovoid and cylindrical variants are represented at Jericho. Bar-Nathan also includes a small, handleless variant with an oval body (her Type 2d), but notes that it probably represents a different type. At Herodian Jericho, most of these jars (her Types 2a, b, c) come from an industrial area dating to the time of Herod, including a structure with miqva'ot (ritual baths). Four examples (three of Type 2a and one of Type 2b) were embedded in the wall of an adjacent storeroom. Another six examples of Bar-Nathan's Type 2d were found in a storeroom for liquids. Bowl-shaped lids are also attested at Herodian Jericho but are not common. One complete ovoid jar with a bowl-shaped lid was found in the corner of an entrance room to one of the Hasmonean twin palaces at Jericho.

A cylindrical jar was reportedly found in a 2nd-century C.E. tomb at Quailba (ancient Abila) in Jordan, although unfortunately it is not illustrated. Bar-Nathan mentions that examples of her Types 2a, 2b, and 2d were found in "Zealot" contexts at Masada (none is illustrated and they are otherwise unpublished). According to de Vaux, no examples of cylindrical jars were found at Ein Feshkha. However, using a broad definition of the type, one ovoid jar and one small cylindrical jar with an everted rim (close to Bar-Nathan's Type 2d) are illustrated from Ein Feshkha (see Fig. 22). Otherwise, no cylindrical jars and no bowl-shaped lids are attested from Ein Feshkha, and there are none from Ein el-Ghuweir. The only other examples of published ovoid jars consist of one from the 1st-century C.E. villa at Ein ez-Zara and another from Ein Boqeq.

To understand why these jars and their bowl-shaped lids are common at Qumran but virtually unattested elsewhere, we must compare them with the storage jars found at other sites in Judea in the 1st century B.C.E. and 1st century C.E. The latter are characterized by the following features: a broad, bag-shaped body with sloping, rounded shoulders that widens towards the bottom; a rounded or slightly pointed base; two vertical ring handles on the shoulders; and a narrow, medium high to tall, vertical neck, often with a slightly everted or thickened rim (see Fig. 22). With minor variations, this remained the dominant type of storage jar in Palestine through the Byzantine period and later. Bag-shaped jars are not uncommon at Qumran, though no examples are published from the scroll caves. Bag-shaped jars are also attested at Ein Feshkha and they represent the only type of storage jar found at Ein el-Ghuweir.

The form of the bag-shaped jars reflects their function. The broad bodies and rounded bases indicate that these jars were used for storage in basements or storerooms. Bag-shaped jars were bulky and awkward to carry or transport, especially when they were full. They would have stood on soft, sandy or dirt floors or were placed on stands. Liquids and grain brought in other containers (such as skins) would have been emptied into the bag-shaped jars for storage. Their relatively tall, narrow necks helped prevent spillage (when tipping or pouring) and were easily corked or sealed. The ring handles on the shoulders were used to grasp the jars when pouring out their contents. In contrast, amphoras, which were used as transport containers (especially on ships), have cylindrical bodies, a pointed base, and large handles. This design enabled amphoras to be easily grasped and lifted (with one hand grasping a handle and the other the pointed base).

The cylindrical and ovoid jars differ fundamentally from the bag-shaped jars. Instead of a rounded base, the cylindrical and ovoid jars have a disc or ring base. Although the ovoid jars are bag-shaped, the body is wider at the top (towards the shoulder) than at the bottom (in contrast to bag-shaped jars). They either have small (pierced) ledge handles on the shoulder or no handles at all (except for the ovoid variant with ring handles on the shoulder). The cylindrical jars have a carinated shoulder. The most distinctive feature of these jars (aside from the cylindrical body) is their short neck and wide mouth. In other words, the cylindrical and ovoid jars are essentially holemouth jars (jars with a large opening). As de Vaux noted, the bowl-shaped lids were designed to be placed over the wide mouths of these jars, fitting snugly on the narrow ledge created by the carinated shoulder. Some of the bowls and jars have matching pierced ledge handles, which could be fastened together. The ring or disc bases enabled the cylindrical and ovoid jars to stand on their own and provided a stability that the bag-shaped jars with their rounded bases lacked. On the other hand, the very short necks and wide mouths of the cylindrical and ovoid jars would not have prevented spillage and could not easily have been sealed.

These differences can perhaps be understood in light of the purity regulations of the community at Qumran, especially those governing the storage and pouring of food and drink (for more on sectarian purity concerns, see Chapter 7). The first relevant regulation appears in the Sabbath code in the Damascus Document (CD 11:9): "He shall not open a plastered vessel on the Sabbath." Lawrence Schiffman has noted that in antiquity jars were normally sealed with clay after filling. The clay would then harden, forming an airtight seal. To open the jar, the clay seal had to be broken. Zvi Gal has distinguished three types of ancient clay stoppers. Conical-shaped stoppers were apparently placed inside the jar's mouth. Since these did not hermetically seal the mouth, Gal has suggested that conical-shaped stoppers were used for jars containing olive oil. The second type of stopper is mushroom shaped. These were made during the sealing process by molding wet clay directly on top of the jar's mouth, hermetically sealing it. Gal believes this type of stopper was used for jars containing grain, which would have needed an airtight seal. The third type of stopper is doughnut shaped, with a hole in the center. These have often been identified as loom weights. Gal has suggested that this type was used for sealing wine jars. The sectarians apparently forbade the breaking of clay stoppers that sealed jars on the Sabbath. Clay stoppers would have been used to seal the narrow necks and mouths of bag-shaped jars. However, because of their wide mouths and short necks, cylindrical and ovoid jars could not have been sealed in this way. Instead, these jars were covered with stone slabs (especially when they were embedded in floors) or were fitted with bowl-shaped lids. In addition, some of the linen cloths from Cave 1 were used as jar covers. This feature of the cylindrical and ovoid jars allowed them to be opened on the Sabbath, thereby circumventing the Sabbath prohibition against the breaking of clay seals.

Another sectarian regulation might help explain the design of these jars. This regulation appears in 4QMMT *(Miqsat Ma'aseh ha-Torah):* "And furthermore concerning the pouring (of liquids), we say that it contains no purity. And furthermore the pouring does not separate the impure {from the pure} for the poured liquid and that in the receptacle are alike, one liquid" (4QMMT B55-58). This passage means that when liquid is poured from a pure (upper) vessel into an impure (lower) vessel, the liquid stream links the two vessels and transmits impurity "upstream" to the pure (upper) vessel. This contrasts with the Pharisaic ruling that liquid does not impart impurity to the vessel from which it is poured. The Mishnah tractate *Yadayim* 4:7 describes the Sadducees objecting to the Pharisaic ruling: "Say Sadducees: We complain against you, Pharisees. For you declare clean an unbroken stream of liquid."

To empty a bag-shaped jar, it was necessary to grasp it by the handles, tilt it, and pour the contents out through the narrow opening. If the pure liquid contents of such a jar were poured into an impure container, the jar and its contents would have been rendered impure according to the sectarian regulations. Although cylindrical and ovoid jars could have been picked up and their contents poured out, their wide mouths would have caused considerable spillage. Spillage could have been reduced by pouring the contents of the jar into a funnel, two examples of which are published from Qumran. However, the short necks and wide mouths of the cylindrical and ovoid jars allowed the contents to be scooped out using another utensil such as a cup, bowl, or dipper (interestingly, a dipper is published from Qumran). That this is the way these jars functioned is suggested by their ring and disc bases, which provided them with a stability that bag-shaped jars did not possess and prevented them from tipping over easily. Removing liquids from the cylindrical and ovoid jars with a cup or dipper circumvented the risk of contaminating the contents by pouring them into another vessel. This feature of their design also made it easy to remove the contents of cylindrical jars embedded in floors, a common phenomenon in the settlement at Qumran. In contrast, it would be almost impossible to empty the contents of a bag-shaped jar embedded in a floor. Finally, the wide mouths of these jars would have allowed their contents to be easily viewed and inspected.

Bar-Nathan correctly noted that the distribution of the cylindrical and ovoid jars indicates they represent a regional type. However, the fact that these jars are much more common at Qumran and the caves than at Jericho, combined with their virtual absence from Ein Feshkha and their complete absence from Ein el-Ghuweir, suggests that they are not simply a regional phenomenon. The community at Qumran obviously preferred the cylindrical and ovoid jars over the usual bag-shaped jars, apparently because of their unique concerns with purity. These jars therefore must have been used to store goods that had a high degree of purity, such as the pure food and drink of the sect, as well as scrolls (and perhaps other goods). Various scrolls document the sect's concern that no impurity come into contact with the pure (solid) food and drink (liquids). For this reason, new members were allowed to partake of the pure food only after more than a year had passed, and with the pure drink only after a second year (because liquids render foods susceptible to impurity, the regulations regarding drink were stricter). The relevant passage from the Community Rule (6:16-21) reads as follows: "And when he draws near to the council of the community he shall not come in contact with the pure food of the community . . . until he completes one full year. . . . Let him not come into contact with the liquid food of the community until he completes a second year. . . ." Members who had violated the penal code were denied access to and contact with the pure food and drink for various lengths of time, depending on the infraction. Similarly, in 4QMMT (B64-65) we read, "And furthermore concerning the lepers, we s[ay that they shall not c]ome (into contact) with the sacred pure food. . . ."

I believe that not only were the cylindrical and ovoid jars preferred because of the sect's unique halakhic concerns, but because their distinctive shape came to signify contents having a high degree of purity. In other words, because their shape was easily identifiable, these jars served as markers to those who were allowed or denied contact with the pure food or drink (or other pure goods) of the sect. Distinctively shaped containers have been used throughout history to signal their contents. For example, in the Hellenistic and Roman periods, wine from different regions of the eastern Mediterranean was shipped in distinctively shaped amphoras. Even today, Coca-Cola bottles have a special shape that we all recognize.

It is difficult to determine whether the presence of cylindrical and ovoid jars at Herodian Jericho and Masada and their absence from Ein Feshkha and Ein el-Ghuweir reflects the presence or absence of sectarians. Perhaps these jars are found at Jericho and Masada because they are a regional type. On the other hand, the fact that at least some of the examples from Jericho were associated with bowl-shaped lids suggests a sectarian-like concern with purity. This means that the discovery of these jars at Jericho could attest to the presence of sectarians or a group with similar purity concerns. Similarly, the appearance of cylindrical and ovoid jars in contexts dating to the time of the First Jewish Revolt at Masada might support Yadin's suggestion that members of the Qumran community joined the rebels there after their own settlement fell to the Romans in 68 c.e. On the other hand, the absence of cylindrical and ovoid jars from Ein Feshkha and Ein el-Ghuweir does not prove that these settlements were nonsectarian or had no connections with Qumran, though this is a possibility (see Chapter 10). Instead, their absence indicates that the pure food and drink (and other pure goods) of the sect were not stored at these sites (perhaps because the communal meals were held at Qumran?).

The large numbers of cylindrical and ovoid jars found in the caves around Qumran indicates that the sectarians stored substantial provisions of pure food and drink (in addition to scrolls) in the caves. The presence of ovoid jars (which appeared before 31 b.c.e.), Hellenistic-type oil lamps (which date to the reign of Herod), and cylindrical jars and wheel-made ("Herodian") oil lamps (which date to the 1st century c.e.) in the caves demonstrates that these jars were deposited throughout Qumran's sectarian occupation (in the pre–31 b.c.e. phase of Period Ib; the post–31 b.c.e. phase of Period Ib; and Period II). Although some of the jars might have been placed in the caves for safekeeping on the eve of the destructions in ca. 9/8 b.c.e. and in

68 C.E., their large numbers and the presence of types that antedate 31 B.C.E. suggest this was an ongoing process. In other words, the sectarians apparently hoarded stores of pure food and drink in the caves on more than one occasion. On the other hand, it is not clear whether scrolls were similarly hoarded in the caves, or whether they were all deposited on the eve of Qumran's destruction in 68 C.E.

One text that might shed light on this phenomenon is 4Q274 3 ii, also designated 4QTohorot A because it deals with purity. Fragment 3, column ii reads as follows:

(2)  . . . those whose impurity [extends over days          ]
(3)  and any (vessel) which has a seal . . . [          shall be unclean]
(4)  for a more (scrupulously) pure person. Any herb [which has no]
(5)  dew moisture on it may be eaten. If it is n[ot eaten, let him put it]
(6)  into the water. For if one [were to put it on]
(7)  the ground and [water] wetted it [when]
(8)  the rain [falls] upon it, if an [unclean person] touches it, let him by no means [eat it]
(9)  in the field during the period [of his purification          ]
(10)  Any earthen vessel [into which a creeping thing] f[a]lls
(11)  [whatever] is in it [ becomes unclean          any]
(12)  liquid be[comes unclean          ]

This text reflects the sectarians' concern with the role of liquids as transmitters of impurity. As a consequence, food stored in open ceramic vessels in a house that is unclean (through the presence of a corpse, for example) becomes unclean. For the more scrupulous, even sealed vessels were not effective barriers against impurity. In addition, food that had been moistened with liquids was rendered susceptible to impurity, as indicated by a passage in the Temple Scroll: "If a man dies in your cities, the house in which the dead man has died shall be unclean for seven days. Whatever is in the house and whoever enters the house shall be unclean for seven days. Any food on which water has been poured shall be unclean, anything moistened shall be unclean. Earthenware vessels shall be unclean and whatever they contain shall be unclean for every clean man. The open (vessels) shall be unclean for every Israelite (with) whatever is moistened in them" (11QT$^a$ 49.5-10). 4Q274 indicates that even falling rain and dew could make food (or at least fruits and vegetables) susceptible to impurity. According to Joseph Baumgarten, "It is likely that Qumran exegesis considered fruits which had been wetted to be susceptible even after the moisture had dried."

These texts suggest that the community at Qumran hoarded stores of pure food and drink in the caves to guard against contact with impurity. This is because they considered even sealed vessels to be susceptible to impurity. This means that pure food and drink stored in sealed vessels in a house or building that became impure would have been rendered impure. Storing pure goods in caves (instead of in the settlement) reduced the risk of contamination through contact with impurity (such as corpse-impurity or other kinds of impurity). The dry conditions inside the caves — the same conditions that preserved the scrolls for 2000 years — also reduced the risk that moisture (such as rain or dew) would come into contact with and contaminate the pure food and drink. This accounts for the design of the bowl-shaped lids, which completely covered the mouths of the jars, fitting snugly over the neck and resting on the shoulder (see Fig. 20). Any moisture (such as rain, dew, bat or bird droppings) that happened to fall on cylindrical jars covered with these lids would have rolled down the sides of the jars and onto the ground. In other words, the lids were designed to prevent moisture from entering the jars. In fact, it could be that the use of bowl-shaped lids not only circumvented the Sabbath prohibition against breaking clay seals but developed out of the sectarians' concern with the transmission of impurity by moisture. As we noted above, bag-shaped jars were usually sealed with wet clay that was molded over the mouth and dried in place. The moisture in the wet clay would presumably have contaminated the contents of jars sealed in this way. Perhaps this is one of the reasons that the cylindrical and ovoid jars and bowl-shaped lids were preferred by the community at Qumran.

As Schiffman has noted, "To a great extent, the sect defined itself as a group maintaining the ritual purity of its food. . . . Indeed, the right to approach the pure food was a step in the process of being accepted as a full member of the sect. But the exclusion from the pure food [for those who violated the ordinances] is even more. It is a consequence of the belief that the offender will defile it, for to the sect, ritual impurity goes hand in hand with moral impurity." The design of the cylindrical and ovoid jars and bowl-shaped lids can be understood as a physical expression of the sect's concern with the purity of food and drink. The hoarding of food and drink in the caves was apparently due to the sectarians' desire to reduce the risk of contamination through contact with impurity and moisture, though some of these stores (and perhaps the scrolls) could have been deposited on the eve of the site's destruction in 68 C.E.

A pseudepigraphical work called the *Assumption of Moses* refers to storing scrolls in jars. At the beginning of the work, Moses tells Joshua that he is about to die, and delivers to him certain books of prophecies, which Joshua is supposed to treat with cedar oil and store in jars in a place appointed by God: "And receive thou this writing that thou mayest know how to preserve the books which I shall deliver unto thee: and thou shalt set these in order and anoint them with oil of cedar and put them away in earthen vessels in the place which He made from the beginning of the creation of the world, that His name should be called upon until the day of repentance in the visitation wherewith the Lord will visit them in the consummation of the end of the days" (1:16-18). Although oil presumably would have been employed to soften and preserve the parchment, the use of the term "anoint" suggests a ritual aspect to its application.

What kind of "earthen vessels" were used to store these scrolls? As we have seen, the narrow openings of bag-shaped jars means they could not have held scrolls. Scrolls could have been placed in other vessels such as large cooking pots (although their globular bodies were not well suited for this purpose) or in broken amphoras or bag-shaped jars. However, the design of the ovoid and cylindrical jars makes them ideally suited for the storage of scrolls as described in the *Assumption of Moses*. The date of this composition (which might have undergone two redactions) is disputed, but the latest identifiable historical allusions suggest that it attained its final form between the years 4 B.C.E. and 48 C.E. Although scholars have noted that the work displays a number of affinities with the Qumran writings, such as a priestly stance and a peculiar eschatological outlook, its apparent absence among the Dead Sea Scrolls suggests that it is not an Essene composition. According to Emil Schürer, "The furthest one can go is to suggest that it derives from a writer sympathetic to Essene ideology."

Because ovoid and cylindrical jars are found mostly in the vicinity of Qumran, I believe it is likely that the author (or redactor) of the *Assumption of Moses* was familiar with and might even have been describing the sectarians' practice of storing scrolls in jars placed in caves. This is admittedly an argument from silence (based on the accident of preservation), since there are no analogous manuscript finds from other sites in Roman Palestine. On the other hand, scrolls from contemporary sites in the region (such as Masada and the Judean Desert caves occupied during the Bar Kokhba Revolt) were not found inside jars and were not associated with ovoid or cylindrical jars (although, as noted above, unpublished cylindrical jars are apparently represented at Masada). However, even at Qumran the only scrolls that were actually found inside jars are apparently those from Cave 1. Nevertheless, these examples provide our only archaeological evidence for the practice described in the *Assumption of Moses*.

There are other ancient reports of scrolls stored inside jars in caves near

Jericho. The early Christian scholar Origen (185-254 c.e.) mentioned that the sixth Greek version of the Psalms he presented in his Hexapla had been found in a jar near Jericho. In describing the same text, the church historian Eusebius (ca. 260-340 c.e.) added that a Greek version of the Psalms and other Greek and Hebrew manuscripts had been found in a jar at Jericho during the reign of Caracalla (*Ecclesiastical History* 6.16.1). In ca. 800 c.e., Timotheus I, the Nestorian patriarch of Seleucia, reported that books of the Old Testament had been found in a cave near Jericho. Of course, we do not know whether these manuscripts were related to the Dead Sea Scrolls. But the nature of the manuscripts (biblical scrolls), the references to locations "near Jericho," and the descriptions of scrolls deposited in jars stored in caves suggest these might represent earlier finds of Dead Sea Scrolls.

If the passage in the *Assumption of Moses* refers to the practice at Qumran, some of the scrolls could have been deposited in the caves before the destruction in 68 c.e. This means that the community at Qumran might have been storing or hoarding scrolls as well as pure food and drink in some of the caves over the course of many years. Jeremiah 32:13-14 indicates that storing scrolls in ceramic jars was an ancient practice going back to biblical times: "And I charged Baruch before them saying, Thus says the Lord of hosts, the God of Israel; Take these documents, this deed of purchase, both that which is sealed, and this open deed; and put them in an earthen vessel, that they may last for many days." This might explain why the community at Qumran, which showed a preference for other biblical Jewish practices such as dining while seated instead of reclining, adopted this practice. It also means that cylindrical jars might originally have been designed or adapted by the sect for the purpose of holding scrolls and then became the preferred containers for storing their pure food and drink as well.

The pottery from Qumran thus sheds a great deal of light on the character of the community. It suggests that the inhabitants practiced a deliberate and selective policy of isolation, manufacturing ceramic products to suit their special needs and concerns with purity. It is clear that they chose to manufacture and use undecorated pottery instead of fine wares. The large number of identical, undecorated plates, cups, and bowls found at Qumran contrasts sharply with contemporary assemblages at other sites in Judea, which are richer and more varied in terms of the types represented. Similar differences are apparent when we compare other aspects of the archaeology of Qumran with contemporary Judean sites.

## Could Qumran Have Been a Country Villa?

Robert Donceel and Pauline Donceel-Voûte have suggested that Qumran was a *villa rustica* (a Roman country villa), not a sectarian settlement. In support of their interpretation, they have cited the "unexpected variety and richness of the objects" from Qumran. More recently, Yizhar Hirschfeld has suggested that Qumran was a "manor house," that is, a wealthy agricultural estate. And finally, according to Jean-Baptiste Humbert, de Vaux's Period Ia continued until the site was destroyed in 57 B.C.E. by Gabinius (a Roman governor of Palestine) or in 31 B.C.E. (during Herod's establishment of control over Jericho and the Dead Sea region). Humbert believes that during Period Ia Qumran functioned as a nonsectarian agricultural settlement. After that, it was taken over by the Essenes and became a cultic center with a permanent population of only 10-15 inhabitants.

However, comparisons between Qumran and contemporary villas in Palestine and elsewhere do not support any of these alternative interpretations. Before considering this evidence, it is important to remember that any comparisons we make should belong to the same period and geographical region — in other words, for Qumran, we need to consider sites in Roman Palestine in general, and especially sites in Judea in the 1st century B.C.E. and 1st century C.E. The more distant the comparisons are in time and space, the less likely they are to be valid. For example, there is no connection in time and space between the Egyptian and Mesoamerican pyramids which, despite their similar appearances, were used for very different purposes. It is also important to remember that for a comparison to be valid, there should be as many points of similarity as possible. In other words, if Qumran was a villa or manor house, it should have more than one or two features in common with contemporary Judean villas and manor houses. This means that we need to compare the layout and design, the interior decoration, and the pottery of Qumran with those of contemporary Judean villas.

For the purposes of comparison, we shall look at four groups of contemporary Judean palaces and villas: (1) the royal Hasmonean and Herodian palaces at Masada, Herodium, and Herodian Jericho; (2) the private, upper-class urban Jewish mansions of the Herodian period in Jerusalem's Jewish Quarter; (3) "Hilkiah's palace," a private, rural villa of the Herodian period in Idumaea; and (4) the recently-published early Roman villas at Horvat 'Eleq and Horvat 'Aqav at Ramat Hanadiv near Caesarea, and at Ein ez-Zara (ancient Callirrhoe) on the eastern shore of the Dead Sea. As we shall see, all of these palaces and villas share certain features that are not found at Qumran (whereas Qumran has certain features that are not found at other sites).

The most extensive remains of Hasmonean palaces have been uncovered by Ehud Netzer in his excavations at Jericho. These palaces typically have a central courtyard surrounded by rooms. A hall that probably functioned as a triclinium (a dining room or reception hall) opened on to the southern side of the courtyard. The opening to the courtyard was through two columns set between the side walls (an arrangement referred to as *in antis*), instead of through a doorway in a wall. This type of hall can be seen in the Hasmonean twin palaces at Jericho and at Masada in the core of the western palace and in Buildings 11, 12, and 13. Other features of the Hasmonean palaces in Jericho include swimming pools, gardens, an elaborate water-supply system, bathhouses, and miqva'ot (ritual baths). At least one building was furnished with stuccoed columns (that is, stone columns covered with molded plaster) in a Hellenized Doric (Greek) order. Remains of wall paintings (frescoes) and floor mosaics were found in several parts of the palace complex, including in one of the bathhouses. Netzer has described the characteristic features of Hasmonean architecture as including "irrigated royal estates, palaces with multiple swimming-pools, bathing facilities and gardens."

The typical features of Herod's palaces followed those of Roman villas. These include a main wing with a triclinium, a peristyle courtyard (that is, an open courtyard surrounded by columns that created a porch around the sides), a bathhouse, and dwelling rooms. The triclinium in Herod's palaces was a large hall with rows of columns surrounding three sides of the room's interior, and a wide entrance on the fourth side opening to the landscape or a courtyard. This type of hall can be seen in Herod's third palace at Jericho and in the circular palace-fortress at Upper Herodium. The triclinium on the lower terrace of the northern palace at Masada differs in having columns around all four sides of the interior. Circular "triclinium-type" halls are found on the middle terrace of Herod's northern palace at Masada and perhaps on the southern mound in Herod's third palace at Jericho. Peristyle courtyards in Herod's palaces typically had rows of columns around all four sides, with double ("heart-shaped") columns at the corners. The columns supported a roofed porch on all four sides, with an open air garden in the center. Peristyle courtyards with interior gardens can be seen in Herod's second and third palaces at Jericho, at Upper Herodium, and perhaps in a modified form on the upper terrace of the northern palace at Masada. Bathhouses or baths are found in all of Herod's palaces at Jericho, at Upper and Lower Herodium, and in the northern and western palaces at Masada. Herod's bathhouses were usually equipped with a Roman-style hypocaust system. In this system, the hot room (steam bath) of the bathhouse had a floor supported by rows of small columns made of bricks or stones (called *suspensura*) (see Fig.

49). The hot air from a furnace in an adjacent room circulated among these small columns and heated the floor. The hot air was also carried along the walls by pipes or flues. Steam was created by splashing water from tubs in the room onto the heated walls and floors. Some of Herod's bathhouses, for example the one in the western palace at Masada, had an older type of heating system with bathtubs containing heated water. Miqva'ot are found in Herod's third palace at Jericho and in the western and northern palaces at Masada.

The extended complexes of Herod's palaces included elaborate entertainment facilities such as large pools for swimming and boating, elaborate gardens, and water channels and installations. Large pools for swimming and boating are found at Lower Herodium and in all three Herodian palaces at Jericho. There is also at least one swimming pool at Masada. Elaborate gardens and landscaping are characteristic features of all of Herod's gardens. Perhaps the best example is the "sunken garden" in Herod's third palace at Jericho, but extensive gardens are found elsewhere in the Herodian palaces at Jericho as well as at Lower Herodium and Masada. Stucco, wall frescoes, floor mosaics, and floor tiles (opus sectile) decorated the interiors of all of Herod's palaces. Stucco was used to create imitation paneling on the walls (this is the First Pompeian Style), to create flutes covering column drums, to cover column capitals, and to imitate other architectural elements (for an example of stucco from Pompeii, see Fig. 50). The frescoes are in the same style (the Second Pompeian Style) as contemporary wall paintings found in Pompeii (see, for example, Fig. 51). In this style, imitation marble or colored stone panels were painted on the surface of the wall. The floor mosaics in Herod's palaces are made of small, black-and-white or colored stone cubes that create geometric or floral designs (see, for example, Fig. 52). The floor tiles were cut into geometric shapes such as triangles and laid in alternating colors (such as black and white) to form decorative patterns. Finally, Herod's palaces (as well as other projects he sponsored) often incorporated Roman architectural elements such as arches, vaults, and domes. In Rome, these curvilinear elements were constructed using brick and concrete. Herod usually used local cut stone for these elements (although he used Roman-type brickwork and imported concrete in his third palace at Jericho and at two other sites in Palestine). An intact masonry (stone) dome survives in the bathhouse at Upper Herodium and intact masonry vaults are found elsewhere at that site.

Although the palaces at Jericho, Herodium, and Masada are the best-known examples of Herod's palaces, these features are found in the other Herodian palace-fortresses around the Dead Sea. For example, frescoes, stucco, and tile floors were discovered at Cypros, which overlooks Herod's palace at Jericho. A peristyle courtyard with heart-shaped columns is visible at Alexandrium-Sartaba in the Jordan Valley north of Jericho. A bathhouse complex has been uncovered at Machaerus on the eastern side of the Dead Sea (in modern Jordan). At Hyrcania, located just to the west of Qumran, rooms grouped around the central courtyard sit on a leveled area supported by masonry vaults. One of the open reservoirs at the foot of the western side of the site might have functioned as a swimming pool.

Scholars who believe that Qumran was a villa might argue that the parallels I have cited so far are not valid, since these sites were royal palaces. However, it is important to consider these parallels because elements of royal architecture and decoration were imitated and used (admittedly on a smaller or more modest scale) by the upper classes of Judean society — that is, by the wealthy members of society who resided in villas. The best examples of contemporary, private, upper-class Judean dwellings (villas) are the Herodian mansions in Jerusalem's Jewish Quarter. The excavator, Avigad, described these mansions as follows:

> Construction in the Upper City was dense, with the houses built quite close together; but the individual dwelling units were extensive, and inner courtyards lent them the character of luxury villas. These homes were richly ornamented with frescoes, stucco work, and mosaic floors, and were equipped with complex bathing facilities, as well as containing the luxury goods and artistic objects which signify a high standard of living. This, then, was an upper class quarter, where the noble families of Jerusalem lived, with the High Priest at their head. Here they built their homes in accordance with the dominant fashion of the Hellenistic-Roman period. It is generally assumed that the Jerusalemite nobility was of the Sadducee faction, whose members included the Hellenizers; the lower classes tended more to the Pharisee faction, which opposed foreign influences. Thus, it can be assumed that this quarter was occupied chiefly by Sadducees. Even so, there is no specific archaeological evidence here to indicate any laxity in their upholding of the traditional precepts of the Jewish religion. On the contrary, the finds indicate that the laws of ritual purity were strictly kept, as were the injunctions against statues and graven images.

This passage highlights two important points. First, the mansions in the Jewish Quarter were urban villas, not located in the countryside like Qumran. In other words, the mansions in the Jewish Quarter were not landed estates. They were built closely together because real estate was at a premium in Jerusalem. Second, these mansions belonged to the uppermost class of contemporary Judean society: the Sadducees. This class included the high priests. Although the Sadducees had a reputation for being Hellenizers (that is, for adopting Greek and Roman culture), the finds from these mansions indicate that the residents strictly observed Jewish law (including purity laws).

Several large houses or parts of houses were uncovered by Avigad. A group of six contiguous or almost contiguous houses is located in the area he referred to as the Herodian Quarter. Another house, in the excavation's Area E, was built in the middle of the 1st century B.C.E. and destroyed at the beginning of the 1st century C.E. when a road was laid over it. This house contained the Hellenistic type lamp that I mentioned above. The "Burnt House," so-called because of the visible signs of fire which destroyed it in 70 C.E., is located in the excavation's Area B, to the north of the Herodian Quarter. In most cases, only the basement stories of the houses are preserved, which contained bathing and storage facilities. At least some of the food was kept in bag-shaped jars or in imported amphoras. Water was stored in cisterns hewn into the bedrock on which the houses were built. The bathing facilities included baths and miqva'ot. Many of the houses contained more than one miqveh, reflecting a concern with purity that we would expect of priestly residents (see Chapter 7). The bath rooms are adjacent to the miqva'ot, and were furnished with bathtubs and paved with colored geometric and floral mosaics. The houses had at least one story above the basement, at ground level, and some might have had a second story. Two of the houses (the "Palatial Mansion" and the "Southern House") are especially large and had an open-air central courtyard surrounded by rooms. One of the mansions (the "House of Columns") had a peristyle courtyard with heart-shaped columns at the corners. The columns were covered with fluted stucco, and two rooms adjacent to the courtyard were paved with floor tiles (opus sectile). The interior decoration of these urban villas included architectural elements made of stucco (including stucco panels), floors paved with tiles or colored mosaics, and frescoes. In fact, the geometric and floral designs in the mosaic floors of these houses are so similar to those in Herod's palaces at Masada that they might have been executed by the same craftsmen or workshops (see Fig. 52). The frescoes include examples of the Second and Third Pompeian Styles (see Fig. 51). However, arches, domes, and vaults are uncommon, and there is no evidence of the use of concrete in these urban villas. Although they were equipped with private baths, these mansions did not have the Roman-type hypocaust system found in most of Herod's palaces. They also lack large swimming pools and landscaped gardens, not surprising in a densely populated urban setting. Thus, the mansions in the Jewish Quarter share some of the features characteristic of Herod's palaces, especially in terms of interior decoration.

If Qumran was a villa, one of the closest analogs should be a rural, Herodian-period villa at Khirbet el-Muraq, ca. 9 mi. west of Hebron. The site was excavated by Emanuel Damati in 1969, who called it "Hilkiah's palace" because of an inscribed stone plaque found in the excavations. This inscription and the presence of stone vessels indicate that the inhabitants were Jewish. The site is located in ancient Idumaea, the district to the south of Judea. Hilkiah's palace was constructed at the end of the 1st century B.C.E. and was destroyed at the time of the First Jewish Revolt against the Romans, probably during Vespasian's campaign to Idumaea in 68 C.E. (the same year Qumran was destroyed). It is situated on a hill some 500 meters above sea level, overlooking the lowlands (Shephelah) of Judea to the west. Important roads lead from the lowlands to the top of the mountain ridge just to the north and south of the site. The villa sat within a fortified enclosure with a square tower on its western side. The tower is constructed of large stones and its walls slope out towards the base. Rooms were ranged along the inner sides of the enclosure, surrounding a large peristyle courtyard. Storage rooms along the southern side of the enclosure were roofed with a barrel vault. Architectural fragments found in the excavations indicate that there was a second-story level. The walls of the villa were constructed uniformly of large stones, roughly square in shape, while ashlars (cut stones) with drafted margins were used for the facades, pilasters, columns, arches, and stylobates. The peristyle courtyard was surrounded by the living rooms of the villa. The unit on the south is described by Damati as the *oikos* or main room of the house, with a *prostas* or entrance room adjoining it to the east. The walls of the *prostas* were covered with stucco molded in geometric patterns. A large, elongated hall on the eastern side of the courtyard is identified as a triclinium. Its walls were decorated with elaborately molded stucco. Two square pillars built of ashlar masonry were located in the hall 4 meters to the north of its south wall. Small niches cut along the length of the southern corners of the pillars and in the walls opposite held wooden partitions that divided the hall into two unequal parts. The villa's bathhouse was located on the northern side of the peristyle courtyard. Its barrel-vaulted steam room was heated by a Roman-style hypocaust system. Remains of a mosaic floor were discovered in the bathhouse. The columns of the peristyle courtyard stood on a nicely cut stone stylobate that was raised slightly above the floor of the courtyard. The decorative elements found in the excavation included stuccoed architectural elements (such as molded panels), mosaic floors, Nabatean-style column capitals, Attic column and pilaster bases (that is, column and pilaster bases carved in a Greco-Roman style called "Attic"), and carved architrave blocks (stone elements belonging to the upper part of the walls).

More recently, the final report on excavations at the early Roman villa at Ein ez-Zara (ancient Callirrhoe) has been published. If Qumran was a villa, Ein ez-Zara should provide a close parallel because it is located by the Dead Sea and dates to the 1st century C.E. The remains at Ein ez-Zara include one building consisting of a large open courtyard surrounded by rooms ("Building A"), and an adjoining building with a plan that resembles the triclinium in Herod's third palace at Jericho. About 20 column drums with different diameters and several column bases made of local basalt were found in various spots around Building A. They apparently originated in a colonnaded courtyard in front of Building B. Unfortunately, little was preserved of these buildings above the foundation level due to reoccupation during the Byzantine period, the plundering of the site for material, the forces of erosion, and recent plowing. It is therefore not surprising that no mosaics or *opus sectile* floors were discovered, aside from one rose-colored paving stone. On the other hand, some finely-molded stucco fragments were recovered. Stone vessels and coins of the First Revolt suggest Jewish presence at the site. However, the only pool discovered shows no evidence of steps and had an outlet to drain the contents, indicating that it was not a miqveh. A comparison between Ein ez-Zara and Qumran reveals some fundamental differences. Unlike Qumran, Ein ez-Zara includes a building with a very large, open courtyard surrounded by a single range of rooms on all sides, and another building that is clearly modeled after the triclinia in Herod's palaces. Although the buildings were almost completely denuded, the stucco fragments suggest that the interiors were richly decorated. On the other hand, despite the evidence for Jewish presence at Ein ez-Zara, there are no miqva'ot.

How does the settlement at Qumran compare with the Hasmonean and Herodian palaces, the mansions in the Jewish Quarters, Hilkiah's palace, and the villa at Ein ez-Zara? In terms of layout and design, the settlement at Qumran has none of the features characteristic of the Hasmonean and Herodian palaces: the hall with two columns *in antis,* the colonnaded triclinium, the peristyle courtyard with garden, the bathhouses, and the large swimming pools and landscaped gardens. It did have an open-air courtyard without a peristyle around which rooms were grouped. Some of these rooms had a second-story level. The plan of the dining room at Qumran (L77) is similar to the triclinia in the Palatial Mansion in the Jewish Quarter and in Hilkiah's palace, though there is no interior decoration at Qumran.

The square towers at Qumran and Hilkiah's palace are also similar. Yizhar Hirschfeld has noted that the layout of the main building at Qumran, which is roughly square and has a fortified tower on the north side, resembles other manor houses in Herodian Palestine, including those at Horvat 'Eleq at

Ramat Hanadiv, Qasr el-Leja in Samaria, and Rujm el-Hamiri southeast of Hebron. Hirschfeld also lists Aroer in the northern Negev, which is a settlement next to a fort, not a manor house or a villa. Based on these comparisons, he believes that Qumran was a manor house.

Hirschfeld and the Donceels have each suggested that the main building at Qumran was the *pars urbana*, that is, the residential part of the villa or manor house, while the surrounding areas and the secondary building were the *pars rustica* or industrial area. However, cooking areas and workshops were located inside the main building (for example, the kitchen in L38-L41 and a dyeing installation in L34), whereas a dining room was located above L111, L120, L121, L122 in the secondary building (see Chapter 6). The service rooms or workshops at other sites are usually segregated from the rest of the palace or villa. In Herod's western palace at Masada, for example, at least some of the service rooms were clustered in a separate wing designated the "Eastern Service Wing" and "Western Service Wing." At Jericho, an extensive area filled with workshops dating from the Hasmonean period to the first half of the 1st century C.E. was discovered some 150 meters to the north of Herod's third palace. At Qasr el-Leja (a rural manor house in Samaria), an oil press and possible workshops or storage rooms were located on the eastern side of the site, while the residential quarters were on the west. A workshop that occupied the basement story of a Herodian mansion called the "Burnt House" in Jerusalem's Jewish Quarter might have produced incense or spice for the use in the temple cult. The living rooms were located on the ground floor and upper story. A stone weight found in the "Burnt House," which is inscribed with the name "Bar Kathros," suggests that the owner belonged to that priestly family. Although Jerusalem was a manufacturing center for stone vessels, painted bowls, and glass ware, there is no evidence for their production in the Herodian mansions in the Jewish Quarter.

An examination of Hirschfeld's final report on his excavations of the fortified early Roman manor house at Ḥorvat 'Eleq reveals significant differences with Qumran. The square tower at Qumran is incorporated into the northern edge of the settlement, whereas a similar tower at Ḥorvat 'Eleq and the other buildings of the settlement are surrounded by a wall with projecting square towers that forms a roughly square, fortified enclosure. A bathhouse of Roman type belonging to the complex (located near a spring outside the enclosure) included a hot room heated by a hypocaust system, rooms with vaulted ceilings, colored marble revetment on the walls, and mosaic floors. Among the finds from Ḥorvat 'Eleq are imported amphoras (including a stamped Rhodian amphora handle of early Roman date), Pompeian red ware (a type of casserole imported from Italy), Roman mold-made discus lamps (including one decorated with the figure of a woman), significant amounts of Eastern Sigillata A, and Cypriot Sigillata and Western Terra Sigillata (including one bowl decorated in relief with a mask and another with a horse). Three fragments of Eastern Sigillata A from Ḥorvat ʿEleq bear inscriptions in Greek that were incised on the vessels after firing. In contrast, no Greek inscriptions were discovered at Qumran.

Hirschfeld excavated another early Roman farmhouse at Ramat Hanadiv. This farmhouse, called Horvat ʿAqav, consists of a roughly square, fortified enclosure containing living quarters, storehouses, cisterns, and agricultural installations (winepresses, an olive press, and a threshing floor). The living quarters and storehouses were located on the eastern side of the enclosure, and the agricultural installations lay in the southwest corner of the enclosure, or outside it. According to Hirschfeld, "a high standard of construction is evident" from the ashlar (cut stone) construction and a finely worked heart-shaped column base. The buildings were covered with tiled roofs. At least some floors were paved with mosaics or with polished stone slabs. The living quarters were provided with one room that contained a built bathtub, and another with a miqveh. The presence of the latter, of course, indicates that the residents of this farmstead were Jewish. The ceramic assemblage includes examples of Eastern Sigillata A, another type of Eastern Sigillata, and Roman mold-made oil lamps with a decorated discus (including one with a griffin).

Despite the similarity between the square towers at Qumran and Horvat ʿEleq and the presence of a miqveh at Horvat ʿAqav, there are many significant differences between the Ramat Hanadiv sites and Qumran. The Ramat Hanadiv sites display a higher quality of construction with finely worked architectural elements: one Roman-type bathhouse with a hypocaust system and one built bathtub; rooms with vaulted ceilings; tiled roofs; colored marble revetment on the walls; mosaic and polished stone floors; and ceramic assemblages that include imports and Eastern Sigillata A, some decorated with figured images. The industrial and agricultural areas are segregated from the spaces with the living quarters. On the other hand, the Ramat Hanadiv sites lack the distinguishing features of Qumran, including the multiplicity of miqvaʾot, the animal bone deposits, and the large adjacent cemetery.

The main problem with Hirschfeld's interpretation is that it is based entirely on a few morphological similarities (similarities in the architectural layout) between Qumran and contemporary manor houses, while ignoring all of the other evidence. This evidence includes differences in interior decoration and the pottery and other finds, as well as Qumran's peculiar features, such as the animal bone deposits, the large number of miqvaʾot, and the adjacent cemetery — none of which is attested at the manor houses mentioned by Hirschfeld or at other contemporary Judean villas and palaces. In analogy, although the facades of many modern banks, train stations, and court houses are constructed in a Classical Greek style, these buildings do not function as Greek temples! Similarly, the presence of a tower and the discovery of arrowheads in the destruction level of 68 c.e. do not indicate that Qumran was a fort. We have seen, for example, that towers are found at manor houses around Roman Palestine, while the arrowheads found at Qumran are associated with the fighting that took place when the Romans conquered the site.

For archaeological interpretations to be valid, they must be based on a thorough consideration of all available evidence and on parallels with contemporary sites in the same geographical region. Of course, the settlement at Qumran shares some features of design with contemporary palaces and villas in Judea and elsewhere in Palestine, since the inhabitants expressed themselves in the architectural vocabulary of their environment. It would be anachronistic to expect the inhabitants of Qumran to build in a style that was completely different from contemporary architecture in Judea. However, these shared features, such as water systems, courtyards without peristyles, and large dining rooms, are too generic and utilitarian to support the identification of Qumran as a villa. To the contrary, it is the differences between Qumran and contemporary villas and manor houses that are significant.

As we have seen, the extensive water system is perhaps the most distinctive feature of Qumran. Elaborate water systems are characteristic of the Herodian palaces. The mansions in the Jewish Quarter contained water facilities in the basements. There was also a system of water channels at Hilkiah's palace, which carried rainwater from the roofs of the buildings to a cistern west of the villa. At Qasr el-Leja, a cistern in the courtyard and two outside of it were supplied with rainwater. However, there is at least one obvious and fundamental difference between the water system at Qumran and those found at the other sites. At Qumran, there are no clearly identifiable bathhouses or built bathtubs, only cisterns and pools, many of which were used as miqva'ot (see Chapter 7). The existence of an extensive water system at Qumran is significant because it indicates that the inhabitants possessed the technology necessary for constructing the kinds of swimming pools and baths found in contemporary villas, but did not do so.

The strongest argument against the identification of Qumran as a villa or manor house lies in the almost complete absence of interior decoration. As advocates of the villa and manor house interpretations have noted, a few architectural elements (such as column drums and bases and voussoir stones) are found at Qumran. These elements apparently belong to one or more structures that stood somewhere in the settlement and were destroyed in the earthquake of 31 B.C.E. (see Chapter 4). In addition, two limestone tiles or flagstones were found in L2, four in L44, and one each in L4 (two fragments), L13, L19 (one fragment), L46 (one fragment), L59, and L61. It is not clear whether these represent *opus sectile* or are just flagstones (for stone tiles from Ein Feshkha, see Chapter 10). Still, the small number of these elements shows that interior decoration is almost completely absent at Qumran. There is no evidence at Qumran for stucco, frescoes, or mosaic floors. This accords well with the ceramic assemblage from Qumran, which yielded no examples of imported Western Terra Sigillata, amphoras, decorated Roman discus lamps, painted Jerusalem bowls, and almost no Eastern Sigillata A. In contrast, nicely-cut stones with dressed margins and frieze blocks with dentilated moldings (that is, blocks carved with rows of projecting teeth along the bottom edge — a decorative element characteristic of Classical architecture) have been discovered at the fortress at Rujm el-Bahr (at the northern end of the Dead Sea) and at the anchorage at Khirbet Mazin (south of Qumran). Frescoes with red and black painted bands were also found at Khirbet Mazin (as well as imported amphoras, as we have seen). On the other hand, just as the settlement at Qumran has a number of peculiar features (such as the animal bone deposits, the large number of miqva'ot, and the adjacent cemetery), its ceramic corpus includes types that are virtually unique to Qumran (such as the cylindrical jars). These comparisons with contemporary sites in Judea support the identification of Qumran as a sectarian settlement.

I hope that this chapter has clarified why the highly-publicized alternative interpretations of Qumran are not supported by the archaeological evidence. In the following chapters, we shall examine the peculiar features of Qumran in light of the information provided by the scrolls and our ancient sources.

## Bibliographical Notes

For a comparison between the ceramic assemblage from Qumran and those from contemporary Judean sites, see Jodi Magness, "The Community at Qumran in Light of Its Pottery," in Michael O. Wise, N. Golb, John J. Collins, and Dennis G. Pardee, *Methods of Investigation,* 39-50. For a discussion of cylindrical jars within the context of sectarian halakhah, see Jodi Magness, "Why Scroll Jars?" in *A Festschrift in Honor of Eric M. Meyers,* ed. Douglas R. Edwards and C. Thomas McCollough (forthcoming). Both of these papers contain references relevant to this chapter; some of the main references are repeated here with additional bibliography. For the Jerusalem painted bowl from Cave 37 near Qumran, see Joseph Patrich, "Khirbet Qumrân in Light of New Archaeological Explorations in the Qumran Caves," in Wise, Golb, Collins, and Pardee, *Methods of Investigation*, 73-95. For the pottery from Ehud Netzer's excavations at Herodian Jericho, see Rachel Bar-Nathan, *The Pottery of Jericho in the Hasmonean Period and the Time of Herod, and the Problem of the Transition from Hasmonean Pottery Types to Pottery Types of the Time of Herod* (M.A. thesis; Jerusalem: Institute of Archaeology at the Hebrew University, 1988 [Hebrew]). For Eastern Sigillata A, see Kathleen Warner Slane, "The Fine Wares," in *Tel Anafa II/I: The Hellenistic and Roman Pottery*, ed. Andrea M. Berlin and Slane (Ann Arbor: Kelsey Museum, 1997), 247-406; John W. Hayes, "Sigillata Orientale A (Eastern Sigillata A)," in *Enciclopedia dell'arte antica, classica e orientale, Atlante delle forme ceramiche 2: Ceramica fine romana nel Bacino Mediterraneo (tardo ellenismo e primo impero)* (Rome: Istituto della Enciclopedia Italiana, 1985), 3-48; Kathleen Warner Slane, J. Michael Elam, Michael D. Glascock, and Hector Neff, "Compositional Analysis of Eastern Sigillata A and Related Wares from Tel Anafa (Israel)," *Journal of Archaeological Science* 21 (1994): 51-64; Jan Gunneweg, Isadore Perlman, and Joseph Yellin, *The Provenience, Typology, and Chronology of Eastern Terra Sigillata*. Qedem 17 (Jerusalem: Hebrew University, 1983).

For Donald T. Ariel's discussion of stamped amphora handles from Jerusalem, see "Imported Greek Stamped Amphora Handles," in *Jewish Quarter Excavations in the Old City of Jerusalem conducted by Nahman Avigad, 1969-1982 1: Architecture and Stratigraphy: Areas A, W and X-2, Final Report*, ed. Hillel Geva (Jerusalem: Israel Exploration Society, 2000), 267-83 (including an Appendix on Amphoras and Ritual Purity); *Excavations at the City of David 1978-1985 Directed by Yigal Shiloh 2: Imported Stamped Amphora Handles, Coins, Worked Bone and Ivory, and Glass*. Qedem 30 (Jerusalem: Hebrew University, 1990), esp. 25-28. Gerald Finkielsztejn has enthusiastically argued that the drop in the number of amphoras imported to Jerusalem in the Hasmonean period is due to the observance of purity laws among the population; see Finkielsztejn, "Hellenistic Jerusalem: The Evidence of the Rhodian Amphora Stamps," in Ingeborg Rennert Center for Jerusalem Studies, *New Studies on Jerusalem: Proceedings of the Fifth Conference, December 23rd 1999*, ed. Avi Faust and Eyal Baruch (Ramat Gan: Bar-Ilan University, 1999), 21*-36*. For the Italian wine and imported fish sauce from Masada, see Hannah M. Cotton and Joseph Geiger, *Masada II: The Yigael Yadin Excavations 1963-1965, Final Reports: The Latin and Greek Documents* (Jerusalem: Israel Exploration Society, 1989), 140-58; Cotton, Omri Lernau, and Yuval

Goren, "Fish sauces from Herodian Masada," *Journal of Roman Archaeology* 9 (1996): 223-38. With the exception of the oil lamps, the rest of the pottery from Yadin's excavations at Masada has not yet been published.

For the 1st–century C.E. villa at Ein ez-Zara, see Christa Clamer, *Fouilles archéologiques de 'Ain ez-Zâra/Callirrhoé, villégiature hérodienne* (Beirut: Institut français d'archéologie du Proche-Orient, 1997) (the ovoid jar is illustrated in Pl. 12:15). For the excavations at Ein Boqeq, see Moshe Fischer, Mordechai Gichon, and Oren Tal, *'En Boqeq: Excavations in an Oasis on the Dead Sea, 2: The Officina, An Early Roman Building on the Dead Sea Shore* (Mainz: Philipp von Zabern, 2000) (the ovoid jar is illustrated there in Fig. 2.7:1). For the cylindrical jar from Abila, see Farah S. Ma'ayeh, "Recent Archaeological Discoveries in Jordan," *Annual of the Department of Antiquities in Jordan* 4-5 (1960): 114-16.

For the results of neutron activation analysis indicating that some of the Qumran pottery is made of Jerusalem clay, see Joseph Yellin, Magen Broshi, and Hanan Eshel, "Pottery of Qumran and Ein Ghuweir: The First Chemical Exploration of Provenience," *Bulletin of the American Schools of Oriental Research* 321 (2001): 65-78. For a typology of clay jar stoppers, see Zvi Gal, "Loom Weights or Jar Stoppers?" *Israel Exploration Journal* 39 (1989): 281-83.

For Andrea M. Berlin's observation that the Jews of Galilee deliberately refrained from using Eastern Sigillata A, see "Romanization and Anti-Romanization in Pre-Revolt Galilee," in *The First Jewish Revolt: Archaeology, History, and Ideology,* ed. Berlin and J. Andrew Overman (New York: Routledge, 2002), 102-30; "The Death of Herod and the New Divide in Galilee," paper presented at the Annual Meeting of the Archaeological Institute of America, Philadelphia, 4 January 2002 (I am grateful to Berlin for providing me with a copy of this paper, and for her permission to cite it).

For the suggestion that after the Roman destruction of the settlement in 68 C.E. members of the Qumran community joined the group at Masada, see Yigael Yadin, *Masada: Herod's Fortress and the Zealots' Last Stand* (New York: Random House, 1966), 174; also see Emanuel Tov, "A Qumran Origin for the Masada Non-Biblical Texts?" *Dead Sea Discoveries* 7/1 (2000): 57-73.

For the sectarian halakhah regarding opening sealed vessels on the Sabbath, see Lawrence H. Schiffman, *The Halakhah at Qumran* (Leiden: E. J. Brill, 1975); also see Hannah K. Harrington, *The Impurity Systems of Qumran and the Rabbis* (Atlanta: Scholars, 1993), 74-75. For discussions of sectarian halakhah regarding the purity of oil and other liquids, see Joseph M. Baumgarten, "The Pharisaic-Sadducean Controversies about Purity and the Qumran Texts," *Journal of Jewish Studies* 31 (1980): 157-70; Schiffman, *Sectarian Law in the Dead Sea Scrolls: Courts, Testimony, and the Penal Code* (Chico:

Scholars, 1983) (esp. 161-73); Baumgarten, "Liquids and Susceptibility to Defilement in New 4Q Texts," *Jewish Quarterly Review* 85 (1994): 91-101; "Torohot," in *Qumran Cave 4 XXV, Halakhic Texts,* ed. Baumgarten et al. *Discoveries in the Judaean Desert 35* (Oxford: Clarendon, 1999), 79-122; the passage from 4QTohorah cited here is from p. 108.

For the Assumption of Moses, see Robert H. Charles, *The Apocrypha and Pseudepigrapha of the Old Testament in English* 2: *Pseudepigrapha* (Oxford: Clarendon, 1913), 407-24; Emil Schürer, *The History of the Jewish People in the Age of Jesus Christ (175 B.C.–A.D. 135)* rev. ed. 3/1, ed. Geza Vermès, Fergus Millar, and Martin Goodman (Edinburgh: T. & T. Clark, 1986), 278-88.

For my discussion of the differences between Qumran and contemporary Judean villas, see Jodi Magness, "A Villa at Khirbet Qumrân?" *Revue de Qumran* 16 (1994): 397-419 (with bibliography; some of the main references are repeated here with additional bibliography); also see "Qumran: Not a Country Villa," *Biblical Archaeology Review* 22/6 (1996): 38-47, 72-73. For *villae rusticae* in Italy, see Roger C. Carrington, "Studies in the Campanian 'Villae Rusticae'," *Journal of Roman Studies* 21 (1931): 110-30. For recent studies of *villae rusticae,* see Roger Ling, "*Villae rusticae* at Boscoreale," *Journal of Roman Archaeology* 9 (1996): 344-50; also see Alfred Frazer, ed., *The Roman Villa: Villa Urbana.* First Williams Symposium on Classical Architecture (Philadelphia: University Museum, 1998). For the relevant publications of Yizhar Hirschfeld and Robert Donceel and Pauline Donceel-Voûte, see the bibliographical notes for Chapter 1. For Herod's palaces at Masada, see Ehud Netzer, *Masada III: The Yigael Yadin Excavations, 1963-1965 Final Reports: The Buildings, Stratigraphy and Architecture* (Jerusalem: Israel Exploration Society, 1991). For the Hasmonean and Herodian palaces at Jericho, see Ehud Netzer, *Hasmonean and Herodian Palaces at Jericho: Final Reports of the 1973-1987 Excavations* 1: *Stratigraphy and Architecture* (Jerusalem: Israel Exploration Society, 2001). For the Hasmonean and Herodian desert palaces in general, see Netzer, *The Palaces of the Hasmoneans and Herod the Great* (Jerusalem: Israel Exploration Society, 2001); Yoram Tsafrir, "The Desert Fortresses of Judaea in the Second Temple Period," in *The Jerusalem Cathedra 2,* ed. L. I. Levine (Detroit: Wayne State University Press, 1982), 120-45. For the Herodian mansions in Jerusalem's Jewish Quarter, see Nahman Avigad, *Discovering Jerusalem* (for the amphoras, see 79, 87-88). For the villa at Khirbet el-Muraq (Hilkiah's Palace), see Emanuel Damati, "Hilkiah's Palace," in *Between Hermon and Sinai, Memorial to Amnon,* ed. Magen Broshi (Jerusalem: Yedidim, 1977), 93-113 (Hebrew); "The Palace of Ḥilkiya," *Qadmoniot* 60 (1982): 117-21 (Hebrew). The results of Pesach Bar-Adon's excavations at Rujm el-Bahr and Khirbet Mazin (Qasr el-Yahud) are published in Hebrew with an

English summary: Pesach Bar-Adon, *Excavations in the Judean Desert.* ʿAtiqot Hebrew series 9 (Jerusalem: Israel Antiquities Authority, 1989), 3-14, 18-29.

The similarities between the layout of Qumran (especially the tower) and other sites such as Rujm el-Qasr were first noted by Shimon Ricklin, "When Did the Essenes Arrive at Qumran? — An Architectural Response," in *Studies in the Settlement of Judea: A Collection of Papers in Historical Geography* 1, ed. Zeʾev H. Erlich (Bnei Brak: Moriah, 1995), 263-66 (Hebrew). For the farmstead at Qasr el-Leja, see Shimon Dar, *Landscape and Pattern: An Archaeological Survey of Samaria 800 B.C.E.–636 CE* (Oxford: BAR International Series 308[i], 1986), 10-12. For Yizhar Hirschfeld's report on his excavations at Ramat Hanadiv (including a chapter on the Hellenistic and Roman pottery by Naama Silberstein), see Hirschfeld, *Ramat Hanadiv Excavations: Final Report of the 1984-1998 Seasons* (Jerusalem: Israel Exploration Society, 2000) (with a discussion of fortified manor houses of the Second Temple period, 684-720; for Qumran, see 716-17).

# CHAPTER 6

# Communal Meals, a Toilet, and Sacred Space at Qumran

Communal meals conducted by the sectarians are mentioned in the scrolls and are described by Josephus. In this chapter, we examine the archaeological evidence for communal meals at Qumran in light of these literary sources. This evidence includes the presence of dining rooms, dining dishes, and the enigmatic animal bone deposits. As we shall see, the distribution of animal bone deposits suggests that the layout of the settlement at Qumran reflects a sectarian concept of sacred space. Rooms associated with varying degrees of purity or impurity seem to have been arranged according to this concept. One of the most interesting installations in the settlement is a toilet in L51, which was apparently associated with impurity. For the concept of purity and impurity among the sectarians and in rabbinic Judaism, see Chapter 7. We begin this chapter by discussing the toilet, before considering the evidence for communal meals and sacred space at Qumran.

## A Toilet at Qumran

De Vaux identified one of the installations he excavated as a toilet. This installation was located in L51, a large room on the eastern side of the main building to the north of the miqveh in L48-L49 (see Figs. 37, 39-41). A terracotta pipe set into a conical, mud-lined pit that was filled with thin layers of coarse, dirty earth was embedded in the floor of this room. In the photographs from de Vaux's excavations, the pipe can be seen set into the dried mud-lining of the pit. One way to confirm de Vaux's identification of this installation as a toilet would be to analyze soil samples from the pit. I do not have access to the material from de Vaux's excavations, and doubt whether soil samples from this pit were saved or are still available for analysis. However, comparisons with toilets in the ancient Mediterranean world suggest that de Vaux's identification is correct. I begin this discussion of the toilet at Qumran by reviewing the archaeological evidence for ancient toilets, and then consider the presence of a toilet at Qumran in light of testimony provided by Josephus and the Dead Sea Scrolls regarding the toilet habits of the Essenes.

Perhaps the best-known examples of ancient toilets are Roman luxury latrines, which were often part of a public bathhouse (see Fig. 42). They were equipped with wooden or stone seats pierced with holes which lined three sides of the room. The arrangement of side-by-side seats means that there was no toilet privacy. The seats were mounted above a constantly running stream of water from the bathhouse, which carried off the sewage. A small gutter on the floor in front of the seats cleaned the spillage. It also carried water for washing the hands and for dipping the sponges on sticks which the Romans used to clean themselves (instead of toilet paper). Examples of luxury latrines can be seen in the Scholastika Baths at Ephesus, at ancient Corinth, and at Ostia (the ancient port of Rome). Roman-Byzantine period luxury latrines are found at Caesarea and Beth Shean in Israel, and there is one in the early Islamic palace at Khirbet el-Mafjar near Jericho. Since these latrines relied on a constant supply of fresh water piped in by aqueduct, they are rarely found outside Roman civic bathhouses or other public establishments.

Sanitary arrangements otherwise varied greatly in the ancient Mediterranean world, even during the time of the Roman Empire. Since many private homes in Roman cities lacked any toilet facilities, residents either had to use a "chamber pot" (such as the bottom half of a broken amphora) or simply went outdoors. The contents of the chamber pots were tossed from the windows of houses on to the street below. This is why better-designed Roman cities such as Pompeii have very high curbs with stepping-stones across the streets (see Fig. 44). The waste was washed away by the overflow from public fountains, which ran through gutters into underground sewers. The lack of concern with toilet privacy is indicated by signs that some shopkeepers at Pompeii put on the outside walls of their shops, requesting that members of the public relieve themselves elsewhere. As John Bodel has observed, "Streets, public reservoirs, doorways, statues, even public and private buildings, not to mention tombs — virtually any outdoor place accessible to the public seems to have been liable to the danger of being fouled with ordure."

When toilet installations are found in Roman houses, they usually consist of a wood or stone seat built over a cesspit for the waste. When the cesspit was full, a manure merchant would be called to carry it away for sale as fertilizer. Sometimes the cesspit was dug in the back yard and connected to the toilet by a terracotta pipe drain. The waste was then "flushed" through the pipe by a bucket of water. However, because of the gentle gradient and the absence of any anti-odor U-bend trap, this arrangement did not represent much of an improvement. This kind of toilet installation is found in many of the houses at Pompeii.

Examples of toilets of Iron Age date have been identified at several sites in Palestine. Close parallels to the toilet at Qumran come from the City of David in Jerusalem, where two stone toilet seats dating to ca. 600 B.C.E. were discovered. Both were made of large, square blocks of limestone pierced with a hole in the center of the concave top. One of the seats was found in a small cubicle at the back of the House of Ahiel, still in its original position over a cesspit (see Fig. 43). An analysis of soil from the cesspit revealed that the inhabitants suffered from intestinal parasites (tapeworm and whipworm) and indicated that their diet included salad plants, potherbs, and spices. Similar stone toilet seats of Iron Age date, sometimes set over cesspits, have been discovered elsewhere in Jerusalem as well as at Buseirah and Tell es-Saidiyeh in Jordan. Late Bronze Age (15th-13th century B.C.E.) examples are known from Egypt. The installation described by de Vaux in L51 at Qumran appears to represent the cesspit of a toilet of this type. Perhaps the pipe set into it was intended to carry waste "flushed" down by pouring in water. Since no seat was found over the pipe and cesspit, it might have been made of wood. However, I believe a pierced stone block that de Vaux found in L44, which is adjacent to and east of L51, could represent a toilet seat. This object, which is described in de Vaux's notes but is not illustrated, was tentatively identified by de Vaux as part of a conduit or chimney flue.

The published plans indicate that the toilet in L51 went out of use after the earthquake of 31 B.C.E. together with the miqveh in adjacent L48-L49. This means that the toilet belongs to the pre–31 B.C.E. phase of Period Ib. The presence of a toilet at Qumran raises the question of the community's rules and regulations regarding purity. The Temple Scroll, War Scroll, and Josephus provide valuable information on sectarian sanitary practices. In contrast, other ancient Roman sources provide little information on Roman toilets and toilet habits. In fact, Alexander Scobie has noted that "Literary evidence concerning sewers and latrines in the Roman world is extremely meagre. . . . [T]here is nowhere extant a description of either a public or private Roman latrine, and no account of their administration."

How do the sanitary arrangements described in the scrolls and by Josephus compare? In the scrolls, latrines are referred to by the Biblical Hebrew term "the hand" or "the place for a hand." In Qumranic Hebrew, the term "hand" *(yad)* means penis (see Chapter 9). The relevant passage from the Temple Scroll (46.13-16) says: "And you shall make them a place for a hand outside the city, to which they shall go out, to the northwest of the city — roofed houses with pits within them, into which the excrement will descend, so that it will not be visible at any distance from the city, three thousand cubits." Yigael Yadin noted that the prohibition and much of the phraseology of this passage are based on the text of Deuteronomy 23:9-14. The War Scroll (1QM 7.6-7) mandates the placement of latrines at a distance of 2000 cubits from the camps, which is 1000 cubits less than the distance from the city prescribed by the Temple Scroll: "There shall be a space between all their camps and the place of the 'hand', about two thousand cubits, and no unseemly evil thing shall be seen in the vicinity of their encampments."

Josephus describes the sanitation practices of the Essenes as follows:

(On the Sabbath they do not) even go to stool. On other days they dig a trench a foot deep with a mattock — such is the nature of the hatchet which they present to neophytes — and wrapping their mantle about them, that they may not offend the rays of the deity, sit above it. They then replace the excavated soil in the trench. For this purpose they select the more retired spots. And though this discharge of the excrements is a natural function, they make it a rule to wash themselves after it, as if defiled. (*War* 2.147-49)

Albert Baumgarten has argued that the sanitation arrangements described in the scrolls and by Josephus differ so fundamentally that they could not reflect the practices of the same sect. He has therefore concluded that the Temple Scroll is not an Essene document or, at least, that the group that lived according to its rules was not the same as Josephus's Essenes. Baumgarten noted that although all these sources describe a practice secluded from the public eye, they differ in the way this was achieved. Whereas the Temple Scroll and War Scroll describe permanent, roofed facilities, Josephus's Essenes dug a new hole in the ground in an open, remote spot each time they had to relieve themselves.

I disagree with Baumgarten's conclusion that this reflects the practices of two different groups or sects because he assumes that our sources provide complete accounts. Instead it appears that only practices which deviated from the norm are described by Josephus and mandated by the Temple Scroll and War Scroll. Furthermore, Baumgarten's chronological argument is flawed. He suggested that the Temple Scroll (which was composed before Josephus wrote) could not represent an earlier stage of the sect than Josephus's Essenes because this would reverse the development of ancient latrines, which were usually a later phenomenon associated with the rise in economic standards. However, as we have seen, private toilets (consisting of a cesspit covered with a seat) are attested in Egypt and Palestine already in the Late Bronze Age and Iron Age.

The textual evidence combined with the presence of the toilet at Qumran indicate that the sectarians attended to their bodily functions in various ways. When they did not have access to built latrines in permanent settlements, they relieved themselves in the manner described by Josephus. The location of the toilet in L51 on the eastern side of the main building suggests that the distance regulations mandated for the toilets in the War Scroll and in the Temple Scroll did not apply to the settlement at Qumran. These sources make a point of requiring the placement of the toilets at minimum distances from the war camps at the end of days and from the ideal city of Jerusalem. In contrast, the silence of ancient Roman sources concerning the placement and construction of domestic latrines reflects a lack of regulation or concern. Similarly, Josephus was struck by the fact that the Essenes secluded themselves when defecating outdoors, in contrast to the usual contemporary practice of openly relieving oneself. This corresponds with the Temple Scroll's requirement that the toilets be located within an enclosed, roofed building, thereby ensuring toilet privacy.

The silence of Roman literary sources including Vitruvius on the subject of the disposal of human wastes in houses and cities may be due to the fact that the presumed knowledge of normal practice made such a discussion unnecessary. In other words, there was no need to mandate or describe normal, accepted practices. In addition, the sectarian concern for toilet privacy reflected in the Temple Scroll and by the testimony of Josephus was exceptional in the Roman world. As Scobie notes, "No extant Roman author gives his impression of a Roman *forica* [luxury latrine], where as many as sixty or more people, men and women, sitting on stone or wooden seats, relieved themselves in full view of each other." The Temple Scroll describes the type of toilet found at Qumran and undoubtedly in other permanent settlements, but it and the War Scroll added a distance regulation because of the state of purity required in the ideal holy city or during the war at the end of days.

Yadin noted that the distances for latrines mandated by the Temple Scroll and War Scroll would have placed them beyond the Sabbath limits. The Sabbath limits *(tehum shabbat)* refers to the maximum distance one is permitted to walk on the Sabbath. In rabbinic Judaism, 2000 cubits is the maximum distance that a person is allowed to walk on the Sabbath. The sectarians permitted a maximum distance of only 1000 cubits, as mandated by the Sabbath Code in the Damascus Document (CD 10.21): "He shall not walk more than one thousand cubits beyond the town." Sectarian law extended the maximum distance to 2000 cubits for the purposes of pasturing an animal (CD 11.5): "No man shall walk more than two thousand cubits after a beast to pasture it outside a town." The fact that the War Scroll mandates the placement of the toilets at a distance of 2000 cubits from the camps and the Temple Scroll mandates their placement at a distance of 3000 cubits from the city of Jerusalem means that these facilities lay outside the Sabbath limits. In other words, the legislation in these documents placed the toilets beyond the maximum distance one was allowed to walk on the Sabbath, thereby making the toilets inaccessible on the Sabbath. Similarly, according to Josephus the Essenes did not defecate on the Sabbath. If this regulation was observed at Qumran, the inhabitants presumably refrained from using the toilet in L51 on the Sabbath.

A fragmentary but significant halakhic (legal) scroll from Cave 4 at Qumran (4Q472 or 4QHalakha C) mentions the same practice of covering excrement that Josephus singled out for description. This fragment reads:

2. ] to cover excrements. If he does not [
3. ] a vessel according to [
4. ] regarding a dee[d

The reference in line 2 to covering excrement recalls Josephus's Essenes, who dig a trench in the ground and, after defecating, "they then replace the excavated soil." Similarly, the Temple Scroll makes a point of mandating that the toilets be pits "into which the excrement will descend." In other words, all of these sources — Josephus, the Temple Scroll, and 4Q472 — document or legislate the unique sectarian concern that excrement be concealed by being buried in a pit. This concern is clearly based on the sectarians' understanding of Deut. 23:12-14, which describes the War Camp: "You shall have a place outside the camp and you shall go out to it; and you shall have a stick with your weapons; and when you sit down outside, you shall dig a hole with it, and turn back and cover up your excrement. Because the Lord your God walks in the midst of your camp, to save you and to give up your enemies before you, therefore your camp must be holy, that he may not see anything indecent among you, and turn away from you."

The sectarians differed from contemporary Jews and non-Jews in regarding defecation as a polluting activity associated with impurity. They also differed in their concern for toilet privacy. This means that unlike everyone else, they did not defecate in view of others. For this reason, the Temple Scroll mandates that the toilets shall be "roofed houses with pits within them, into which the excrement will descend." This document describes enclosed (indoor) toilet facilities in a permanent settlement or urban context. Interestingly, the toilet at Qumran corresponds with this description, for de Vaux's notes indicate that L51 was roofed. The fact that the only doorway in L51 opened on to a room with a miqveh (L48-L49) recalls Josephus's description of the Essene custom of washing themselves as if defiled after attending to their bodily functions.

Because of their concern with modesty, Essene men wore loincloths even when immersing themselves in a miqveh and took care not to expose their genitalia to others (see Chapter 9). This concern for toilet privacy explains the placement of the toilet in L51 at the extreme western end of the room. Not only was this toilet located in a "roofed house," but it would not have been visible to passersby. In fact, the only way to view the toilet from outside L51 would be from the eastern wall of L52, a spot that no one was likely to pass by casually. When the sectarians did not have access to permanent toilet facilities, they apparently relieved themselves by digging a hole in the ground. Josephus singled this practice out for description because in contrast with the contemporary custom of defecating in view of others, the sectarians made a point of finding a secluded spot and wrapping their cloaks around themselves. De Vaux tentatively suggested that an iron tool found in Cave 11 represents the kind of hatchet that was presented to new initiates into the sect and used for digging a hole in the ground (see Fig. 45).

The evidence we have reviewed here indicates that the sectarians attended to their bodily needs in various ways depending on the available facilities. Because of their belief that defecation is a polluting activity, the sectarians washed themselves after defecating and required the placement of latrines at a certain distance from their ideal holy city of Jerusalem and the war camps at the end of days. On the Sabbath, they refrained from defecating altogether. Our modern Western obsession with toilet privacy and hygiene has obscured the fact that the sectarian practices were the exception rather than the norm in antiquity. In my opinion, modern scholars have overlooked some of the peculiar practices of the Essenes described by Josephus because they sound normal to us: for example, finding a secluded spot when defecating and washing afterwards, or being served food on individual dishes instead of eating with others out of a common dish (see below). The sectarians developed these habits out of concern with the transmission of impurity, not because they were concerned with sanitation or hygiene in the modern sense of the word. Josephus singled these practices out for description precisely because they differed from the norm.

In rabbinic Judaism, defecation is not considered a polluting activity: "These do not become unclean and do not impart susceptibility to uncleanness: 1) sweat, 2) stinking pus, 3) excrement, 4) blood which exudes with them, and 5) liquid [which is excreted with a stillborn child] at the eighth month" (Misnnah *Makhshirin* 6:7). According to the Mishnah, excrement can be used to seal a clay vessel (Mishnah *Kelim* 10:2; for general background on the Mishnah and rabbinic Judaism, see Chapter 7). In the Palestinian Talmud, Rabbi Jose ruled that defecation is associated with cleanliness instead of with impurity: "And is excrement [a matter of ritual] impurity; is it not merely [rather a matter of] cleanliness [being considered filth]?" (*Pesaḥim* 7:12). I believe the Mishnah provides the key to understanding why the sectarians differed from other Jews in associating defecation with impurity: "This governing principle applied in the temple: Whoever covers his feet [and defecates] requires immersion . . ." (Mishnah *Yoma* 3:2). This passage refers to the toilet used by the priests in the Jerusalem temple. After using the toilet, the priests were required to immerse themselves in a miqveh. Because the sect extended the temple purity laws to its members, they viewed defecation as a polluting activity and required immersion afterwards (as Josephus reports). Another passage from the Mishnah explains why the Temple Scroll mandates the placement of the toilets to the northwest of the city of Jerusalem. The miqveh associated with the toilet used by the priests in the temple was located in the Chamber of Immersion. The toilet and immersion facilities were located in underground rooms beneath the northwest side of the temple courtyard: "Through that [room in the Beit Hamoked, the Chamber of the Hearth] on the northwestern side do they go down to the room for immersion" (Mishnah *Middot* 1:6). The Temple Scroll mandates the placement of toilets in the ideal city of Jerusalem to the northwest of the city because the toilet facilities in the Second Temple were located to the northwest of the temple. Similarly, the sectarian concern with toilet privacy or modesty can be understood in light of the temple arrangements described in the Mishnah: "[If] one of them should have a nocturnal emission of semen, he goes out, proceeding along the passage that leads below the building — and lamps flicker on this side and on that — and he reaches the immersion room, and there was a fire there, and a privy in good taste. And this was its good taste: [if] he found it locked, he knows that someone is there; [if he found it] open, he knows that no one is there. He went down and immersed, came up and dried off, and warmed himself by the fire" (Mishnah *Tamid* 1:1). In other words, the room containing the toilet used by the priests serving in the temple had a door that could be closed or locked to ensure privacy. Because the toilet in L51 could not have served the needs of the entire community, most of the members must have relieved themselves outside the settlement, either in built facilities or in the manner described by Josephus. If built facilities existed outside the settlement, they may have been located to the northwest. In this case, the miqveh at the northwest corner of the site (L138) might have been used by these members before entering the settlement, as we shall see.

Because the sectarians viewed themselves as a replacement for the temple and created by means of the sect a substitute for the sacrificial cult, temple purity laws were transferred to the lives of the members. The requirement of immersion after defecation and concern for toilet privacy among the priests serving in the temple were therefore made universal. Similarly, male members wore white linen garments (including a linen loincloth) like those worn by the priests serving in the Jerusalem temple (see Chapter 9).

Based on his study of the Temple Scroll, Yadin suggested that during the Second Temple period there were two basic positions regarding the application of the purity regulations found in the Pentateuch: a minimalist position, which limits the laws of purity to the area of the temple and its priests, and a maximalist position, which extends the laws of purity to all of Israel. The sectarians represented the maximalist position. The life of the sect was therefore conducted as if the community were a virtual temple. We shall return to this issue when we consider the miqva'ot at Qumran (Chapter 7).

## Communal Meals: The Literary Evidence

The sectarians envisaged future, eschatological meals over which a priestly messiah and a messiah of Israel would preside. These messianic banquets are described in the Messianic Rule (also called the Rule of the Congregation, Hebrew *serekh ha'edah;* 1QSa 2.11-22). Other evidence from the Dead Sea Scrolls and from Josephus indicates that the sectarians regularly conducted real banquets or communal meals similar to the future messianic banquets. The nature of these communal meals is disputed. Lawrence Schiffman, for example, believes that they were eschatalogical in nature. Sinners were excluded, as they would be from the banquet and community of the future age. This reflects the group's expectation that it lived in the eschaton; the present banquets represented a sort of preparation for the messianic banquets. According to Schiffman, although the communal meals at Qumran had clear messianic overtones, they were not sacral meals. This means that the group did not view these meals as a substitute for the temple sacrifices and, by way of extension, there is no analogy between these meals and the Christian Eucharist.

However, many scholars believe that the communal meals of the sectarians were sacral or religious in nature. Hartmut Stegemann, for example, describes them as common ritual meals that were modeled after those held in the temple on the occasion of the pilgrimage festivals. The restrictions on participation in the communal meals of the sectarians correspond with the Torah's stipulation that only Israelite men ages 20 and up who were free of physical handicaps and were in a state of ritual purity could take part in the ritual meals in the temple. The communal meals might have been considered substitutes for the temple sacrifices, in which the sectarians did not participate. Mathias Delcor noted that the communal meals are characterized by the same acts required of or performed by priests in the Jerusalem temple, including the pronouncement of blessings, the wearing of white robes, and immersion in miqva'ot prior to the meals (or, in the case of the temple, before the sacrifices). Priests seem to have been responsible for preparing the food and drink for the communal meals just as they were for preparing the sacrifices in the temple. In fact, Josephus explicitly compared the communal dining room of the Essenes to "a holy precinct." According to James VanderKam, the messianic character and eschatological associations of these meals as well as the prominence of bread and wine and the fact that they were repeated regularly recall elements found in the New Testament descriptions of the Lord's Supper. Stegemann believes that the meals were ritual but not sacramental like the Eucharist. Moshe Weinfeld has noted the connection or overlap between the communal meals of the sectarians on the one hand and their assemblies or sessions on the other. In this regard the sect resembles other guilds in the Greco-Roman world, where the banquet (symposium) was an occasion for libations, sacral meals, chanting of hymns, and celebrating festivals. A fixed seating order was a feature of the communal meals and other assemblies of these guilds.

According to the Community Rule, communal meals were held with at least 10 members present, arranged by rank and presided over by a priest: "And when [the table has been prepared for eating or the n]ew wine [for drinking, the] priest shall [be first to stretch out his hand to bless the firstfruit of the bread] and of the wine" (Community Rule [1QS] 6.4-6). As Schiffman has noted, the reference to bread and wine is symbolic of a meal that included food and drink, since bread was a staple. It also reflects the fact that it was specifically the bread and wine that were blessed. The order of blessing the bread first and then the wine in this passage of 1QS follows Genesis 14:18 (the blessing of Melchizedek) and is the same in the Synoptic Gospels' account of

Jesus' last supper. In Jewish tradition today this order is reversed. Because the *tirosh* consumed by the sectarians at their communal meals was a newly pressed wine, it had a much lower alcoholic content than regular wine, which underwent a longer period of fermentation. The consumption of *tirosh* at these meals parallels the sacrificial ceremonies conducted in the Jerusalem temple for which the priests were required to remain sober. The priest (or in the case of the future banquets, the messiah) offered blessings and prayers before the meal. In contrast with the scrolls, where the priest (or messiah) made a blessing only at the beginning of the meal, Josephus refers to blessings at the beginning and end of the meal. According to the initiation process of the sect, new members were admitted to the communal meals in stages. At first, they were allowed to partake only of the pure food of the sect, which was considered less susceptible to defilement than liquids. Only in a more advanced stage of initiation could they partake of the pure drink of the sect. These restrictions were necessary to maintain the absolute purity of these meals. As Per Bilde has noted, "participation in the common meal is the primary expression of full membership in the community."

Josephus's relatively detailed account of the communal meals of the Essenes complements and supplements the information provided in the scrolls:

> . . . they reassemble in the same place and, girded with linen loin-cloths, bathe themselves thus in cold water. After this purification they assemble in a special building to which no one is admitted who is not of the same faith; they themselves only enter the refectory if they are pure, as though into a holy precinct. When they are quietly seated, the baker serves out the loaves of bread in order, and the cook serves only one bowlful of one dish to each man. (*War* 2.129-31)

The following observation by Johannes van der Ploeg highlights the similarities between the communal meals of the Essenes and those of Christian monks:

> It is quite natural that the Essenes, whom Josephus describes as working on the land during the morning hours, took off the clothes in which they had laboured, washed themselves before their meals, took other clothes, to put them off when they returned to the land, after leaving the refectory. In modern Christian monasteries of our time, especially those in warm countries, exactly the same is done: the monks have clothes in which they work in the field, in the monastery, etc., and special, better and cleaner ones, in

which they appear in the church and in the refectory. Before and after the meal, the monks and other religious of various orders are accustomed to sing and to pray; a priest pronounces the blessing over the simple food, which nobody may touch before the blessing has been given. During the meal it is not permitted to anyone to speak. In this, everything is the same as in the description of Josephus.

However, van der Ploeg noted that in contrast to Christian monks, the immersion required before communal meals reflects a uniquely sectarian concern with purity. Other requirements, including pure food and drink (and presumably, pure dishes), reflect this same concern.

## Archaeological Evidence for Communal Meals at Qumran

The corpus of ceramic vessels from Qumran provides one type of archaeological evidence for communal meals. As Magen Broshi has noted, the presence of a potters' workshop with two kilns throughout the existence of this small settlement reflects a concern with ritual purity. In other words, the inhabitants produced their own pottery to ensure its purity. This is why the ceramic corpus from Qumran consists largely of the same, undecorated types of cups, bowls, and plates used for dining, which appear to have been manufactured at the site. A store of over 1000 dishes, lying neatly stacked but broken where they had fallen on the ground, was discovered in L86 (the "pantry") (see Fig. 30). Nearly all of these vessels represent dishes used for dining, such as plates, cups, and bowls. They include 279 shallow, carinated bowls with flaring rims, 798 hemispherical cups, and 150 deep cups with thin walls and flaring rims (and one example of a similar but carinated cup). There are also 37 large, deep bowls or kraters which could have been used for mixing wine and water or for serving food, 11 table jugs for pouring wine, and eight large jars for storing food or drink. In other words, this assemblage represents a complete table service. The absence of cooking pots indicates that the food was cooked elsewhere in the settlement. The large number and uniformity of the dishes points to communal meals with many participants as well as a concern with purity. This accords with Josephus's testimony that each member received an individual plate with a serving of food, in contrast to the usual custom of sharing common dishes: "the cook serves only one bowlful of one dish to each man" (*War* 2.130). In ancient Palestine, light meals typically consisted of bread dipped into a wine-based vinegar, while the main meal was usually a lentil or vegetable stew served in a large bowl and sopped up with bread. Josephus's account and the large number of individual cups, bowls, and plates at Qumran indicate that the inhabitants did not follow the usual custom of eating out of common dishes. This practice undoubtedly stems from their belief that impurity could be transmitted through food and drink. The morphology (shapes) of these vessels confirms de Vaux's suggestion that they were broken as a result of the earthquake of 31 B.C.E., which means they belong to the pre-31 phase of Period Ib.

Because L86 opened onto the largest room in the settlement (L77), de Vaux concluded that the latter served as a communal dining room and assembly hall. He noted that the inhabitants deposited what appear to be the remains of religious or ritual meals in the spaces around the outside of the buildings. These deposits consisted of animal bones that were placed between large potsherds or inside jars, either flush with or on top of the ancient ground level (see Figs. 24, 25). They were covered with little or no earth. Analyses have indicated that the bones belonged to adult sheep and goats, lambs or kids, calves, and cows or oxen. No single deposit contained the complete skeleton of any animal. Instead, the bones had been taken apart and the flesh was no longer attached to them when they were collected. Many of the bones appear to have been broken or fragmentary before they were deposited. Twenty-six out of the 39 deposits that Frederick Zeuner examined contained bones from a single animal or species, while the others included bones from up to four different animals. In cases where more than one species were present in a single deposit, one species predominated and the others were represented by odd scraps. Zeuner calculated that the minimum number of individuals represented among the approximately 500 specimens he examined were distributed as follows: 5 goats, 5 sheep, 26 sheep or goats, 10 kids or lambs, 4 oxen or cows, 6 calves, 1 other. These specimens came from 22 deposits in L130, 8 deposits in L132, and 7 deposits in the South Trench. De Vaux noted that the bones must be the remains of meals, since all were clean but some were charred, indicating that the meat was boiled or roasted on a spit. Interestingly, several bones appear to have been lying in a fire before being deposited. In other words, these bones were carefully collected and deposited, although the fact that they were lying in a fire means they could not have been eaten as part of a meal. Zeuner noted that the presence of beef indicates these could not be the remains of Passover meals. In addition, most of the deposits that included only one or two species (which are the majority) contained some bones on which there was no flesh to eat. Zeuner observed that "The fact that it was considered worth while to place in a pot and then to bury scraps of a meal that were useless for human consumption strongly points to a ritual character of the custom. More than that, it suggests that the ritual had already become a matter of form, the original sacrificial effort having been replaced by a symbolic act."

Most scholars including de Vaux believe that these remains do not represent the victims of ritual sacrifice. This is because no remains of an altar have been found at Qumran, and the scrolls provide no clear indication that this community offered animal sacrifices outside the Jerusalem temple. According to this view, the sect did not reject animal sacrifices altogether but refused to participate in the cult in the Jerusalem temple because they considered it impure. As Schiffman has stated, "It must be emphasized that the sectarians did not offer sacrifices at Qumran." Magen Broshi has expressed to me the opinion that "The Qumranites, in whose library Deuteronomy was the most popular biblical book, could not have sacrificed outside Jerusalem." Moshe Weinfeld has noted that the Qumran sect differed conspicuously from other Greco-Roman associations in the complete absence of ordinances in the scrolls regarding sacrifice, oblations, and convocations in temples on holidays. In fact, the Community Rule (9.4-5) states that members of the sect shall atone for their sins by offering prayers instead of animal sacrifices. Similarly, a passage from Proverbs (15:8) that is cited in the Damascus Document was altered slightly to make prayer preferable to impure sacrifice: "No man shall send to the altar any burnt-offering, or cereal offering, or incense, or wood, by the hand of one smitten with any uncleanness, permitting him thus to defile the altar. For it is written, *The sacrifice of the wicked is an abomination but the prayer of the just is as an agreeable offering*" (CD 11.18-21). Since meat was rarely consumed by most people in antiquity, the animal bones at Qumran might therefore represent the remains of occasional sacral or ritual meals that were nonsacrificial. In this case, they could represent the remains of meals consumed during the annual Feast of the Renewal of the Covenant, which might have been held at Qumran. According to Josephus, the Essenes gathered twice a day for communal meals. It is impossible to determine whether the sectarians considered all or only some of their communal meals to be sacral or ritual. We also do not know on which occasions meat was consumed at Qumran, although it was presumably not a frequent occurrence.

On the other hand, a few scholars have interpreted the animal bone deposits as evidence for a sacrificial cult at Qumran. For example, Frank Moore Cross has noted that the sectarian rewording of a passage from Ezekiel (44:15) in the Damascus Document (CD 3.18–4.4) seems to allude to animal sacrifices. In it, the sect is identified with "the priests and the Levites and [sic!] the sons of Zadok who kept the office of my sanctuary when the children of Israel went astray from me, they shall bring me fat and blood." In fact, the Damascus Document contains several laws relating to animal sacrifice (such as CD

11.17-21), although some scholars have suggested that these are survivals from a period when the sectarians still participated in the cult in the Jerusalem temple. The War Scroll (2.5-6) refers to "the men who shall attend at holocausts and sacrifices to prepare sweet-smelling incense for the pleasure of God, to atone for all his congregation." This indicates that the sectarians anticipated offering animal sacrifices during the coming apocalyptic war.

Our ancient sources provide conflicting or unclear testimony regarding the offering of animal sacrifices by the Essenes. Philo (*Every Good Man is Free* 75) states that the Essenes did not offer animal sacrifices: "Indeed, they are men utterly dedicated to the service of God; they do not offer animal sacrifice, judging it more fitting to render their minds truly holy." On the other hand, in a confused passage Josephus seems to indicate that the Essenes offered animal sacrifices privately: "They send offerings to the temple, but perform their sacrifices using different customary purifications. For this reason, they are barred from entering into the common enclosure, but offer sacrifice among themselves" (*Ant.* 18.19; the epitome of Josephus and the Latin version express this passage in the negative: "offer no sacrifices since the purifications to which they are accustomed are different").

Because the sectarians viewed themselves as a substitute temple it might have been a logical step for them to offer animal sacrifices by themselves. As we have seen, however, there is no evidence that the sectarians offered animal sacrifices outside the Jerusalem temple, and there are no remains of an altar at Qumran. It is more likely that just as the sectarians considered their communal meals to be a substitute for participation in the Temple cult, they treated the animals consumed at these meals in a manner analogous to the Temple sacrifices, although they were not technically sacrifices. This alternative is attractive because the level of purity required by the sectarians for participation in the communal meals and the manner in which these meals were conducted paralleled the cult in the Jerusalem temple. The food and drink consumed at the communal meals were at the highest level of purity, like the sacrifices offered in the temple. For this reason, the remains of animals consumed at the communal meals were disposed of in a manner analogous to the sacrifices offered in the temple. This explanation seems best in light of the following characteristics of the animal bone deposits at Qumran: (1) the species represented correspond in type and proportions to those sacrificed in the Jerusalem temple; (2) the fact that the meat was boiled or roasted corresponds with the treatment of temple sacrifices that were consumed; (3) the manner in which these bones were carefully placed on the ground around the buildings (see below) is otherwise difficult to explain; (4) the fact that these deposits include meatless bones and bones that had been lying in a fire (which means they had not been eaten as part of a meal) is also otherwise inexplicable.

Schiffman has noted that 4QMMT (Hebrew *Miqsat Ma'aseh Ha-Torah*) may shed light on the animal bone deposits. The relevant passage states: "And {dogs} are not to be brought to the sacred camp for they may eat some of the bones from the Sanctuary to which meat is still attached. For Jerusalem is {the sacred camp} . . ." (4Q397:58-59). According to Schiffman, this passage indicates that the authors of the document were displeased that dogs were allowed in Jerusalem because they might scavenge the bones of sacrificed animals. Since animal bones are described as a source of corpse-impurity elsewhere in this text and in the Temple Scroll, he has suggested that the sectarians at Qumran buried them to prevent dogs or other animals from scattering them throughout the settlement and potentially defiling the members. This raises two obvious questions. First, if the bones were considered a source of potential defilement, why did the community keep them in the area of the settlement? After all, they lived in the midst of a wilderness, not in an urban center, and could easily have discarded the bones elsewhere (such as throwing them over the edge of the cliff into Wadi Qumran). Second, if the community wanted to keep the bones for ritual reasons but considered them a potential source of defilement, why did they not bury them in deep pits that would have been inaccessible to dogs?

I therefore do not accept Schiffman's interpretation, although I believe that the passage from 4QMMT sheds light on the animal bone deposits from Qumran. In it, Jerusalem is referred to as the "sacred camp," as opposed to the temple ("Sanctuary"). The holocausts (Hebrew *'olah*) offered in the Jerusalem temple, which were completely consumed by fire, left only ashes and bits of bone. But in other types of sacrifices, such as the *zevach* and *pesach*, the animals were either wholly or partly consumed by the priests and people. After the sacrifice, the flesh of the animal was generally boiled and any other remains were burned. This seems to correspond with the physical evidence from Qumran, where most of the meat was boiled and some was roasted. The objection raised by the author of 4QMMT suggests that in the city of Jerusalem (the "sacred camp") dogs scavenged the bones of sacrificed animals, presumably either after the meat had been consumed by banqueters and while the bones were awaiting burning and disposal, or after the bones had been burned. Since dogs had access to them, the bones were not buried in deep *favissae* (sacred pits), but must have been buried in shallow pits or piled on the ground.

David Wright has discussed the disposal of the *hattat*, a type of sacrifice that belonged to the priests. The Hebrew Bible specifies that the skin, meat, head, legs, entrails, and excrement of the hattat are to be taken to an ash dump outside the camp (that is, outside the Temple enclosure) and burned. This ash dump was also used for the disposal of other cultic refuse, including the ashes from the altar of burnt offerings. Although the ash dump was located outside the camp (outside the Temple enclosure), it was still considered a "pure place," as opposed to other disposal sites outside the camp which were considered impure. This is because, although they were not impure, the remains of the hattat were still considered holy. Depending on their level of holiness or importance, the leftovers of different kinds of sacrifices offered in the Jerusalem temple had to be burned within one or two days. Wright has demonstrated that this method of disposal was intended to prevent the profanation of the remaining portions of the bones and carcass. He has also noted that this process of disposal included the breaking of pottery.

The animal bones deposited in or under potsherds and pots outside the buildings at Qumran apparently represent the remains of communal meals at which meat was consumed. Because the sectarians considered these meals to be a substitute for participation in the sacrifices in the Jerusalem temple, they disposed of the remains of the animals they consumed in a manner analogous to those sacrificed in the temple. They carefully deposited the remains of these animals in or under potsherds and pots outside buildings in the settlement, which corresponds with the area of the "camp" in Jerusalem. Many of the pottery vessels used in these meals seem to have been deliberately broken before being placed with the animal bone deposits. Because of this practice, as well as the sectarian belief that food and drink transmit impurity (requiring separate dishes for each member), the community needed hundreds of ceramic dishes, as seen in L86 and L114.

Another piece of physical evidence suggests a correlation between the animal bone deposits at Qumran and the remains of sacrificial banquets in ancient Jerusalem. According to de Vaux, the animal bone deposits at Qumran were found "with varying frequency in almost all the open spaces of the Khirbeh." This gives the impression that these deposits were widespread. In fact, according to de Vaux, these deposits were found in only eight loci: in Period Ib, L23, L65, L80, L92, L130, and L135; and in Period II, L73, L80, L130, and L132 (refer to the site plan in Fig. 5). Animal bone deposits were also discovered in two trenches excavated along the inner face of the wall that encloses the esplanade to the south of the settlement (the "South Trench"). Magen Broshi has informed me that animal bone deposits were also discovered by Yitzhak Magen in excavations he recently conducted on the esplanade to the south of the site. Instead of being distributed throughout the settlement, the loci with the animal bone deposits form two distinct clusters: one in L130, L132, and L135 at the northern end of the site; and the other in L65, L73, L80, and L92 at the southern and eastern ends of the site. The only locus that falls outside these two clusters is L23 in the courtyard in the center of the main building. This means that all of the loci with animal bones (except L23) are located on the fringes of the settlement, outside the buildings. In other words, the animal bones were deliberately deposited outside the buildings, not simply in the open spaces around them. As we shall now see, the two clusters appear to correspond with the location of communal dining rooms inside the settlement. We begin with the southeast cluster (L65, L73, L80, L92), which surrounds the communal dining room in L77.

L77 is the largest room at Qumran (see Fig. 28). The adjacent pantry (L86) containing a store of over 1000 dishes collapsed in the earthquake of 31 B.C.E. and was subsequently buried. During Period Ib, the floor sloped gently down from the western end of the room to a doorway in the southeast wall and from there rose slightly to the east. A water channel that opened through the doorway in the northwest wall allowed the floor to be washed, with the water draining through the doorway in the southeast wall. After the earthquake, the roof of L77 had to be rebuilt. Three square pillar (pier) bases were erected in a row on top of the Period Ib floor at the eastern end of the room, ending with a pilaster (a square pillar) base abutting the east wall. The bases were made of mud brick covered with plaster. Wooden posts placed on these bases supported the ceiling beams. The door opening onto the southern esplanade was blocked, and the water channel leading through the north doorway of the room was diverted. Because of this and because the floor was now leveled (with a step at its eastern end), the room could no longer be washed in the same way as before. According to de Vaux, the presence of a few dishes on the floor, especially in the southwest corner, indicates that L77 still functioned as a dining room in Period II. Although this is correct, it is not accurate. The archaeological evidence suggests that after the earthquake of 31 B.C.E., the dining room was transferred to an upper floor (a second-story level) above L77. This is indicated by construction of a spiral staircase with a square central pillar in L35, in the southeast corner of the central courtyard of the main building, to the north of L77 (see Fig. 15). De Vaux's notes (published by Humbert and Chambon) describe this staircase as having been constructed over the water channel that supplied the miqveh in L48-L49, which was destroyed by the earthquake and subsequently abandoned. This means that the staircase was constructed after the earthquake. Since the areas surrounding the staircase to the west, north, and east were open to the sky when it was constructed (these areas are the central courtyard in L25, L37, and the courtyard that replaced the damaged miqveh in L48-L49), the staircase must have provided access to a second-story level to the south, above L67, L54-L58, and L77. The construction of a wall dividing the pool in L56-L58 into two after the earthquake and the erection of the pillar bases at the east end of L77 were necessary to support this new second-story level. Perhaps the plastered rectangular platform in L81 that abutted the outside of the western wall of L77 was also a pillar base (in Humbert and Chambon's volume it is attributed to Period II). The buttressing added around the outside of the eastern and southern walls of L89 and the burnt wooden ceiling beams discovered lying on the Period II floor of L86 suggest that the second-story level extended above this room. An intact cylindrical jar with a Hebrew name painted in red on the shoulder was set into one of the basins in L34 (apparently a dyeing installation), and a stone disc that covered it lay on the ground nearby (see Fig. 16). If this jar belongs with the basins, it would provide an example of a cylindrical jar of pre–31 B.C.E. date since these basins went out of use after the earthquake. However, I believe that this jar should be associated with Period II, for it was embedded in the Period II floor that covered the basins (that is, its rim was flush with the floor), as indicated by the stone disc and burnt wood roof beams lying on the floor nearby. The beams must be from the burning of the roof at the end of Period II, because this area was open to the sky before the earthquake of 31 B.C.E., when the basins were located here (L34). These beams indicate that this area was roofed in Period II. The fact that the dining room moved upstairs also explains why the water channel that facilitated the washing of the floor at the ground level went out of use and the doorway in the southeast wall was blocked up after the earthquake.

Although the pantry of dishes in L86 is associated with the pre–31 B.C.E. phase of Period Ib, other evidence indicates that L77 functioned as a dining room after the earthquake (although it moved upstairs). The first piece of evidence consists of a pottery deposit found in the fill of pool L58 (a pool without steps created after the division of L56-L58 into two). Although this deposit included several storage jars, it consisted mainly of cooking pots and tableware (cups, bowls, plates, jugs and juglets; de Vaux collected sherds belonging to about 30 restorable vessels). According to de Vaux, these vessels were thrown into the pool when the site was destroyed in 68 C.E. at the end of Period II. They must come from the second-story level of L77, which overlooked the pool. The second piece of evidence consists of the kitchen in L38-L41, a large room along the northern side of the central courtyard in the main building. This room contained three ovens (or cooking hearths), a paved area with signs of burning, and a mud-brick platform. Because these installations appear to have been constructed after the earthquake, it is unclear whether this room functioned as a kitchen before 31 B.C.E. A doorway in the southwest wall of L38-L41 opened onto the northwest side of the central courtyard. The staircase in L35 was located diagonally across from it, on the southeast side of the courtyard. The staircase was accessed on its north side (from the direction of the kitchen) through two long, narrow, side-by-side passages, each of which could be closed by a door at the end (at the entrance to the stairs) (see Fig. 15). This suggests that one doorway was used as an entrance and the other as an exit by those climbing up and down the stairs. Such an arrangement is described in the Temple Scroll in relation to the rotation of the priestly courses in the temple: ". . . the second (= incoming) [priestly course] shall enter on the left . . . and the first (= outgoing) shall leave on the right. They shall not mingle with one another nor their vessels" (11QT$^a$ 40.1-4). The two long, narrow passages were apparently meant to ensure the separation of those entering and exiting the staircase (see Chapter 7).

De Vaux suggested that the nicely cut architectural elements found around the site (see Chapter 4) originated in an arcade to the south of L49 and L52 (an area that was later extensively remodeled) or in a colonnade that stood on a stylobate separating L49 from L35 which was covered by a wall in Period II. I believe these elements originated in a structure that was destroyed by the earthquake of 31 B.C.E. In one of his preliminary reports, de Vaux attributed the stylobate to the period immediately preceding the earthquake. This structure was probably located in the area of the staircase in L35, as de Vaux proposed. Although the evidence indicates that there was a dining room in the second-story level of L77 during Period II, it is not clear whether one existed in this locus during the post–31 B.C.E. phase of Period Ib. There is no evidence that this locus functioned as a dining room during this phase, since all of the published dishes belong either to the pre–31 B.C.E. phase of Period Ib or to Period II. Perhaps during the post–31 B.C.E. phase of Period Ib (that is, from 31 to ca. 9/8 B.C.E.), the community's dining room was located elsewhere — above L111, L120, L121, L122, and L123, as we shall see.

Although L77 was the only communal dining room identified by de Vaux, the northern cluster of animal bones (in L130, L132, L135) points to the existence of a dining room in the secondary building. This is also indicated by the presence of a store of dining dishes in L114, next to the round cistern (see Fig. 33). Stacks of dishes were found lying broken on the ground, just as in L86 (see Fig. 34). They included 39 shallow, open bowls with incurved rims, 111 hemispherical cups, 9 deep cups or bowls with flaring walls, one cup or bowl with a ledge rim, one large, deep bowl or krater, one table jug, two jugs or juglets with rounded bases, and three wheel-made (or "Herodian") oil lamps. There was also a large quantity of potsherds.

Because of the wheel-made ("Herodian") lamps, de Vaux initially assigned this assemblage to Period II. However, he later reassigned it to Period Ib, since the wheel-made lamps looked rougher and earlier than the typical "Herodian" lamps, and because this deposit was covered by Period II. I believe de Vaux's confusion stems from the fact that this deposit should be assigned to the post–31 B.C.E. phase of Period Ib, a phase he did not recognize. In other words, this represents an assemblage dating to the reign of Herod the Great, as opposed to the assemblage from L86, which antedates the earthquake of 31. This makes sense for two reasons. First, the rough appearance of the wheel-made lamps can be explained by the fact that this type appeared only shortly before Herod's death. Second, the northern cluster of animal bone deposits and the ceramic assemblage in L114 must be associated with a communal dining room located nearby. Although some of these deposits dated to Period II, de Vaux noted that most belonged to Period Ib. However, the Period Ib deposits are all described as having been covered in the sediment of the water that flooded the site after its abandonment, including two pots containing animal bones that were carried away by the flood. The abandonment and flooding of the site occurred after Qumran was destroyed by fire in ca. 9/8 B.C.E. Another deposit of dishes from L126 (a small room to the north of L110) might be associated with the dining room in this area. De Vaux mentioned that a great deal of pottery including bowls and plates was found in L126. The only two pieces published (which are described as coming from Period II) are a basin or krater and a handleless jar.

The pottery published from L130 and L135 includes some of the same types as in L114. The assemblage from L130-L135 contains at least four oil lamps of Hellenistic inspiration, a type that dates to the post–31 B.C.E. phase of Period Ib (see Chapter 5). The fact that many of the vessels illustrated from L130-L135 appear to be slightly earlier in date than those from L114 reflects the fact that they were deposited here over the course of at least 20-30 years, whereas the assemblage from L114 represents the dishes in use at the time of the settlement's destruction in ca. 9/8 B.C.E.

Is it possible to identify the communal dining room where these cooked animals were consumed and the dishes from L114 were used? It could not lie to the north, east, or south of the pantry in L114 and the round cistern next to it (L110), as this area was occupied by miqva'ot and workshops (see Fig. 31). Interestingly, the latter included a large baking oven (in L105). Instead, the dining room should be sought in the complex of rooms immediately to the west of L110 and L114, that is, in L111, L120, L121, L122, and L123 (see Fig. 32). However, the partition walls and installations in these loci make them unsuitable candidates for a communal dining room. Instead, I believe that the dining room was located in the second-story level above these loci. The existence of a second-story level in this area is attested by a staircase in L113 (see Fig. 35). Because the five surviving stone steps rise towards the south, de Vaux assumed that they led to a second story above L101. However, the staircase must have turned 180 degrees at a landing on the south side of L109 and L113 and continued up along the west side of L113 to the area above L111, L120, L121, L122, and L123. It is paralleled by the staircase in L13 in the main building, which also turned 180 degrees at a landing and provided access to the second-story level of the tower and the rooms above L1, L2, and L30 (see Fig. 12). According to de Vaux, L111 was originally an open-air courtyard (see Fig. 32). After the earthquake of 31 B.C.E. its eastern wall was doubled and it was roofed over. The staircase in L113 appears in the published plans of Period II but not in Period Ib. Its construction is apparently contemporary with the roofing of L111 and dates to the post–31 B.C.E. phase of Period Ib. In other words, all of the available evidence suggests that after the earthquake of 31 B.C.E., a new dining room was constructed in the secondary building above L111, L120, L121, L122, and L123. The dishes were stored in L114, and the animal bones from some of the meals consumed were buried just to the north of and outside this building.

It is impossible to determine whether both this dining room and the one in L77 were used during the post–31 B.C.E. phase of Period Ib, although, as we have seen, it is possible that only the former functioned during this period. However, the fact that animal bone deposits were found in Period II contexts in both clusters suggests that both were used as dining rooms during the final phase of the site's occupation, that is, during the 1st century C.E. The absence of evidence for benches used as dining couches accords with Schiffman's observation based on the scrolls that the participants in the messianic banquets were to eat sitting instead of reclining, following the biblical Jewish rather than the Greco-Roman custom. This suggests that during their communal meals at Qumran the sectarians followed the same custom of dining while seated. This corresponds with Josephus's testimony regarding the communal meals of the Essenes, whom he describes as sitting (kathisanton) instead of reclining (War 2.130). In contrast, according to Philo, the Therapeutae conducted their communal meals while reclining on rough couches (On the Contemplative Life 69). The fact that the Essenes drank non-intoxicating amounts of new wine and therefore remained quiet and sober during their communal meals contrasts with Greek and Roman symposia, which were characterized by the consumption of large quantities of wine and loud, boisterous behavior (see Fig. 36). This too is singled out for description by Josephus (War 2.132-33).

## The Concept of Space at Qumran

Another feature of the dining rooms at Qumran corresponds with the testimony of Josephus and the scrolls. As I mentioned above, members were required to immerse themselves in a miqveh before participating in the communal meals. It is therefore not surprising to find a large miqveh (L56-L58) outside the entrance to the dining room in L77 and two more (L117-L118) to the east of the dining room above L111, L120, L121, L122, and L123 (refer to the plan of the site in Fig. 5). Although miqva'ot are scattered throughout the settlement, their distribution does not appear to be random. Instead, they seem to be associated with areas where purity was required or in areas where impurity was incurred. For example, miqva'ot are located at the entrances to the communal dining rooms, at the entrance to the room with the toilet (L48-L49), and in areas with workshops (in L71, which is next to the potters' workshop). Another miqveh is located in L138 by the northwest entrance to the site.

The locations of the toilet, the miqva'ot, and the animal bone deposits seem to reflect a sectarian concept of pure versus less pure and impure space. Discussions of the architecture of Qumran have focused on the two parts of the settlement: the main building and the secondary building. The main building has been viewed as an integral unit consisting of a square marked by the tower on the north. Yizhar Hirschfeld has claimed that because this layout displays similarities with rural villas elsewhere in Roman Palestine, Qumran was a manor house, not a sectarian settlement (see Chapter 5). However, the inhabitants of Qumran apparently conceived of their settlement as a series of spaces with varying degrees of purity or impurity. The miqveh in L48-L49 was associated with the toilet in L51. The very large miqveh at the southeastern end of the site (L71) must have served the potters' workshop and been used by those entering the settlement from the east (by L84), where the cemetery is located. The large miqva'ot in L56-L58 and L117-L118 must have been used for purification before entering the communal dining rooms.

This brings us back to the animal bone deposit in the open courtyard in the center of the main part of the settlement (L23). As we noted above, this is the only deposit that lies outside the two clusters. The presence of this deposit suggests that the eastern part of the main building was considered an impure space. The toilet in L51 was also associated with impurity. The distribution of the animal bone deposits supports Schiffman's suggestion that the sectarians considered animal bones to be a source of impurity, although they were apparently placed on the ground just outside the main buildings because of their association with the communal meals. The animals consumed in these meals were disposed of in a manner analogous to sacrificial remains from the Jerusalem temple. All of these areas were served, at least before the earthquake of 31, by the miqveh in L48-L49. This means that the eastern part of the main building was occupied by workshops and installations that were associated with some degree of impurity, paralleling the arrangement of rooms in the secondary building.

The fact that all of the animal bones were deposited in or around the outside of these impure areas may be a physical expression of the concept of the "temple" (the areas requiring the greatest degree of purity) versus the "sacred camp" (the areas with lesser degrees of purity or with impurity). The disposition of space at Qumran seems to correspond with a passage in the Temple Scroll: "And you shall make three places to the east of the city, separated one from another, into which shall come the lepers and the people who have a discharge and the men who have had a nocturnal emission" (Temple Scroll 46.15). Yadin noted that there are also a number of rabbinic regulations prohibiting the location of workshops to the west of Jerusalem, perhaps because the prevailing winds in Jerusalem are westerly. The arrangement of the settlement at Qumran seems to reflect this kind of spatial concept. The western half of each part of the settlement contains the rooms with the greatest degree of purity including the communal dining rooms and in the main part of the settlement, the "scriptorium" (L30) and a possible meeting room (L4), paralleling the "temple." The eastern half of each part of the settlement contains workshops and, in the main building, a toilet. The animal bones were deposited in and around these eastern halves. These areas seem to parallel the "sacred camp" referred to in 4QMMT and other documents. Finally, the cemetery, which was associated with the greatest degree of impurity lies to the east, completely outside the boundaries of the settlement (perhaps mirroring the location of the traditional Jewish burial ground in Jerusalem on the slopes of the Mount of Olives, to the east of the walled city).

The arrangement of space at Qumran is therefore reminiscent of the passage from 4QMMT, with the western half of each part of the settlement symbolizing the "temple" and the areas around them corresponding with the "sacred camp." In the Temple Scroll, the temple city is made equivalent to the wilderness camp of Deuteronomy 23; just as the latter surrounded Mount Sinai during the revelation, so the former surrounds the temple. This means that the laws of a sacred camp apply to the temple city. Some scholars believe that the "temple" (Hebrew 'ir ha-miqdash, or "city of the sanctuary") in the Temple Scroll refers to the entire city of Jerusalem, while according to others it refers only to the area of the Temple Mount. Either way, the plan of the temple as conceived of in the Temple Scroll created a compound of concentric zones of holiness emanating from the Divine Presence in the center. As the holiness radiated outward, so the levels of purity progressed inward. The settlement at Qumran seems to have been laid out along similar lines.

An analogous arrangement of sacred space (or "cultic topography") has been noted by Wright in Priestly legislation regarding Jerusalem. The relevant passages in the Hebrew Bible describe a graduated system with the sanctuary (temple enclosure) in the center. The sanctuary has the highest degree of purity and is described as a "holy place." The city surrounding the sanctuary is called a "pure place" because it is generally pure, although some types of impurity (such as the disposed remains of sacrifices) are allowed. The area outside this, which is called an "impure place," is both pure and impure. Wright has also noted that there is a functional distinction or segregation between different types of impurity, depending on whether they are communicable or noncommunicable.

Interestingly, the toilet in L51 and the adjacent miqveh in L48-L49 went out of use and do not appear to have been replaced after the earthquake of 31 B.C.E. Presumably the members now had to leave the settlement altogether to use toilet facilities or relieve themselves in the manner described by Josephus. Perhaps these facilities were located to the northwest of the settlement, an arrangement that would parallel the location of the toilets mentioned in the Temple Scroll, "to the northwest of the city." Yadin suggested identifying "the place called Betsoa" [the house of excrement], which Josephus describes as having been located on the northwest side of Jerusalem, with an Essene toilet. He noted that the Gate of the Essenes, which is also mentioned by Josephus, was located nearby. Yadin proposed that this gate became associated with the Essenes because they used it to gain access to their toilet facilities and perhaps chose to live in its vicinity.

Before entering the settlement at Qumran, members would have immersed themselves in the miqveh in L138 at the northwest entrance to the site (see Fig. 23). The existence of a toilet within the settlement at Qumran suggests that at least until 31 B.C.E. the eastern half of the main building did not strictly correspond with the "temple city" or wilderness camp of the Temple Scroll, which prohibits toilets within the city. Similarly, the only animal bone deposit attested within the settlement (in L23) dates to Period Ib (it is not clear whether it belongs to the pre- or post-earthquake phase of Period Ib). Perhaps the disappearance of toilet facilities and animal bone deposits within the settlement at Qumran after Period Ib (either after the earthquake of 31 B.C.E. or after 9/8 B.C.E.) reflects a reorganization of space more literally along the lines of the sectarian ideal Jerusalem.

## Communal Meals at Qumran and Josephus's Essenes

Let us now reconsider Josephus's description of the communal meals of the Essenes in light of the archaeological evidence from Qumran:

> . . . they reassemble in the same place and, girded with linen loin-cloths, bathe themselves thus in cold water. After this purification they assemble in a special building to which no one is admitted who is not of the same faith; they themselves only enter the refectory if they are pure, as though into a holy precinct. When they are quietly seated, the baker serves out the loaves of bread in order, and the cook serves only one bowlful of one dish to each man." (*War* 2.129-31)

According to this passage, only members of the community were allowed to participate in the communal meals. Before entering the dining room, they immersed themselves in a miqveh for the purposes of purification. They then put on special clothes for the meal, as indicated by this same passage: "Afterwards they lay aside the garments which they have worn for the meal, since they are sacred garments" (*War* 2.131). (For sectarian clothing, see Chapter 9.)

Josephus's description of the dining room as a "holy precinct" and of the "sacred" garments worn by the Essenes during their communal meals corresponds with other evidence that the sectarians considered these meals to be a substitute for participation in the temple sacrifices. Like priests serving in the temple, the sectarians drank new wine *(tirosh)* in measured amounts that were not intoxicating. In contrast to Greek and Roman symposia, which were characterized by the consumption of large quantities of wine and noisy, boisterous (drunken) behavior, the sectarians remained sober and quiet during their communal meals, as Josephus noted: "When they are seated quietly . . ." (*War* 2.130). Because his non-Jewish audience would have found this behavior peculiar, Josephus provided an additional explanation: "No shouting or disturbance ever defiles the house; they allow each other to speak in turn. To those outside, this silence of the men inside seems a great mystery; but the cause of it is their invariable sobriety and the fact that their food and drink are so measured out that they are satisfied and no more" (*War* 2.132-33).

The sectarians also rejected the Greco-Roman custom of reclining while dining, and instead ate while seated: "When they are quietly seated . . ." (*War* 2.130). This is supported by the lack of evidence for couches in the dining rooms at Qumran. In contrast to the ancient custom of eating out of common dishes, each member received an individual serving, apparently because of the concern that food and drink could transmit impurity. The fact that members were served individual portions of food and drink explains the discovery of hundreds of identical plates, cups, and bowls in L86 and L114 at Qumran. Josephus's description of the communal meals of the Essenes corresponds closely with the archaeological evidence from Qumran, suggesting that the Qumran community is the focus of this passage.

## Bibliographical Notes

For my discussion of the toilet at Qumran, see Jodi Magness, "Two Notes on the Archaeology of Qumran," *Bulletin of the American Schools of Oriental Research* 312 (1998): 37-44 (with bibliography; some of the main references are repeated here). For the toilet from the City of David in Jerusalem, see Jane Cahill, Karl Reinhard, David Tarler, and Peter Warnock, "It Had to Happen: Scientists Examine Remains of Ancient Bathroom," *Biblical Archaeology Review* 17/3 (1991): 64-69. For Albert Baumgarten's views on the toilet practices of the Essenes, see "The Temple Scroll, Toilet Practices, and the Essenes," *Jewish History* 10 (1996): 9-20. For a fascinating discussion of sanitation (or lack thereof) in the Roman world, see Alexander Scobie, "Slums, Sanitation, and Mortality in the Roman World," *Klio* 68 (1986): 399-433. For Roman luxury latrines, see Richard Neudecker, *Die Pracht der Latrine: Zum Wandel öffentlicher Bedürfnisanstalten in der kaiserzeitlichen Stadt* (Munich: Verlag Dr. Friedrich Pfeil, 1994). Also see John Bodel, "Graveyards and Groves: A Study of the *Lex Lucerina*," *American Journal of Ancient History* 11 (1986 [1994]) (the sentence quoted is from p. 33); A. Trevor Hodge, *Roman Aqueducts and Water Supply* (London: Duckworth, 1992). For the iron pick from Cave 11, see Roland de Vaux, "Une hachette essénienne?" *Vetus Testamentum* 9 (1956): 399-407.

For a detailed study of the War Scroll, see Yigael Yadin, ed., *The Scroll of the War of the Sons of Light against the Sons of Darkness* (Oxford: Oxford University Press, 1962); for the passage regarding the placement of the toilets in relation to the camps, see 290. For a detailed study of the Temple Scroll, see Yadin, ed., *The Temple Scroll* 1-3 (Jerusalem: Israel Exploration Society, 1977-1983). For a popular account, see Yadin, *The Temple Scroll: The Hidden Law of the Dead Sea Sect* (New York: Random House, 1985); for the passage regarding the placement of the toilets in relation to Jerusalem, see 178. For a recent discussion of the Temple Scroll with updated bibliography, see Sidnie White Crawford, *The Temple Scroll and Related Texts* (Sheffield: Sheffield Academic, 2000). Josephus's passage describing the toilet habits of the Essenes (*War* 2.147-49) is from the Loeb edition: Josephus, *The Jewish War, Books I-III*, ed.

Henry St. John Thackeray (Cambridge, Mass.: Harvard University Press, 1976), 379-81. For a discussion of the Sabbath Code in the Damascus Document, see Lawrence H. Schiffman, *The Halakhah at Qumran*. The translation of the passage from the Palestinian Talmud Pesahim is from Baruch M. Bokser and Schiffman, *The Talmud of the Land of Israel: A Preliminary Translation and Explanation* 13: *Yerushalmi Pesaḥim* (Chicago: University of Chicago Press, 1994). For 4Q472, see Torleif Elgvin, "472a. 4QHalakha C," in Joseph Baumgarten et al., *Qumran Cave 4 XXV* (Oxford: Clarendon, 1999), 154-55.

For an analysis of the animal bone deposits, see Frederick E. Zeuner, *Palestine Exploration Quarterly* 92 (1960): 27-36 (see 28-30). My views on communal meals and the animal bone deposits at Qumran are published in Jodi Magness, "Communal Meals and Sacred Space at Qumran," in *Shaping Community: The Art and Archaeology of Monasticism*, ed. Sheila McNally (Oxford: BAR International Series 941, 2001), 15-28 (with bibliography; some of the main references are repeated here with additional bibliography).

For sectarian views on the temple and sacrifices, see Lawrence H. Schiffman, "Community Without Temple: The Qumran Community's Withdrawal from the Jerusalem Temple," in *Gemeinde ohne Tempel, Community without Temple: Zur Substituierung und Transformation des Jerusalemer Tempels und seines Kults im Alten Testament, antiken Judentum und frühen Christentum*, ed. Beate Ego, Armin Lange, and Peter Pilhofer (Tübingen: Mohr Siebeck, 1999), 267-84 (Schiffman's quote regarding the lack of evidence for animal sacrifices at Qumran is on 272); Robert A. Kugler, "Priesthood at Qumran," in *The Dead Sea Scrolls After Fifty Years: A Comprehensive Assessment* 2, ed. Peter W. Flint and James C. VanderKam (Leiden: E. J. Brill, 1999), 93-116 (for sacrificing priests, see 111); John Bowman, "Did the Qumran Sect Burn the Red Heifer?" *Revue de Qumran* 1 (1958): 73-84; Jean Carmignac, "L'utilité ou l'inutilité des sacrifices sanglants dans la 'Règle de la Communauté' de Qumrân," *Revue Biblique* 63 (1956): 524-32; Joseph M. Baumgarten, "Sacrifice and Worship Among the Jewish Sectarians of the Dead Sea (Qumrân) Scrolls," *Harvard Theological Review* 46 (1953): 141-59. For an interpretation of Josephus, *Ant.* 18.19, see Albert I. Baumgarten, "Josephus on Essene Sacrifice," *Journal of Jewish Studies* 45 (1994): 169-83. Baumgarten interprets Josephus's reference to Essene sacrifices as meaning they offered the red heifer on their own.

For Schiffman's views on communal meals at Qumran, see "Communal Meals at Qumran," *Revue de Qumran* 10 (1980): 45-56; *Sectarian Law in the Dead Sea Scrolls*, 191-210; *The Eschatological Community of the Dead Sea Scrolls* (Atlanta: Scholars, 1989), 53-67; *Reclaiming the Dead Sea Scrolls*, 333-38.

For David P. Wright's discussion of the disposal of sacrifices and the system of sacred space in Priestly writings, see *The Disposal of Impurity: Elimination Rites in the Bible and in Hittite and Mesopotamian Literature* (Atlanta: Scholars, 1987).

For the views of other scholars on the communal meals of the Essenes and the animal bone deposits at Qumran, see Johannes van der Ploeg, "The Meals of the Essenes," *Journal of Semitic Studies* 2 (1957): 163-75; Edmund F. Sutcliffe, "Sacred Meals at Qumran?" *Heythrop Journal* 1 (1960): 48-65; Mathias Delcor, "Repas cultuels, esséniens et thérapeutes, thiases et haburoth," *Revue de Qumran* 6 (1968): 401-25; Roger T. Beckwith, "The Qumran Calendar and the Sacrifices of the Essenes," *Revue de Qumran* 7 (1969-1971): 587-91; Moshe Weinfeld, *The Organizational Pattern and the Penal Code of the Qumran Sect* (Göttingen: Vandenhoeck & Ruprecht, 1986); Per Bilde, "The Common Meal in the Qumran-Essene Communities," in *Meals in a Social Context*, ed. Inge Nielsen and Hanne S. Nielsen (Aarhus: Aarhus University Press, 1998), 145-66. For the suggestion that the animal bone deposits represent the remains of meals eaten at Qumran during the annual Feast of the Renewal of the Covenant, see Jean-L. Duhaime, "Remarques sur les dépôts d'ossements d'animaux a Qumrân," *Revue de Qumran* 9 (1977-78): 245-51; Geza Vermès, *The Complete Dead Sea Scrolls in English*, 44-45. Vermès believes that the female skeletons found in the western sector of the cemetery at Qumran represent the remains of women sectarians who perished during this festival (see Chapter 8). For the view that the animal bone deposits at Qumran represent the remains of sacrifices, see Frank Moore Cross, *The Ancient Library of Qumran*, 84-86.

CHAPTER 7

# Miqva'ot at Qumran

One of the controversies surrounding the settlement at Qumran concerns its elaborate water system (described in Chapter 4). De Vaux characterized this system, with its numerous pools connected by channels, as the most striking feature of Qumran. Many scholars believe that some of the pools were Jewish ritual baths (Hebrew *miqveh;* plural *miqva'ot*) used for the purposes of purification by immersion. However, because there are no sources of fresh water in the immediate vicinity of Qumran, some scholars believe that the inhabitants would have needed all of the water stored in the pools just to survive in the arid desert environment (in which case, the water stored in the pools was used only for drinking, watering animals, and other utilitarian purposes). De Vaux rejected the identification of the pools at Qumran as miqva'ot: "We have seen that there are a considerable number of cisterns at Khirbet Qumran, but the ordinary needs of any relatively numerous community living in a semi-desert region would be sufficient to explain the installation of a water system of this kind." At the time de Vaux wrote, however, little was known about ancient miqva'ot in Palestine. Much progress has been made in this field in the last decade. As we shall see, the evidence now available indicates that many of the pools at Qumran were used as miqva'ot, reflecting a concern with purity on the part of the site's inhabitants. We begin this chapter with a review of the literary sources on purity and miqva'ot in rabbinic and sectarian Judaism.

## Purity and Miqva'ot in the Hebrew Bible
## and in Rabbinic Judaism

The concept of purity in rabbinic Judaism is distinct from a state of physical cleanliness or freedom from sin in the Christian sense. Since impurity is contracted through natural processes and not human will, in rabbinic Judaism it is not a moral category. Most impurities are contracted during the normal course of living, and once a person contracts impurity, he/she can become purified through mechanical means. Although it is not a sin to become impure, the failure to purify oneself is considered a sin and contaminates the temple. The Hebrew Bible (Leviticus) lists the following sources of impurity: unclean animals, childbirth, certain skin diseases, "diseases" (such as mildew) on the walls of houses, bodily discharges, sexual misconduct (illicit sexual relationships), and contact with a corpse. Impurity can be contracted by humans, vessels or utensils, and food and drink. The biblical usages of purity and impurity occur mainly in priestly documents, reflecting the need for priests to maintain purity for the purposes of the sacrificial cult in the Jerusalem temple. The practical consequence of being impure was that one could not participate in the temple cult. This was a central concern of Judaism before the destruction of the Second Temple in 70 C.E. However, the purity laws not only applied to the temple cult but affected all aspects of Jewish life, from diet to sexual relations.

According to the Priestly Code in the Hebrew Bible, living water (spring water) could remove impurity. By the end of the 1st century B.C.E., still water stored in a miqveh came to be accepted as the single most important medium of purification. This water could come from a spring or from rainfall. Immersion in water had the power to remove most types of impurity from people and utensils. According to Pharisaic halakhah (based on Leviticus 22:6-7), after immersion but before sunset, an impure person (designated a *tebul yom*) was considered pure enough to consume pure but nonsacramental food and drink (such as *ma'aser sheni*, second tithes). Other groups, including the author of the Temple Scroll and the community at Qumran, considered the *tebul yom* completely impure until the sun set. This position is expressed by the author of 4QMMT (4Q394 3-7 i 13-16): "{And concerning the purity of the heifer of the sin-offering}, he who slaughters it and he who burns it and he who collects {its ashes and he who sprinkles the} [water] of purification — all these {are to be pure} at sunset so that the pure shall sprinkle the impure." The removal of corpse-impurity (which was the highest degree of impurity) was achieved by sprinkling the affected person with living or flowing spring water mixed with the ashes of an unblemished red heifer. Strict regulations governed this procedure, which is based on Numbers 19. The author of Hebrews (9:14) emphasized the superiority of Jesus' sacrifice in the heavenly sanctuary to the Levitical priests' sacrifice of the earthly red heifer. According to the Christian view, since Jesus is the sacrificial animal, his blood purifies.

Because contact with sources of impurity is inevitable, frequent and repeated immersion is necessary for purification. One of the obstacles to determining the function of the Qumran pools is the lack of contemporary literary sources that describe installations used for ritual bathing or immersion. As we shall see, several passages in the Dead Sea Scrolls refer to the cleansing of impurity through immersion in water. However, the single most important literary source for ancient miqva'ot is the Mishnah, a six-part law code that was compiled ca. 200 C.E. by Rabbi Judah ha-Nasi (Judah the Prince). The Mishnah is also referred to as the Oral Law because it represents the interpretations of the Written Law (Pentateuch) that were passed down orally from successive generations of teachers to their disciples. The six parts of the Mishnah are devoted to: (1) agricultural rules; (2) laws governing appointed seasons (such as the Sabbath and festivals); (3) laws on the transfer of women and property; (4) the system of civil and criminal law; (5) laws for the conduct of the cult and the temple; (6) laws on the preservation of cultic purity in the temple and under certain domestic circumstances.

The Sixth Division of the Mishnah includes a tractate (treatise) entitled *Miqva'ot.* There are at least three methodological problems with using this tractate in relation to the pools at Qumran: (1) although many of the laws contained in the Mishnah represent an oral tradition going back to the Second Temple period, it is difficult to pinpoint their date of origin; (2) the Mishnah reflects a Pharisaic tradition, which sometimes differs from the Qumran community's interpretation of Jewish law; (3) there is much disagreement on the extent of the influence of the rabbinic sages in contemporary Jewish society in Judea. Despite these problems, the Mishnah is an indispensable source for a discussion of the Qumran pools. Although the individual passages can be difficult to date, many reflect traditions going back to the Second Temple period (as indicated by the inclusion of laws dealing with the temple cult). In addition, the Qumran community observed the same purity laws as other Jewish groups, but disagreed on the interpretation and application of certain points. In general, the Qumran community was stricter in its interpretation of Jewish law than other groups.

According to the Mishnah, miqva'ot must meet a number of criteria. They must be wholly or partially hewn or dug into the ground, like natural pools, and cannot be built above ground, like bathtubs. Miqva'ot do not have drains, which means that to change the water or clean the pool the contents must be removed manually. Miqva'ot must contain a minimum amount of 40 seahs of still, undrawn water (estimates of this amount range from 250 to 1000 liters; 500 liters = ca. 125 U.S. gallons). This means that although the water can be led into the pool through human agency (for example, by an aqueduct or channel), it must originate in natural sources (such as rain water or spring water) instead of being carried or drawn. No manmade vessel can be used to gather or collect the rain water or spring water. As long as a miqveh contains at least 40 seahs of undrawn water, unlimited amounts of drawn water can be added without negating its purity. To be purified, a person must be immersed fully in the miqveh, up to the fingertips. This can be done in various positions (including reclining), as long as the water reaches all of the body surfaces.

## Purity and Miqva'ot in the Dead Sea Scrolls and among the Essenes

Several passages in the Dead Sea Scrolls indicate that the sectarians practiced immersion in water for the purposes of purification. According to the Community Rule (1QS 3.4-6), those who rejected the covenant were denied admission to the community: "He shall not be reckoned among the perfect; he shall neither be purified by atonement *(kippurim)*, nor cleansed by purifying waters (or sprinkling waters; *mei niddah*), nor sanctified by seas and rivers, nor washed clean with any ablution (or bathing waters; *mei rahatz*). Unclean, unclean shall he be. For as long as he despises the precepts of God he shall receive no instruction in the Community of His counsel."

The next passage describes admission to the community: "For it is through the spirit of true counsel concerning the ways of man that all his sins shall be expiated. . . . And when his flesh is sprinkled with purifying water *(mei niddah)* and sanctified by cleansing water *(mei doche)*, it shall be made clean by the humble submission of his soul to all the precepts of God" (1QS 3.7-9).

These passages indicate that the Qumran community associated external cleansing with the spiritual transformation demanded of its members. This means that the sectarians did not distinguish between cultic and moral impurity. The community's laws treat transgressing divine law not as a metaphor for becoming unclean, but as an actual source of impurity. If a member transgressed any part of the community's laws, he was excluded from the "purity" (that is, the pure food or drink) of the sect and required a rite of purification. To the sectarians, purity and impurity were manifestations of the moral state of the individual. For example, passages in several scrolls (such as

4QThrA1 and 1QH 1:32) attest to their belief that skin disease (Hebrew *sara'at*) is caused by sin or an evil spirit. The sectarian view that anyone who transgressed divine law was impure is expressed elsewhere in the Community Rule (5.13-14): "They shall not enter the water to partake of the pure Meal of the men of holiness, for they shall not be cleansed unless they turn from their wickedness: *for all who transgress His word are unclean*" (my emphasis). For the sectarians, immersion for the purposes of purification was ineffective unless it was accompanied by spiritual repentance. Many scholars have noted the similarities between sectarian views of purification and those associated with John the Baptist, who was active in the vicinity of Qumran during the 1st century and might even have been a member of the community at some point (though this is a matter of controversy). However, in Christianity baptism became a one-time penitential purification, as opposed to the repeated immersions and other purification rites required in Judaism.

The employment of different terms (such as sprinkling waters, bathing waters) in 1QS3.4-9 indicates that the sectarians had different categories of water for purification. The "sprinkling water" used for the purification of novices in 1QS 3.9 suggests that they were held to be defiled to the same degree as someone who had contracted corpse-impurity. The association of sprinkling waters with the holy spirit is suggested by another passage from the Community Rule (4.21): "He [God] will cleanse him of all wicked deeds with the spirit of holiness; like purifying waters *(mei niddah)* he will shed upon him the spirit of truth (to cleanse him) of all abomination and injustice." A fragmentary scroll from Cave 4 (4Q284, line 5) mentions "sprinkling waters to [clea]nse (themselves)." In normative Judaism, water mixed with the ashes of a red heifer was sprinkled only on someone who had contracted corpse-impurity. However, Joseph Baumgarten has noted that the Qumran community required the sprinkling of this water *(mei niddah)* after immersion in a pool for those who had contracted other types of impurity.

Purification through immersion in water (as opposed to sprinkling) is mentioned in other Qumran texts. The Temple Scroll requires bathing and the washing of garments (and sometimes sprinkling) for those who have contracted certain types of impurity including seminal discharges, corpse-impurity, and contact with some living creatures (Temple Scroll 49-51). The Damascus Document (CD 10.11-14) states that "No man shall bathe in dirty water or in an amount too shallow to cover a man. He shall not purify himself with water contained in a vessel. And as for the water of every rock pool too shallow to cover a man, if an unclean man touches it he renders its water as unclean as water contained in a vessel." These regulations correspond closely with those in the Mishnah, according to which the pool must contain enough water to completely cover a person (which the Mishnah specifies as a minimum of 40 seahs). Similarly, according to the Mishnah, under some circumstances if the color of the water changes, the miqveh is unfit for use until the original color is restored (Tractate *Miqva'ot* 7:3-5). Most scholars understand the reference to unclean "water contained in a vessel" in this passage of the Damascus Document as meaning that the sectarians prohibited the addition of any amount of drawn water to a fit immersion pool (that is, a pool containing the required minimum amount of undrawn water). In contrast, Pharisaic halakhah allowed drawn water to be added, though with some restrictions. The term "rock pool" used in this passage could denote a natural rock pool or a pool dug into the ground (that is, a manmade miqveh).

A passage from the Sabbath code in the Damascus Document (CD 11.1) permits someone who is standing in the water of a pool on the Sabbath to drink from it: "If he is on a journey and goes down to bathe, he shall drink where he stands, but he shall not draw water into a vessel." The use of the term "bathe" *(rahatz)* instead of "immerse" *(tabal)* means that this passage (like the passage from CD 10.11 discussed above) could refer to someone who is washing in an immersion pool but is not fully immersed. The point of this legislation is that the bather is forbidden to carry water drawn in a vessel (for example, in a cup or pitcher) on the Sabbath. Drawing drinking water from pools used for washing or for purificatory immersion (natural pools and perhaps manmade miqva'ot as well) must have been common since it is taken for granted in this passage. On weekdays, the water could have been drawn out with a vessel.

The reference in this passage of the Damascus Document to a bather standing in the water is paralleled in a scroll called 4Q512 (fr. 10-11 x 2-5). This scroll describes the immersion required of a *zab* (one who has had a seminal discharge): "[And when] he [has complet]ed the seven days of [his purifi]cation [ ], [then] he shall launder his garments in wa[ter and bathe his flesh in water] and cover (himself with) his garments and bless wh[ere he stands saying, 'Blessed are you] God of Isra[el' ]." This passage indicates that the sectarians recited a blessing after immersion, while still standing in the water. In contrast, rabbinic halakhah calls for the recitation of blessings before immersion, except in the case of proselyte immersion (because liturgical recitations are not required of non-Jews, converts recite the blessing after immersion). The requirement that the bather cover himself with clothes while still standing in the water (for the purposes of modesty) recalls Josephus's descriptions of the Essenes: ". . . and, girded with linen loin-cloths, [they] bathe themselves thus in cold water" (*War* 2.129); "The women bathe wearing a dress, whereas the men wear a loin-cloth" (*War* 2.161; I have translated *endymata* as dress instead of linen, as Vermès and Goodman have it). Because of this concern with modesty, the sectarians secluded themselves when defecating and were forbidden to wear torn or tattered clothing that exposed their genitalia (see Chapter 9).

Josephus describes how the Essenes purified themselves through immersion before participating in their communal meals: "Then, after working without interruption until the fifth hour, they reassemble in the same place and, girded with linen loin-cloths, bathe themselves thus in cold water. After this purification they assemble in a special building to which no one is admitted who is not of the same faith; they themselves only enter the refectory if they are pure, as though into a holy precinct" (*War* 2.129). Here Josephus emphasizes the fact that the sectarians required a state of purity for participation in the communal meals. This corresponds with the cult in the Jerusalem temple, where the priests were required to immerse themselves before the sacrifices. Similarly, a scroll from Cave 4 (4Q512 11, frg. 9) requires that a *zab* purify himself before eating and drinking, although it pertains to individual meals instead of communal meals.

We have seen that because the sectarians viewed themselves as a replacement for the temple and created by means of the sect a substitute for the sacrificial cult, they extended the temple regulations to all of their members. Like the priests in the Jerusalem temple, they immersed themselves in a miqveh after defecating (see Chapter 6). The male members wore white linen garments (including a linen loincloth) similar to those worn by the priests serving in the temple (see Chapter 9). Another expression of this universalist attitude is the sectarian practice of sprinkling water mixed with the ashes of a red heifer on those who had contracted types of impurity other than corpse-impurity (mentioned above). This apparently derives from the use of sprinkling water for the purification of Levites that is described in Numbers 8:7.

The sect also ranked its members according to their level of purity in a manner that recalls the regulations pertaining to the temple cult. The Mishnah tractate *Ḥagigah* (2:6) describes immersion to attain various levels of purity prior to consuming different kinds of foods, offerings, and sacrifices:

> He who immerses for the eating of unconsecrated food and is thereby confirmed as suitable for eating unconsecrated food is prohibited from eating tithe. [If] he immersed for eating tithe and is thereby confirmed as suitable for eating tithe, he is prohibited from eating heave offering. [If] he immersed for eating heave offering and is thereby confirmed as suitable for eating heave offering, he is prohibited from eating food in the status of Holy Things. [If] he immersed for eating food in the status of Holy Things

and is thereby confirmed as suitable for eating food in the status of Holy Things, he is prohibited from engaging in the preparation of purification water. . . .

As we have seen, the Community Rule (5.13-14) prohibits nonmembers from immersing in the water used by the community. Josephus describes this kind of situation in relation to Essene candidates who have passed their first year of initiation: "Having proved his continence during this time, he draws closer to the way of life and partakes of the purer waters of purification . . ." (*War* 2.138). This indicates that access to the water was dictated by the status of the individual within the sect. Similarly, Josephus describes the initiation process of the Essenes as follows: "They are divided into four lots according to the duration of their discipline, and the juniors are so inferior to their elders that if the latter touch them they wash themselves as though they had been in contact with a stranger" (*War* 2.150). This passage indicates that the Essenes divided members into groups according to their level of initiation, which corresponded with their degree of purity or impurity.

The process of initiation and system of ranking are also described in a number of sectarian documents, in particular the Community Rule and the Damascus Document. Nonmembers were impure at the highest level of impurity; only a corpse had greater impurity. For this reason, during the first year of initiation, a candidate was considered impure in the first degree and was prohibited from touching the pure food and drink of the sect: "After he has entered the Council of the Community he shall not touch the pure Meal of the Congregation until one [full] year is completed, and until he has been examined concerning his spirit and deeds; nor shall he have any share of the property of the Congregation" (CD 6.17). During the second year, the candidate could touch the pure food but not the pure drink of the sect. Only after becoming a full member was the candidate considered entirely pure and allowed to touch both the pure food and drink of the sect. This system of initiation reflects the sectarian belief that liquids contract and impart impurity more easily than solids.

The four "lots" or groups described by Josephus recall the Mishnah's four gradations among those who observed the laws of purity: (1) those who kept apart from the ordinary people *(ammei ha'aretz)* and ate their ordinary food in purity; (2) priests and their households who ate the heave-offerings; (3) those permitted to eat of the sacrifices; and (4) those involved in the preparation of the ashes of the red heifer (Mishnah Ḥagigah 2:7). Joseph Baumgarten has observed that, "While we cannot equate these four stages with those of the *Mishnah,* we may presume that the fully initiated Essenes observed a standard of purity equivalent to the highest rabbinic gradation, that required for the preparation of the ashes of the red heifer. If any of these touched even unclean foods or liquids, which normally only defile the hands, they were held to be completely defiled."

The manner in which a member's status or rank in the sect was equated with his level of purity recalls the plan of the temple as conceived of in the Temple Scroll. This plan creates a compound of concentric zones of holiness, in which the holiness emanated outward from the Divine Presence in the center. As the holiness radiated outward, the levels of purity increased towards the center. The author of the Temple Scroll added a third (outermost) court, which was not a feature of any other ancient Jewish temple, to allow Israelite women, children, and proselytes (that is, the group with a lesser degree of purity) to participate in the festivals from a suitable distance. We have seen that it might be possible to detect this concept of radiating zones of purity in the layout of the settlement at Qumran (Chapter 6).

## Miqva'ot of the Second Temple Period: The Archaeological Evidence

Although the literary sources indicate that the sectarians practiced immersion and sprinkling for the purposes of purification, they provide little information about the installations used for storing this water. One exception is the Damascus Document (CD 10.14), which as we have seen mentions water in a rock pool. Ronny Reich has written the most comprehensive study of miqva'ot in Second Temple period Palestine, focusing especially on examples from Jerusalem (in particular, the Herodian villas in the Jewish Quarter), the Hasmonean and Herodian palaces at Jericho and other Judean sites (such as Masada), and Qumran. More recently, David Amit identified a series of miqva'ot in the Hebron hills (Har Hevron). Reich noted that stepped pools are widespread in Judea during the 1st century B.C.E. and 1st century C.E., but are rare or unattested before and after that. Apparently, in earlier periods immersion for purification was carried out mostly in natural bodies of flowing water or rock pools containing rain water. Even in the Second Temple period, most of our sources in the Greek language (such as Josephus and Philo) refer to immersion in natural bodies of water.

Immersion in water was necessary to maintain the purity required for participation in the cult in the Jerusalem temple. Because rain falls in small amounts only during certain months of the year and natural sources of water are scarce in Judea, it became common during the 1st century B.C.E. and 1st century c.e. to dig pools (miqva'ot) in the ground to hold water for the purposes of purification. It is not a coincidence that the 1st-century B.C.E. and 1st-century C.E. miqva'ot discovered to date are concentrated in Jerusalem and its environs, including along the pilgrimage routes in the Hebron hills. They are especially common in the villas in Jerusalem's Jewish Quarter, at Herodian Jericho, and at Qumran. After the destruction of the Second Temple in 70 c.e. and the cessation of the sacrificial cult, manmade purifactory pools of this type became rare or disappeared altogether.

According to Reich, the presence or absence of steps constitutes the basic criterion for distinguishing between pools used for storing drinking water (cisterns) and pools used for purificatory immersion (miqva'ot) at Qumran as well as at other Judean sites. Cisterns do not have steps, whereas miqva'ot are stepped pools. Although there can be exceptions, and pools with narrow steps can be identified as either a cistern or a miqveh, this criterion is fairly consistent. Why is the presence or absence of steps significant? Broad sets of steps (that is, steps occupying the pool's entire width) are unnecessary and even wasteful in cisterns, which are designed to hold and store drinking water. Broad steps take up precious volume and reduce the pool's storage capacity. In addition, hewing regularly measured and spaced steps (like those in miqva'ot) adds to the labor and cost. For these reasons, cisterns often lack steps (as in the case of the round Iron Age cistern [L110] at Qumran). Very large cisterns such as those in Herod's palaces at Masada sometimes have a narrow set of steps attached to one wall to provide access as the water level dropped. Such steps also allowed the clearing of silt that washed in with the water and was deposited at the bottom of the cistern. In contrast, broad sets of steps were obviously intended to provide easy access in and out of the pools. For this reason, most miqva'ot have broad sets of steps. In addition, the rabbinic prohibition against jumping or diving into a miqveh would have necessitated the provision of steps: "He who jumps into an immersion-pool, lo, such a one is blameworthy" (Tosefta *Miqva'ot* 5:14).

However, although all miqva'ot have steps, not all stepped and plastered pools (even those which held 40 seahs of undrawn water) are miqva'ot. Sometimes stepped and plastered pools are cold-water plunge baths in bathhouses, and large ones could be swimming pools. The identification of stepped pools as miqva'ot must be made on the basis of their context as well as on the presence of additional features such as partitions (see below). Cold-water plunge baths (*frigidaria* in Latin) are one component of a bathhouse. Some of the bathhouses in Judea, such as the Hasmonean palaces at Jericho and Herod's palaces at Masada, also have miqva'ot in or next to the bathhouse. However, there is no evidence for a bathhouse at Qumran. Swimming pools in Second Temple period Judea have been discovered only at some of the Hasmonean and Herodian palaces (for example, at Jericho, Masada, and Herodium). Conversely, Reich noted that there are no references in rabbinic literature to a cistern being used as a miqveh. This is because the absence of steps would have made it impossible to immerse in the cistern without jumping or diving.

Small plastered pools with a narrow set of steps attached to one wall represent a type of miqveh that is common in the Hasmonean palaces of Jericho. Because they are concentrated in an industrial area at Jericho, Reich has suggested that these pools were used for the immersion of utensils and domestic items such as tents and bedding. Examples of this type of miqveh are also represented at Qumran (L83, L69; see below). All manmade miqva'ot were hewn into the bedrock or dug into the ground and covered with thick layers of plaster to prevent water seepage. Because the water had to be still rather than flowing, ancient miqva'ot never have tesselated (mosaic) floors, which would have allowed leakage through cracks between the stone cubes. The thick layers of plaster covering the floors, steps, and sides of the miqva'ot were rounded at the corners to prevent injury to the barefoot bathers.

Some of the miqva'ot at Qumran and other Judean sites have additional features, including alternating steps (that is, steps with alternating deep and normal treads); a bottom step with a high rise that created a deep basin at the bottom; a small auxiliary step in the middle or bottom of the staircase; and double doors and/or low partitions running down the steps. No single pool contains all of these features, and they are not present in every miqveh. In other words, the absence of all or any of these features does not mean the pool was not a miqveh. This is because the only requirements for a manmade miqveh in the Second Temple period were that it must be a plastered pool that is dug or hewn into the ground, with steps that allow the bather to immerse without jumping or diving in, and it must hold a minimum amount of undrawn water (according to the sectarian literature, there had to be enough undrawn water to completely cover the bather's body; in rabbinic halakhah, this amount was determined to be a minimum of 40 seahs of undrawn water). On the other hand, the presence of one or more of these additional features can indicate that the pool is a miqveh.

Some miqva'ot have steps with alternating treads that are normal (25-30 cm.) and deep (40-70 cm.) in height, usually with one deep tread placed after groups of two to four normal treads. This arrangement is sometimes found in public buildings of the Second Temple period and in water installations, such as the swimming pools in the Hasmonean and Herodian palaces at Jericho. In miqva'ot, these alternating steps were apparently intended to allow immersion at different levels according to the amount of water present. When the miqveh was full, the bather could stand on a step with a deep tread midway up the staircase (which created a landing) instead of descending to the bottom. This feature could also have been used as a measuring device to indicate whether the water level was dropping to dangerously low levels, since the owners/users probably knew which level (perhaps signaled by one of the deep treads) marked the minimum of 40 seahs. In many miqva'ot, the last tread is often deeper than the others, creating a basin at the bottom that could be used for immersion when the water level dropped. There is often a small step added to the corner of the deep last tread (or sometimes to a deep tread in the middle of the staircase) to help the bather get in and out of the pool. These small auxiliary steps are found only in miqva'ot, not in other types of water installations.

Some of the miqva'ot at Qumran and other Judean sites have one or more low, plastered partitions running vertically down the uppermost steps (see Fig. 39). Perhaps some of the partitions guided the flow of water into the pools, as de Vaux suggested. However, the fact that partitions are not found in all miqva'ot indicates that they must have been intended primarily to serve the symbolic purpose of separating the impure from the pure (in other words, if this was simply a functional feature to channel the water into the pool, we would expect all pools with broad steps to have it). An impure person would have descended into the miqveh on one side of the partition, immersed himself or herself, and ascended the steps in a purified state on the other side of the partition.

This kind of separation between impure and pure is described in the Temple Scroll (45.4-5) in relation to the rotation of the priestly courses: ". . . the second (= incoming) [priestly course] shall enter on the left . . . and the first (= outgoing) shall leave on the right. They shall not mingle with one another nor their vessels" (see Chapter 6 for a discussion of this passage in relation to the dining room in L77). A Greek apocryphal gospel written on parchment (probably composed in the 2nd or 3rd century c.e.) and found in 1905 in Oxyrhynchus (pronounced Ox-see-reen-kus) in Egypt contains a reference to a priest bathing in a miqveh with this arrangement. In the relevant passage, a high priest who is identified as a Pharisee tells Jesus that "I am pure, for I have washed myself in the pool of David, and having descended by one staircase I came up by another. . . ." The Mishnah describes how unclean vessels are carried down into a miqveh on one "path" and brought up on another: "All utensils found in Jerusalem, on the path down to an immersion pool, are assumed to be unclean. [If they are found] on the path up from the immersion pool, they are assumed to be clean" (*Sheqalim* 8:2).

A similar arrangement is described in another passage in the Mishnah in relation to the entrances to the Temple Mount: "All those who enter the Temple Mount enter at the right, go around, and leave at the left" (*Middot* 2:2; mourners and those who were excommunicated went in the opposite direction). In fact, this arrangement can be seen in the Hulda gates, the two sets of gates at the southern end of the Temple Mount that served as the main pilgrim thoroughfares. Pilgrims presumably entered the Temple Mount through the right-hand (eastern) gate and exited via the left-hand (western) gate. The staircase in front of the left-hand gate has alternating deep and normal treads similar to those found in some miqva'ot, a device which may have been intended to slow the pace of those entering or leaving the Temple Mount. A Hellenistic (2nd-century B.C.E.) work by a Jewish writer, which is entitled the Letter of Aristeas, describes a similar arrangement of steps in Jerusalem: "For the ground ascends, since the city is built upon a mountain. There are steps too which lead up to the cross roads, and some people are always going up, and others down and they keep as far apart from each other as possible on the road because of those who are bound by the rules of purity, lest they should touch anything which is unlawful."

Some miqva'ot have double (side-by-side) doorways which, like partitions, separated those entering from those exiting. Miqva'ot with partitions or double doorways are relatively uncommon, occurring mainly in the area of Jerusalem and the Hebron hills to the south. According to Eyal Regev, only about 50 out of 300 miqva'ot that Reich counted (most of which are in the Jerusalem area) have this feature. Approximately one-third of the miqva'ot that David Amit identified in the Hebron hills have partitions or double doorways. Because of their pattern of distribution and the care taken to separate the impure from the pure, Regev has suggested that miqva'ot with partitions or double doorways were intended for use by priests, who had to maintain a higher degree of purity (and were therefore more concerned with purity laws) than other Jews. For example, priests were required to immerse themselves before consuming different kinds of offerings and sacrifices. If Regev is correct, the multiplicity of miqva'ot with partitions at Qumran should be understood in light of the priestly orientation of the sect. However, Amit disagrees with Regev's interpretation. He believes that the variety of miqva'ot in Judea (including different sizes, sets of broad or narrow steps, and the presence or absence of such features as partitions or double doorways, or alternating deep and normal treads) should be attributed to a number of factors. For example, miqva'ot can vary depending on their physical setting: in residential contexts, in agricultural contexts (especially in association with wine and oil presses), along pilgrimage routes (that is, in association with the cult in the Jerusalem temple), and near cemeteries. In addition, the purity laws were observed (albeit with differences) by many groups of Jews and not only by priests during the late Second Temple period. The variety of miqva'ot could also reflect their use for immersion by those who had contracted different kinds of impurity. According to Amit, therefore, the differences in size, features, and arrangement of miqva'ot in Judea should be attributed to a variety of factors.

## Miqva'ot at Qumran: The Archaeological Evidence

According to de Vaux, during Period Ib (that is, the pre–31 B.C.E. phase of Period Ib), the hydraulic system of Qumran was greatly expanded. Flash-flood waters were now brought by aqueduct from Wadi Qumran. The aqueduct entered the settlement at its northwest corner, where the water spread out into a broad, shallow decantation basin. This basin served as a settling tank for the silt carried by the flash-flood waters. From here the water flowed south through a channel, with tributaries filling the pools around the settlement. Additional decantation basins were located in front of each pool or group of pools. Because there are no sources of spring water in the immediate vicinity of Qumran (the closest springs are located 2 miles to the south at Ein Feshkha), and rainfall is minimal (only 1-2 inches per year), the inhabitants would have needed to store enough water for drinking and other utilitarian purposes as well as for purification.

Bryant Wood calculated that the pools at Qumran had a total capacity of 577,800 liters of water. However, the only two large pools without steps (L110 and L91) held 259,000 liters of water. L58, which was created in Period II when the stepped pool L56 was divided in two, also lacks steps. According to Wood, these two pools (L110 and L91) would have provided enough water for a community of 200 people and pack animals to survive during the eight-month-long dry season (from mid-March to mid-November). In other words, according to Wood's calculations, the pools at Qumran contained an excessive amount of water even for a community of 200 living in the desert, and therefore some of them must have been used as miqva'ot.

Reich identified 10 of the 16 pools at Qumran as miqva'ot: L138, L118, L117, L85, L83, L56 (which in Period Ib = L56 + L58), L48 (= L48 + L49), L68, L69, L71 (refer to the plan of the site in Fig. 5). Of these, eight have broad sets of steps: L138, L118, L117, L85, L56, L48, L68, and L71. We shall now examine these pools in greater detail, following Reich's order and the flow of water from northwest to southeast.

L138 is located outside of and to the northwest of the settlement, by the sluice-gate through which the water brought by the aqueduct entered the site (see Fig. 23). Because almost the entire area of this small, rectangular pool is occupied by steps, de Vaux identified it as a "bath," although he hesitated to assign it any ritual function. The main entrance was by means of a broad set of steps on the northwest side of the pool. Long, narrow steps created a shelf on either side of the broad steps. Two additional but narrower sets of steps led into the pool from entrances in the northeast and southwest corners. According to Reich, these two entrances represent a later addition, while the shelves flanking the broad set of steps are the result of the widening of the original pool. The placement of this pool suggests that it was used for purification by those entering the site. This could include members who had used the toilet, if we assume that after the earthquake of 31 and the destruction of the toilet in L51 these facilities were now located to the northwest of the settlement, following the regulations for Jerusalem in the Temple Scroll (see Chapter 6; it could also include those who had attended to their bodily needs outside the settlement even before the earthquake of 31). This might account for the modifications to the original pool noted by Reich.

L117 and L118 are located in the western sector (secondary building) of the settlement (see Fig. 31). L118 is adjacent to and north of the round Iron Age cistern (L110), and L117 lies on the eastern side of the Iron Age cistern. These two pools were apparently built together as a pair with a shared entrance room or vestibule in the vicinity of the decantation basin in L119 *bis* (as previously noted, de Vaux sometimes used *bis* to indicate a subdivision of a locus). In other words, L118 was entered from the south and L117 was entered from the north. The decantation basin (L119 *bis*) and the channel and tributaries that wind through this sector and supplied these pools were originally covered. The decantation basin was presumably covered by wooden planks, while the channel and its tributaries were covered with stone slabs that formed part of a paved area on the eastern side of the round Iron Age cistern. A few of the stone cover slabs are visible in the plans and photographs from de Vaux's excavations. L117 and L118 have very similar layouts, dimensions, and capacities. L118 has a deep tread that creates a landing before the two normal treads at the bottom. L117 had two partitions (only one of which is preserved) at the top of the steps. The partitions terminated at a deep tread that creates a landing about one-third of the way down. This pool also has a small auxiliary step in the middle of the deep last tread, which facilitated access to the basin at the bottom when the water level dropped.

Reich noted that pairs of miqva'ot are common in Jerusalem. He suggested that these pairs might have been used for immersion by different groups, such as men versus women; adults versus children or members of the family versus servants; or for different degrees of purity (for example, for those eating heave offerings versus those eating Holy Things); or for different groups among those who observed the laws of purity (such as priests versus other Jews). It is also possible that when miqva'ot occur in pairs both were not used at the same time. For example, one miqveh could have been used first and, when during the course of the long dry season it became too dirty to use or the water level dropped, the second miqveh could have been opened. Since access to immersion water depended on a member's status in the Qumran community, the miqva'ot in L117 and L118 might have been used by members of different ranks. If this is the case, L117, which differs from L118 in having partitions and an auxiliary step at the bottom, might have been restricted to priests or members of higher rank who had to maintain a greater degree of purity.

L85 and L83 are two small pools at the southern end of the site, to the west of the pantry of dishes in L86. L85 has broad steps leading to a deep basin at the bottom. According to de Vaux's notes, this basin formed a landing at the bottom of L85. The landing provided access to L91, a large reservoir without steps located immediately to the south. However, as Reich noted, it is not clear whether L85 was connected with L91, because de Vaux left this area untouched to preserve a later Roman channel built over it. If the two were connected, L85 represents the staircase leading into cistern L91. In this case, the steps might have continued below the unexcavated fill into cistern L91. If the two were unconnected, L85 represents a miqveh. L83 is a pool with a narrow set of steps attached to the west wall, which adjoins L85 on the east. Interestingly, the two pools are connected by a channel about 3 feet above the floor level of L83. In addition, only L83 was fed by the main water-supply channel, while L85 was filled by the channel connecting it with L83. Reich noted that side-by-side miqva'ot with narrow sets of steps and miqva'ot connected by a pipe are common in the Hasmonean palaces in Jericho. However, most of the Qumran pools have features that are characteristic of miqva'ot in Jerusalem, including broad sets of steps, alternating deep and normal treads, and a small auxiliary step by the deep bottom tread.

L56 is a pool with broad steps located to the north of the communal dining room in L77. In Period Ib it formed one large miqveh together with L58. After the earthquake of 31, the pool was divided by a wall into a large unstepped reservoir to the east (L58), which was apparently now used as a cistern, and a smaller but still spacious stepped pool to the west (L56). L56 has one deep tread forming a landing after every group of four normal treads. A small auxiliary step adjoins one side of the lowest tread. Two low partitions run down the uppermost three steps at the western end of L56, terminating at the base of a deep tread that formed the first landing. Water was channeled into the pool between these two partitions.

L48-L49 (L48 designates the steps of pool L49) is located on the eastern side of the settlement, to the south of the toilet in L51 (see Figs. 37, 39). Its broad steps, which were accessed from the south, were damaged during the earthquake of 31. The pool subsequently went out of use and was filled in. Three low partitions run down the uppermost five steps. The westernmost partition was connected with the water channel to the south and was apparently intended to guide the flow of water into the pool. Interestingly, an additional entrance to the pool, which was separated from it by a partition, was appended to the eastern side of the broad steps. Perhaps this reflects segregated access to the pool for different groups or members of different ranks among the community. Because L48-L49 was damaged in the earthquake, it provides evidence that miqva'ot with broad sets of steps and partitions existed in Judea in general and at Qumran in particular prior to 31 B.C.E. The presence of this miqveh also reflects a concern with purity laws on the part of the inhabitants during the pre-31 phase, indicating (together with other evidence such as the communal dining room in L77 and the pantry of dishes in L86) that Qumran was a sectarian settlement even before 31 B.C.E.

L68, L69, and L71 are located at the southeastern end of the site, to the south of the potters' workshop. L68 is a small plastered pool that is almost completely occupied by steps. As with L138, de Vaux identified L68 as a "bath." This pool has two sets of broad steps, one descending from the west and the other from the east. Reich believes that this pool originally had two entrances (one on the east and one on the west), one of which was later blocked. He noted the similarities between the double staircase in this pool and those in the miqva'ot in the Hasmonean palaces at Jericho. L69 is another small pool adjacent to the western side of L71. Like L68, L69 has a double staircase, but its steps are narrow and are attached to the eastern wall of the pool. The steps were accessed from the north and south sides of the pool. Two auxiliary steps adjoin the bottommost step of the pool. The upper auxiliary step is divided by a low partition. L71 is a very large pool with broad steps that were accessed from the north. It has alternating deep and normal treads, with a deep tread creating a landing after every group of five regular treads. A small auxiliary step is appended to one side of the bottom step. Two partitions run down the uppermost steps. The western partition terminated after four steps, and the eastern one terminated after five steps, at a deep tread that formed the first landing. The partitions have no connection to the water channel that fed the pool (supporting the view that the partitions found in some pools are not simply a functional feature to help direct the flow of water).

## Conclusions

Of the 10 pools at Qumran that Reich identified as miqva'ot, only L138 and L68 (which de Vaux described as "baths") lack additional features such as partitions, alternating deep and normal treads, and small auxiliary steps. Eight of the 10 pools have broad sets of steps (the exceptions are L83 and L69, which are small pools with narrow sets of steps attached to one wall).

The only pair of miqva'ot found at Qumran are L117 and L118. Was there a physical connection between these two pools? According to Pharisaic halakhah, if the water in a miqveh becomes impure (for example, by falling below 40 seahs), it can be purified through contact with pure water stored in an adjacent pool. In Hebrew, this procedure is called *hashakah* ("tangency"), and the adjacent pool is referred to as an *otsar* ("treasury"). The contact with the pure water in the adjacent pool could be effected by unplugging a small aperture in a common wall. Perhaps the best-known example of this arrangement is found in the miqveh in a room on the southeast side of Masada, which was added by the Jewish rebels who occupied the site during the First Jewish Revolt against the Romans. The sages allowed pure water to be piped into an impure miqveh, as described in Mishnah *Miqva'ot* 6:8: "They clean immersion pools: a higher pool by the lower pool, and a distant [pool] by a nearby [pool]. How so? One brings a pipe of earthenware or lead, and puts his hand under it until it is filled with water, and draws it along and makes it touch."

There are cases (for example in Jerusalem) where one miqveh in a pair was apparently used as an *otsar* for the other. Do the miqva'ot in L117 and L118 reflect such an arrangement? Apparently not, since according to sectarian halakhah not only was impure water in a miqveh not purified through contact with pure water in an adjacent pool, but the contact between them would have contaminated the pure pool. This is because the sectarians believed that impurity could be conveyed upstream by liquids. In other words, if a liquid was poured from a pure container into an impure one, the impurity was transmitted by the stream of liquid, rendering the pure container (and its contents) impure. The sectarian view is expressed in 4QMMT (4Q397 6-13): "And furthermore the pouring does not separate the impure {from the pure} for the poured liquid and that in the receptacle are alike, one liquid." Amit has noted, however, that this passage does not explicitly refer to miqva'ot. In addition, pairs of miqva'ot that could be connected by a pipe (such as those found in Jerusalem) are no more than 1 meter apart. In contrast, the miqva'ot in L117 and L118 are over 5 meters apart (measuring from the southeast corner of L118 to the northwest corner of L117), which is too great a distance for connection by a pipe. In light of the sectarian belief that liquids transmit impurity upstream, it is not surprising that at Qumran there are no examples of an *otsar* or pairs of miqva'ot that could be connected by a pipe.

The archaeological evidence contradicts de Vaux's assumption that the pools at Qumran were uncovered and open to the sky. For example, the published plans indicate that the walls of the pools are the same thickness as those of the other rooms at the site. In the photographs from de Vaux's excavations, the walls of most of the miqva'ot appear to be preserved to about the same height as the rest of the walls in the settlement. In addition, the span of the largest pools (L91, L56, L71) is no greater than that of the largest roofed rooms (such as L77, L121, L130, L4, L1, L51). This is significant because at Qumran and other ancient sites in Palestine the maximum span of a room could not exceed the length of the wooden beams that could be obtained for the roofing. The maximum span of a room could be increased by using columns to support the wooden ceiling beams. Apparently, the pools at Qumran were enclosed with walls and roofed with wooden beams covered with layers of rushes, reeds, and mud like the other rooms in the settlement. Enclosing and roofing the Qumran miqva'ot would have greatly reduced the rate of evaporation during the long, hot dry season. Furthermore, the miqva'ot found at contemporary sites (such as those in the basements of the villas in Jerusalem's Jewish Quarter) were enclosed in roofed structures. The Qumran miqva'ot have always seemed anomalous because scholars assumed they were not enclosed. Presumably the roofing of the pools was not preserved because whatever materials were not burned when the site was destroyed collapsed into the pools and rotted in the water and silt.

There is no evidence for second-story rooms above the miqva'ot except in the case of L56-L58, where there must have been a passage (perhaps on a roof terrace) leading from the staircase in L35 to the second-story level of the dining room in L77 (after the earthquake of 31; see Chapter 6). Some of the differences between the miqva'ot at Qumran and those at other sites reflect the local geological conditions. In Jerusalem, the miqva'ot are hewn into the hard bedrock (limestone) below the houses. These miqva'ot tend to be smaller and narrower than those at Qumran, which are cut into the soft marl of the terrace (and were revetted along the sides and bottom with stones covered with plaster). Because space was at a premium in the urban setting of the Jerusalem villas, the miqva'ot are hewn into the bedrock of the basements beneath the houses. The miqva'ot in the Hebron hills are hewn into the local hard bedrock (limestone) slopes outside of and adjacent to the houses, as there was plenty of room to spread out in this rural area. Because Qumran is built on a terrace of soft, crumbly marl, the buildings had no basements. The pools were therefore accessed at the ground level. As we have seen, some of the rooms in the settlement — including the communal dining rooms above L77 and above L111, L120, L121, and L122, and the "scriptorium" in L30 — were located at the second-story level. In other words, although there is no basement story at Qumran, the layout is analogous to other settlements, where the miqva'ot were at the lowest level and the rooms used for living, dining, and meeting purposes were located above. Reich has demonstrated that the amount of space occupied by the pools in relation to the total size of the settlement at Qumran is proportionate to that occupied by miqva'ot in contemporary villas in Jerusalem's Jewish Quarter. The fact that the pools at Qumran appear to occupy a disproportionate amount of space relative to the rest of the settlement is probably due to their placement at ground level among the other buildings instead of in the basement story, as in the Jerusalem villas.

Most of the miqva'ot at Qumran (especially L56 and L71) are larger than those in the villas in Jerusalem's Jewish Quarter and even those in the Hasmonean and Herodian palaces of Judea. The miqva'ot at Qumran are also distinguished by the large basins at the bottom of the last step. These features reflect the fact that the miqva'ot at Qumran served the needs of a community instead of individual households. They were designed to accommodate dozens of members, many of whom would have had to immerse themselves at the same time of day (for example, before the communal meals) or on the same occasions (for example, on certain holidays and festivals). In fact, Josephus's description of the communal meals of the Essenes suggests that miqva'ot were located in proximity to the dining rooms: "Then, after working without interruption until the fifth hour, they reassemble in the same place and, girded with linen loin-cloths, bathe themselves thus in cold water. After this purification they assemble in a special building to which no one is admitted who is not of the same faith; they themselves only enter the refectory if they are pure, as though into a holy precinct" (*War* 2.129).

In light of Josephus's testimony, it is not surprising that some of the largest miqva'ot at Qumran are located by the entrances to the communal dining rooms: L56-L58 by L77, and the pair of miqva'ot in L117 and L118 by L111, L120, L121, L122, and L123. The miqveh in L56-L58 shared a common entrance hall or vestibule with the communal dining room in L77 (before the earthquake of 31; after the earthquake the dining room was relocated to the second-story level of L77 and was accessed via the spiral staircase in L35; see Chapter 6). The miqva'ot in L117 and L118 were entered through an entrance hall or vestibule in the area of decantation basin L119 *bis*. This basin and the rest of the area on the east side of the round Iron Age cistern (L110) was paved. This paved space provided access to the staircase in L113 on the south side of the round cistern, which led to the dining room at the second-story level above L111, L120, L121, L122, and L123.

It is not a coincidence that the largest miqveh (L71) is located at the southeastern edge of the settlement. This miqveh served the potters' workshop in L64 and must also have been used by those entering the settlement from the direction of the cemetery. As we have seen, the inhabitants of Qumran apparently manufactured much of their own pottery to ensure its purity. The Mishnah describes immersion in connection with the firing of ceramic vessels used for purificatory rites involving the ashes of the red heifer: "He who brings a clay utensil for the purification [rite] immerses and spends the night [watching over] at the furnace. R. Judah says, 'Even from the house does he bring [it], and it is suitable.' For all are believed [to preserve cleanness] concerning the purification [rite]" (*Parah* 5:1). The miqveh in L71 must also have been used by those entering the site in the area of the potters' workshop (L84) from the direction of the cemetery. Esther Eshel has noted that the Temple Scroll (11QT$^a$ 49) and a halakhic-liturgical text from Cave 4 (4Q414) require immersion in a miqveh on the first, third, and seventh days after the defilement for someone who contracted corpse-impurity. In contrast, rabbinic halakhah requires immersion for this kind of impurity only on the seventh day. Eshel has suggested that the halakhah requiring immersion on the first day after contracting corpse-impurity was observed in a few places in Judea where miqva'ot are found adjacent to a cemetery (including two miqva'ot at the Tomb of Queen Helena of Adiabene or so-called Tombs of the Kings in Jerusalem and one miqveh in the courtyard of a burial cave in the necropolis at Jericho). In my opinion, this halakhah accounts for the placement of the largest miqveh at Qumran next to the gate that provided access to and from the direction of the cemetery.

Could the stepped pools at Qumran have been multi-functional, as Patricia Hidiroglou has suggested? It is possible that the water in some of the miqva'ot at Qumran was, on at least some occasions (for example, in times of drought), utilized for everyday purposes such as drinking. However, the presence of steps and additional features (such as partitions) indicates that these pools were designed to serve primarily (if not always) as miqva'ot. We have seen that the legislation in the Damascus Document permits someone washing (or perhaps immersing) in a pool on the Sabbath to drink the water as long as he did not carry it in a vessel. On other days, water could have been drawn out with a vessel and used for drinking or other purposes. However, the restricted access to immersion water described in the sectarian scrolls and by Josephus means that pools could not have functioned simultaneously as a miqveh *and* as a community cistern (or as a community bath for secular purposes). For only those individuals who were permitted access to the miqva'ot could drink from them; others would have been denied access to the water in those pools. No such restrictions applied to cisterns and other pools that were not used for purificatory purposes. The absence of heated pools or steam rooms (and systems for heating the water), mosaic floors, and built-up bath-tubs indicates that the pools at Qumran were not part of a bathhouse.

A comparison with water installations at contemporary sites in Pales-tine that were inhabited by non-Jewish populations — specifically, by Phoe-nicians and Nabateans — highlights the unique nature of the pools at Qumran. The first site we shall consider is Tel Anafa in the Hula Valley of Is-rael's Upper Galilee. Excavations at Tel Anafa revealed the remains of a large and elaborate building dating to the Late Hellenistic period (ca. 125 B.C.E.–70 B.C.E.). This building was a villa with two stories of rooms arranged around a central courtyard. Because of the painted and gilded stucco (molded plaster) that decorated the walls of the rooms, the excavators called this villa the "Late Hellenistic Stuccoed Building." There are no stepped and plastered pools in the villa. Instead, a three-room bath complex occupied its entire eastern side. The two northern rooms were paved with mosaics. A large plastered basin (that is, a large built-up, plastered bathtub with no steps) was found by the southern wall of the central room. The southern room contained two stone-lined fire pits, one of which was built into the wall next to the plastered basin, to heat the water. Interior drains connected all three rooms, and the plastered basin was equipped with a drain. Based on the architectural style, the nature of the ceramic assemblage, and parallels with bathhouses at Punic sites, the excavators have identified the occupants of the Late Hellenistic Stuccoed Building as Phoenicians.

Stepped and plastered pools are also unattested at contemporary Nabatean sites. One such site is Mampsis (Arabic Kurnub; Hebrew Mamshit), a small town located in Israel's northern Negev. T. E. Lawrence ("Lawrence of Arabia") and Sir Leonard Woolley visited and mapped Mampsis during their survey of the region in 1914. In the 1960s and 1970s Avraham Negev con-ducted extensive excavations at the site. In the Middle and Late Nabatean pe-riods (that is, from the late 1st century B.C.E. to the 2nd and 3rd centuries C.E.), the inhabitants of Mampsis constructed sturdy, spacious houses or vil-las of stone. The houses had two stories of rooms surrounding a central courtyard. The floors of the rooms were paved with flagstones, and the walls were plastered and (at least sometimes) painted.

Like Qumran, Mampsis is located in an arid desert environment with no freshwater springs nearby. The inhabitants of Mampsis therefore con-structed a series of dams in the dry riverbed (Naḥal Mamshit) below the site.

These dams trapped the flash-flood waters that flow through the riverbed on rare occasions in the winter. The water stored in the pools behind the dams supplied most of the town's water. The water was brought up manually (in buckets or skins, by hand or on pack animal) and emptied into a large public reservoir. The reservoir, which is rectangular in shape and was plastered but has no steps, was covered with a roof made of wooden beams and palm branches. The water from the dammed pools in Naḥal Mamshit was also used to fill the large, plastered cisterns in the town's houses. These underground cisterns were located in the courtyards of the houses and sometimes even in the middle of streets. In addition, every drop of rain water that fell inside the town was caught by channels and gutters and channeled into the cisterns, which were roofed structures with no steps. The water was drawn by dropping a bucket or skin through a stone head with an opening at ground level, above the middle of the cistern.

There is also a bathhouse adjacent to the public reservoir at Mampsis. A hypocaust system heated the caldaria (steam rooms). The frigidarium contained two plastered pools that were used as cold water plunge baths, one semicircular and the other octagonal. Both pools were sunk into the floor with walls built up above the ground. Each was provided with a step on the outside to provide access to the pool. Each pool also had a bench covered with polished stone slabs along one inner wall. The pools were drained by pipes located at the base of the benches.

Other examples of Nabatean private houses of 1st- to early 2nd-century C.E. date have been uncovered at ez-Zantur in Petra. Petra, located in Jordan (southeast of the Dead Sea) is famous for the elaborate tomb facades carved by the Nabateans into the red sandstone cliffs (the best-known tomb, called the Khazneh or "Treasury," was featured in the movie *Indiana Jones and the Last Crusade*). The houses at ez-Zantur, like those at Mampsis, were spacious stone structures. They were paved with flagstones and the walls were decorated with painted plaster and stucco. The water-supply system in these houses is similar to the arrangements at Mampsis, with channels and gutters connected to underground cisterns. There are no examples of stepped and plastered pools.

This review has indicated that stepped and plastered pools are unattested in the Phoenician villa at Tel Anafa and in the Nabatean houses at Mampsis and ez-Zantur at Petra. The comparisons between Qumran and Mampsis are especially instructive, given their physical proximity. Both sites are located in an arid desert environment with no freshwater springs in the vicinity, and their inhabitants relied on stored flash floods for most of their water supply. However, the elaborate system of stepped and plastered pools, which de Vaux described as Qumran's most striking feature, is not paralleled at Mampsis. These pools were designed as miqva'ot and should be understood within the context of the community's concern with purity.

Amos Kloner has claimed that the Hellenistic period site of Marisa (Arabic Tell Sandahannah; Hebrew Mareshah) in Idumaea provides evidence for the use of stepped and plastered pools by a non-Jewish population in Palestine. After the kingdom of Judah was conquered by the Babylonians in 586 B.C.E., the Edomites (who inhabited the region on the southeast side of the Dead Sea) moved into southern Judea. Their descendants were called Idumaeans, and the region of southern Judea became known as Idumaea. Marisa flourished during the Hellenistic period (3rd and 2nd centuries B.C.E.), thanks largely to an economy based on pigeon raising and the production of olive oil. Spacious stone houses were constructed on the summit ("Upper City") and slopes ("Lower City") of the Iron Age tel. The Hellenized inhabitants of the town (consisting of Idumaeans and Phoenicians from Sidon) carved underground caves into the soft chalk on which the tel sits. The chalky rock quarried from the caves was used for the construction of the houses. Caves located beneath the houses were used as cisterns or for storing food, since they retained their coolness even in summer. The cisterns are distinguished by their bell-shaped interiors, which narrow towards the top. They often have a narrow set of steps attached to the wall and winding around the interior. Other caves cut into the chalky slopes contained olive presses, columbaria (dovecotes), and tombs. One famous burial cave is decorated with wall paintings depicting, among other things, a series of exotic and imaginary animals.

According to Kloner, who conducted excavations at Marisa in 1989 and 1991, stepped and plastered pools found inside some of the houses (not in the underground caves) represent ritual baths. Kloner claims that these pools are even found in houses that antedate the conquest of Marisa by the Hasmonean king John Hyrcanus I in 112 B.C.E. and the subsequent conversion of the Idumaean population to Judaism. If this is the case, the local population might have practiced some kind of purification rites similar to those required in Judaism even before their conversion. Kloner has suggested that perhaps these rites originated among the Judean Jews who remained in the area and were absorbed into the Idumaean population during the Persian and Hellenistic periods. However, Gerald Finkielsztejn, who was an area supervisor during Kloner's excavations in the Lower City, disagrees with Kloner. He believes that the stepped pools at Marisa postdate John Hyrcanus's conquest of the town. This means that there is currently no definite evidence for the use of stepped immersion pools among the non-Jewish population of Hellenistic

Marisa. This is hardly surprising in light of the fact that stepped and plastered pools developed in response to Judaism's purity requirements, which centered around the temple cult.

The large size and number of miqva'ot at Qumran are a physical expression of the community's unique concerns regarding purity. This archaeological evidence complements Joseph Baumgarten's observation about the scrolls: "Among the Qumran fragments concerned with religious law, those which deal with Tohorah, ritual purity, are salient both because of their relative abundance and because of the importance of purity in the life of the community."

## Bibliographical Notes

De Vaux's quote about the water system at Qumran is from *Archaeology and the Dead Sea Scrolls,* 131. Basic works on purity and miqva'ot in rabbinic Judaism include: E. P. Sanders, *Jewish Law from Jesus to the Mishnah* (Philadelphia: Trinity, 1990); Jacob Neusner, *The Idea of Purity in Ancient Judaism; Purity in Rabbinic Judaism: A Systematic Account* (Atlanta: Scholars, 1994); Hannah K. Harrington, *The Impurity Systems of Qumran and the Rabbis* (Atlanta: Scholars, 1993). For an English-language commentary on the tractate *Miqva'ot,* see Neusner, *A History of the Mishnaic Law of Purities* 13-14 (Leiden: Brill, 1976). The translation of the passage from the Palestinian Talmud Pesahim is from Baruch M. Bokser and Lawrence H. Schiffman, *The Talmud of the Land of Israel* 13. The translation of the passage from the Tosefta is from Neusner, *The Tosefta Translated from the Hebrew, Sixth Division, Tohorot (The Order of Purities)* (New York: KTAV, 1977). For discussions with references on the influence of the sages in Judean society in the 1st century C.E., see Lee I. Levine, *The Ancient Synagogue: The First Thousand Years* (New Haven: Yale University Press, 2000), 440-41; Martin Goodman, *The Ruling Class of Judaea: The Origins of the Jewish Revolt against Rome, A.D. 66-70* (New York: Cambridge University Press, 1995), 23-24, esp. n. 39.

For discussions of purity concerns among the Qumran community, see Joseph M. Baumgarten, "The Essene Avoidance of Oil and the Laws of Purity," *Revue de Qumran* 6 (1967-69): 183-92 (my translation of Josephus's *War* 2.138 loosely follows that on 190, n. 35; Baumgarten's observation regarding the four gradations is from 190); Sidney B. Hoenig, "Qumran Rules of Impurities," *Revue de Qumran* 6 (1967-69): 559-67; Baumgarten, "The Purification Rituals in *DJD 7,*" in Devorah Dimant and Uriel Rappaport, *The Dead Sea Scrolls: Forty Years of Research,* 199-209 (the translations of 4Q284, line 5 and

4Q512 Col. XI, fragment 9 in this chapter are from this article); *Jewish Quarterly Review* 85 (1994): 91-101; "The Red Cow Purification Rites in Qumran Texts," *Journal of Jewish Studies* 46 (1995): 112-19; "The Purification Liturgies," in Peter W. Flint and James C. VanderKam, *The Dead Sea Scrolls After Fifty Years,* 2:200-12 (the passage from 4Q512 fragments 10-11 cited in this chapter is from 206); "Torohot," in *Qumran Cave 4 XXV,* 79-122 (for a critique of E. P. Sanders' skepticism regarding the observation of purity laws in everyday life, see 80); "The Use of *Mei Niddah* for General Purification," in Lawrence H. Schiffman, Emanuel Tov, and VanderKam, *The Dead Sea Scrolls Fifty Years After Their Discovery,* 481-85 (Baumgarten's quote at the end of this chapter is from 481); Hannah K. Harrington, "The Nature of Impurity at Qumran," in Schiffman, Tov, and VanderKam, *The Dead Sea Scrolls Fifty Years After Their Discovery,* 610-16. The Sabbath Code in the Damascus Document is discussed in Schiffman, *The Halakhah at Qumran.* For 4Q414 see Esther Eshel, "4Q414 Fragment 2: Purification of a Corpse-Contaminated Person," in *Legal Texts and Legal Issues.* Proceedings of the Second Meeting of the International Organization for Qumran Studies, Cambridge 1995, ed. Moshe Bernstein, Florentino García Martínez, and John Kampen (Leiden: E. J. Brill, 1997), 3-10; "414. 4QRitual of Purification A," in Joseph Baumgarten, *Qumran Cave 4 XXV*135-54. Eshel notes that the use of confessional words in 4Q512 (such as "I have sinned") reflects the sectarian view that purity and impurity were manifestations of the moral state of the individual.

Much of the literature concerning the archaeology of ancient miqva'ot in Judea is in Hebrew. The basic archaeological study of miqva'ot of the Second Temple period in Judea is Ronny Reich's Hebrew-language, unpublished dissertation, *Miqva'ot in the Second Temple Period and Period of the Mishnah and Talmud* (Jerusalem: Institute of Archaeology, Hebrew University, 1990). His views on the Qumran pools are summarized in "Miqwa'ot (Ritual Baths) at Qumran," *Qadmoniot* 114 (1997): 125-28 (Hebrew). For his English-language publications on this subject, see "Archaeological Evidence of the Jewish Population at Hasmonean Gezer," *Israel Exploration Journal* 31 (1981): 48-52; "More on Miqva'ot," *Biblical Archaeology Review* 13/4 (1987): 59-60; "The Hot Bath-House (balneum), the Miqweh and the Jewish Community in the Second Temple Period," *Journal of Jewish Studies* 39 (1988): 102-7; "The Great Miqveh Debate," *Biblical Archaeology Review* 19/2 (1993): 52-53; "*Miqwa'ot* at Khirbet Qumran and the Jerusalem Connection," in Schiffman, Tov, and VanderKam, *The Dead Sea Scrolls Fifty Years After Their Discovery,* 728-31; "They Are Ritual Baths: Immerse Yourself in the Ongoing Sepphoris Mikveh Debate," *Biblical Archaeology Review* 28/2 (2002): 50-55. For recently identified miqva'ot in the Hebron Hills with an update of Reich's discussion of miqva'ot, see the unpublished, Hebrew-language M.A. thesis by David Amit, *Ritual Baths (Miqva'ot) from the Second Temple Period in the Hebron Mountains* (Jerusalem: Institute of Archaeology, Hebrew University, 1996). This work includes a critique of E. P. Sanders' discussion of miqva'ot. For a shorter, published version of Amit's thesis, see Amit, "Ritual Baths (Miqva'ot) from the Second Temple Period in the Hebron Mountains," in *Judea and Samaria Research Studies, Proceedings of the 3rd Annual Meeting-1993*, ed. Ze'ev H. Ehrlich and Ya'akov Eshel (Kedumim-Ariel: The Research Institute, The College of Judea and Samaria, 1994), 157-89 (Hebrew). For an English-language article by Amit about a miqveh complex in the Hebron Hills, see "A Miqveh Complex near Alon Shevut," *'Atiqot* 38 (1999): 75-84. For the miqva'ot in the Hasmonean and Herodian palaces at Jericho, see Ehud Netzer, "Ancient Ritual Baths (Miqvaot) in Jericho," *The Jerusalem Cathedra* 2, ed. Louis I. Levine (Detroit: Wayne State University Press, 1982), 106-19. Netzer has now published the final report on the excavation of these palaces: *Hasmonean and Herodian Palaces at Jericho.*For a possible connection between the miqva'ot at Jericho and priestly presence, see Joshua Schwartz, "On Priests and Jericho in the Second Temple Period," *Jewish Quarterly Review* 79 (1988): 23-48.

For the steps in front of the Hulda Gates in Jerusalem, see Meir Ben-Dov, *In the Shadow of the Temple* (New York: Harper & Row, 1985), 113.

The apocryphal gospel from Oxyrhynchus was published by Bernard P. Grenfell and Arthur S. Hunt, *The Oxyrhynchus Papyri* 5 (London: Egypt Exploration Fund, 1908). For the most recent discussion of this document, including the translation cited here, see François Bovon, "*Fragment Oxyrhynchus 840*, Fragment of a Lost Gospel, Witness of an Early Christian Controversy over Purity," *Journal of Biblical Literature* 119 (2000): 705-28. Bovon suggests that this document reflects the controversy between Christian groups during the 2nd and 3rd centuries over the necessity of water baptism. He notes that the procedure of going up and down steps could refer to immersion in a Christian baptistery instead of a miqveh. The translation of the passage from the Letter of Aristeas is from Robert H. Charles, *The Apocrypha and Pseudepigrapha of the Old Testament in English* 2: *Pseudepigrapha* (Oxford: Clarendon, 1913), 105.

For the identification of the stepped pools at Qumran as miqva'ot, see Bryant G. Wood, "To Dip or Sprinkle? The Qumran Cisterns in Perspective," *Bulletin of the American Schools of Oriental Research* 256 (1984): 45-60. In contrast, Patricia Hidiroglou believes that the pools at Qumran were multifunctional; "L'eau et les bains à Qoumran," *Revue des etudes juives* 159 (2000): 19-47. For a critique of the "maximalist" position of E. P. Sanders and Ronny Reich regarding the identification of stepped pools as miqva'ot, see

Benjamin G. Wright III, "Jewish Ritual Baths — Interpreting the Digs and the Texts: Some Issues in the Social History of Second Temple Judaism," in *The Archaeology of Israel: Constructing the Past, Interpreting the Present,* ed. Neil A. Silberman and D. Small (Sheffield: Sheffield Academic, 1997), 192-214. Wright understands the passage from CD 10.11-14 as meaning that in cases where the water in a rock pool is insufficient to cover a person, it is considered unclean, like water stored in a vessel (in which a person is prohibited from immersing himself or herself).

For the suggestion that miqva'ot with partitions or double doorways were used by priests and those with an *otsar* were associated with Pharisees, see Eyal Regev, "Ritual Baths of Jewish Groups and Sects in the Second Temple Period," *Cathedra* 79 (1996): 3-20 (Hebrew). The story of the identification of the stepped pools at Masada as miqva'ot was recounted by Yigael Yadin in his popular book, *Masada: Herod's Fortress and the Zealots' Last Stand,* 164-67. For detailed descriptions of the stepped pools and other water installations at Masada, see Ehud Netzer, *Masada III.* Asher Grossberg has suggested that the miqveh in the southeastern casemate room at Masada functioned in a different manner than Yadin suggested; "How were the Miqva'ot at Masada Made Fit?" *Cathedra* 85 (1998): 33-44 (Hebrew).

For the excavations at Tel Anafa, see Sharon C. Herbert, *Tel Anafa* 1/1-2: *Final report on Ten Years of Excavation at a Hellenistic and Roman Settlement in Northern Israel* (Ann Arbor: Kelsey Museum, 1994). For a brief and popular overview of the results of the excavations at Tel Anafa, see Andrea M. Berlin, "Between Large Forces: Palestine in the Hellenistic Period," *Biblical Archaeologist* 60 (1997): 2-51 (for the Late Hellenistic Stuccoed Building, see 26-27). For Mampsis, see Avraham Negev, *The Architecture of Mampsis: Final Report* 1: *The Middle and Late Nabatean Periods.* Qedem 26 (Jerusalem: Hebrew University, 1988). For the houses at ez-Zantur in Petra, see Rolf A. Stucky et al., *Petra ez-Zantur* 1: *Ergebnisse der Schweizerisch-Liechtensteinischen Ausgrabungen 1988-1992* (Mainz: Philipp von Zabern, 1996). Houses at ez-Zantur that are decorated with wall paintings are described by Bernhard Kolb, "Die Patrizierhauser von ez-Zantur," *Welt und Umwelt der Bibel* 19 (2001): 52-53. For Amos Kloner's identification of ritual baths among the non-Jewish population at Marisa, see "Mareshah (Marisa), The Lower City," in Ephraim Stern, *The New Encyclopedia of Archaeological Excavations in the Holy Land,* 3:951-53; "Underground Metropolis, The Subterranean World of Maresha," *Biblical Archaeology Review* 23/2 (1997): 24-35, 67 (see the diagram of "a model home" on 29). For the dating of the miqva'ot at Marisa to after Hyrcanus's conquest of the site, see Gerald Finkielsztejn, "More Evidence on John Hyrcanus I's Conquests: Lead Weights and Rhodian Amphora Stamps," *Bulletin of the Anglo-*

*Israel Archaeological Society* 16 (1998): 33-63 (for the ritual baths, see 47-48). Finkielsztejn argues that Hyrcanus conquered Marisa in 111/110 B.C.E. (not 112). For a useful collection of references to excavated pools in Palestine that are identified as miqva'ot, see Hanan Eshel, "A Note on 'Miqvaot' at Sepphoris," in *Archaeology and the Galilee: Texts and Contexts in the Graeco-Roman and Byzantine Periods,* ed. Douglas R. Edwards and C. Thomas McCollough (Atlanta: Scholars, 1997), 131-33.

# CHAPTER 8

# Women and the Cemetery at Qumran

The question of women's presence at Qumran is related to the controversies surrounding the interpretation of the site. For example, if Qumran was a villa or manor house, women must have lived there. However, even among scholars who accept the identification of Qumran as a sectarian settlement there is no consensus regarding the presence of women. This is due largely to different information provided by our literary sources about the role or status of women in this sect. In this chapter, we examine the archaeological evidence for the presence of women at Qumran. We begin with a brief review of the literary sources.

## Literary Sources on Female Sectarians/Essenes

The field of Dead Sea Scrolls studies was long dominated by male scholars with an androcentric approach. This was due partly to the fact that de Vaux and some of the other members of the original publication team were Catholic priests (and all of them were men). In addition, our information about the Essenes is provided by males with misogynistic tendencies (Josephus, Philo, and Pliny). The fact that most modern scholars have assumed that the community at Qumran consisted of adult celibate men did not encourage the introduction of feminist or gender studies into the field. As Eileen Schuller has noted, "Certainly the standard view which depicts the authors of the scrolls as 'monks,' male celibates living in isolation in the desert, has not suggested to scholars that there is anything here of particular interest for the study of women in antiquity, except perhaps by way of a negative example of misogyny carried to its logical conclusion." This attitude has begun to change within the last decade, thanks to the work of Schuller and other scholars, including Lawrence Schiffman, Linda Bennett Elder, and Joan Taylor.

Both Philo and Pliny describe the Essenes as a community of adult celibate men. This reflects the negative attitude towards women and the admiration for an ascetic and celibate lifestyle held by many Hellenistic and Roman writers (especially philosophers). Pliny describes the Essenes as "a people unique of its kind and admirable beyond all others in the whole world, without women and renouncing love entirely. . . . Owing to the throng of newcomers, this people is daily re-born in equal number; indeed, those whom, wearied by the fluctuations of fortune, life leads to adopt their customs stream in in great numbers. Thus, unbelievable though this may seem, for thousands of centuries a race has existed which is eternal yet into which no one is born . . ." (*Natural History* 5.73).

Philo's misogynistic bias is evident in the following passage, in which he uses the celibacy of the Essenes as an excuse to launch into a diatribe against the evils of women and marriage:

> On the other hand, shrewdly providing against the sole or principal obstacle threatening to dissolve the bonds of communal life, they banned marriage at the same time as they ordered the practice of perfect continence. Indeed, no Essaean (Essene) takes a woman because women are selfish, excessively jealous, skillful in ensnaring the morals of a spouse and in seducing him by endless charms. Women set out to flatter, and wear all sorts of masks, like actors on the stage; then, when they have bewitched the eye and captured the ear, when, that is to say, they have deceived the lower senses, they next lead the sovereign mind astray. On the other hand, if children are born, they then declare with audacious arrogance, and swollen with pride and effrontery, what they were formerly content to insinuate hypocritically by means of allusions, and shamelessly employ violence to commit actions all of which are contrary to the good of the common life. The husband, bound by his wife's spells, or anxious for children from natural necessity, is no more the same towards the others, but unknown to himself he becomes a different man, a slave instead of a freeman. (*Hypothetica* 11.14-17)

At the beginning of his description of the Essenes, Josephus reveals a similar bias: "The Essenes renounce pleasure as an evil, and regard continence and resistance to the passions as a virtue. They disdain marriage for themselves, but adopt the children of others at a tender age in order to instruct them; they regard them as belonging to them by kinship, and condition them to conform to their own customs. It is not that they abolish marriage, or the propagation of the species resulting from it, but they are on their guard against the licentiousness of women and are convinced that none of them is faithful to one man" (*War* 2.120-21). Elsewhere he states that, "In addition, they take no wives and acquire no slaves; in fact, they consider slavery an injustice, and marriage as leading to discord" (*Ant.* 18.21).

In these passages, Pliny, Philo, and Josephus seem to indicate that the Essenes were celibate men who adopted children or were joined by new members from outside the sect. However, Josephus, who is the only one of these three writers with a first-hand knowledge of the Essenes, indicates that at least some Essenes were married and had families. First, in *War* 2.120-21 he qualifies his statement that the Essenes "disdain marriage for themselves," by saying that "It is not that they abolish marriage . . . but are on their guard against the licentiousness of women. . . ." Later in *War*, Josephus describes an "order" of married Essenes:

> There exists another order of Essenes, who, although in agreement with the others on the way of life, usages, and customs, are separated from them on the subject of marriage. Indeed, they believe that people who do not marry cut off a very important part of life, namely, the propagation of the species; and all the more so that if everyone adopted the same opinion the race would very quickly disappear. Nevertheless, they observe their women for three years. When they have purified themselves three times and thus proved themselves capable of bearing children, they then marry them. And when they are pregnant they have no intercourse with them, thereby showing that they do not marry for pleasure but because it is necessary to have children. The women bathe wearing a dress, whereas the men wear a loincloth. (*War* 2.160-61)

Josephus's testimony indicates that the group or groups our ancient sources describe as Essenes included men who practiced celibacy (at least occasionally if not permanently) as well as married members. As we shall see, the archaeological evidence suggests that the community at Qumran consisted mostly of adult men. This community (or less likely, a similar one) seems to have been the focus of Pliny's, Philo's, and much of Josephus's descriptions. These writers characteristically focused on those practices of the Essenes that were different and exotic. Not only did the celibacy practiced by at least some Essenes attract their attention, but it fed into the authors' misogynistic biases and was part of the ascetic lifestyle they considered to be virtuous. As David Goodblatt has pointed out to me, Philo describes the virtues of female members (especially the "aged virgins") of the Therapeutae. The fact that he does not mention female Essenes suggests that the community at Qumran was the focus of his description. Josephus admits that some Essenes were married, but explains that this was only for the purposes of "the propagation of the species." Whether this was indeed the case or represents Josephus's opinion (perhaps invented to explain why there were married Essenes), the fact remains that at least some Essenes were married. In addition, Josephus's testimony indicates that the women observed at least some of the Essenes' purity regulations, including immersion in ritual baths (while wearing a dress to ensure modesty).

The Dead Sea Scrolls provide similarly ambiguous (or at least mixed) information regarding women in the sect. The Community Rule (Manual of Discipline; 1QS), which many scholars consider to be a sort of constitution for the community at Qumran and includes the community's penal code, contains no references to women (except for the biblical idiom "one born of woman," 1QS 11.21) or legislation concerning sexual relations, marriage, and children. Because of the community's concern with ritual purity, these omissions suggest that women were not present at Qumran. On the other hand, Elder has pointed out that "no published text from Qumran mandates celibacy." Geza Vermès concurs, but argues that the omissions in the Community Rule indicate that the Qumran community consisted of male celibates: "The evidence here [in the Community Rule] is not obvious in that no regulation directly states that all the members were forbidden to marry. But in this document, to use an oxymoron, the argument from silence speaks loud and clear."

The Community Rule contrasts with other sectarian documents which contain references to or legislation concerning women and children. The Damascus Document describes a society in which marriage and families were the norm. One passage specifically refers to married groups living in "camps" (CD 7.6-9): "And if they live in camps according to the rule of the Land, marrying and begetting children, they shall walk according to the Law and according to the statute concerning binding vows, according to the rule of the Law which says, *Between a man and his wife and between a father and his son*" (Numbers 30:17[Eng. 16]). This document also includes legislation regarding marriage, divorce, and oaths given by women: "And each man marries the daughter of his brother or sister, whereas Moses said, *You shall not approach your mother's sister; she is your mother's near kin* (Leviticus 18:13). But although the laws against incest are written for men, they also apply to women. When, therefore, a brother's daughter uncovers the nakedness of her father's brother, she is (also his) near kin" (CD 5.7-11). "Inasmuch as He said, *It is for her husband to cancel her oath* (Numbers 30:9), no husband shall cancel an oath without knowing whether it should be kept or not" (CD 16.10-11). "Likewise he who marri[es]} a woma[n] . . . advice. Likewise he who divorces (his wife)" (CD 13.16-17). One passage in the Damascus Document refers to punishment given to members for "murmuring" against the "Fathers" and "Mothers," suggesting that there were women of relatively high status in the sect (although of lower status than the "Fathers"): "[If he has murmured] against the Fathers, he shall leave and shall not return [again. But if he has murmured] against the Mothers, he shall do penance for ten days. For the Mothers have no *rwqmh* (distinction?) within [the Congregation" (4Q270, fr. 7, 13-14).

A scroll called the Rule of the Congregation or Messianic Rule (1QSa) includes women and children in its description of the sectarian community at the End of Days: "When they come, they shall summon them all, the little children and the women also, and they shall read into their [ears a]ll the precepts of the Covenant . . ." (1QSa 1.4-5). In the War Scroll (1QM 7.3), women and children (as well as men who are crippled or impure) are excluded from the camps, suggesting that they were ordinarily part of the community: "No boy or woman shall enter their camps, from the time they leave Jerusalem and march out to war until they return." Similarly, the Temple Scroll contains legislation for marriage, sexual relations, childbirth, and purity laws relevant to women. For example, it strictly separates impure menstruating women from the rest of the community. In the ideal temple as described in the scroll, pure women would be allowed to enter the outermost of the three courts. Although it might not be a sectarian composition, this document was apparently considered authoritative by the sect. One passage in the Temple Scroll mentions that women who have been captured in war and married their captor "may not touch your pure food for seven years. Nor shall she eat a whole-offering until seven years pass; then she shall eat (it)" (11QT$^a$ 63.14).

Despite Josephus's testimony and the references to and legislation concerning women in some of the sectarian scrolls (including women who were called "Mothers"), it is unclear whether (or how) women were initiated into the sect and what status they could attain. The issue we shall consider here is not whether there were married (or female) Essenes in general (which depends on the evaluation of the literary sources), but whether there is archaeological evidence for the presence of women at Qumran. Archaeological evidence has been cited both to support and deny the presence of women at Qumran. This evidence falls into two main categories: (1) the human remains from the cemetery; and (2) the finds from the settlement. We begin with a review of the human remains from the cemetery.

## The Cemetery

A large cemetery is located some 30-40 meters to the east of Qumran, separated by the boundary wall on the eastern side of the settlement (see Figs. 46, 47). The cemetery is spread over the top of the plateau (this is the "western sector," which de Vaux considered to be the main part of the cemetery), with extensions (or "secondary cemeteries") on hills to the north, east, and south (including to the south of Wadi Qumran). Here I refer to the cemetery at Qumran in the singular, although it is perhaps more accurate to refer to cemeteries, as some scholars have suggested. The cemetery is estimated to contain 1100 to 1200 graves (those excavated by de Vaux were numbered serially and designated "T" for *tombe*). All of the graves in the western sector (except for T4) are arranged in neat rows with a uniform orientation, with the head laid to the south and the feet to the north. The graves are marked by heaps of small stones, with a large headstone at each end. They are arranged in three groups that are separated by two broad east-west paths. Most of the graves on the hill to the southeast (the "southern extension") and all of the graves in the southern cemetery (to the south of Wadi Qumran) are oriented east-west, with the heads of the deceased laid to the east.

The 19th-century explorers Clermont-Ganneau and Condor and Tyrwhitt-Drake excavated two of the graves on top of the plateau (see Chapter 2). Clermont-Ganneau observed that the burials could not be Muslim due to their north-south orientation. Muslim burials in Palestine are usually oriented east-west, with the head laid to the east and the face turned south towards Mecca. Over the course of several seasons, de Vaux excavated 43 graves in the cemetery (including in the "extensions") at Qumran. The graves are dug into the marl of the terrace to an average depth of 1.5–2.0 meters, and most contain a single inhumation (that is, one whole body with the flesh still intact was laid in the grave). Four graves contained two burials each: T16, T24, T37 in the western sector, and T3 in the southern cemetery. Three graves contained apparent reinhumations (T11, T24, T37; a reinhumation means that a body was buried a second time, after it was buried elsewhere and the flesh had decomposed). The bodies were apparently wrapped in linen shrouds and some were perhaps placed in wooden coffins (as suggested by fragmentary wood remains and iron nails found in T17, T18, and T19). At the bottom of each grave, a niche or "loculus" was dug along the length of the shaft. The body was placed in this loculus, which was sealed by stone slabs or mud bricks. The shaft was then filled with earth (see Fig. 48).

Except for those in the southern cemetery, the graves contained virtually no burial goods or gifts. In a few cases, potsherds were mixed with the fill of the shaft. As an aside, I note that in his preliminary report in the *Revue Biblique* 61 (1954): 215, de Vaux stated that a bag-shaped jar similar to the one illustrated there in Fig. 1:4 was found in the fill of T4. However, in Humbert and Chambon's volume (p. 346), the jar from the fill of T4 is described as a *jarre cylindrique* (a cylindrical jar), and an oil lamp of unspecified type is said to have been found in the fill of T26.

The lack of associated goods makes it difficult to date the burials. Because of the proximity of the cemetery to the settlement, scholars have assumed that they are contemporary. As we shall see, however, not all of the graves are necessarily associated with the settlement. Unfortunately, recent attempts to radiocarbon date the material from the graves have failed to yield results. This is because not enough collagen is preserved in the skeletons and there is too little carbon to allow even for accelerator mass spectroscopy (AMS) analysis. The wood from the coffins cannot be radiocarbon dated because it is saturated with paraffin, which was applied as a preservative after the excavations.

The skeletons excavated by de Vaux were preliminarily identified at the time of the excavations by Henri-Victor Vallois and Gottfried Kurth. Those from T1, T2, T9, T14, and T17 are now missing (that is, their whereabouts are currently unknown). In addition, the nine skeletons from 10 graves excavated by Solomon Steckoll in 1966 and 1967 are now lost. Because of this and because of Steckoll's highly speculative and controversial interpretations of the skeletons he excavated (including the identification of one as a "scribe" and another as a "horseman"), I do not include his material in this discussion.

Of the skeletons excavated by de Vaux whose whereabouts are known, 22 are now in Munich, nine are in Jerusalem, and eight are in Paris. Some of the skeletons ended up in Europe because they were taken by Vallois and Kurth to France and Germany for further study. The 22 skeletons in Kurth's collection in Munich were recently reexamined by Kurth's assistant, Olav Röhrer-Ertl (in collaboration with Ferdinand Rohrhirsch and Dietbert Hahn). Röhrer-Ertl has identified nine of the 22 skeletons as adult males, eight as adult females, and five as children. However, of the skeletons from the western sector (where all of the excavated graves except T4 were aligned in rows oriented north-south), Röhrer-Ertl has identified nine as adult males and two as adult females. These 11 skeletons came from 10 graves: T20, T21, T22, T23, T24a-b, T26, T28, T29, T30, T31; the females were in T22 and T24b. In addition, Vallois identified the skeleton from T7 in the western sector of the cemetery as a female (this skeleton is not among those reexamined by Röhrer-Ertl, but is part of Vallois's collection, now in Paris; see below). The other females and all of the children were buried in the extensions, which de

Vaux considered to be secondary. These extensions are: the central extension (with one excavated grave [T11], containing an adult male [see below]); the southern extension (with six excavated graves [T32-T37], apparently containing six adult females and one child); and the southern cemetery, located on the south side of Wadi Qumran (with four excavated graves [T1-T4] containing one adult female and four children; for the northern cemetery and northern extension, see below).

Joseph Zias, a physical anthropologist based in Israel, has challenged the identifications of the skeletons made by Röhrer-Ertl. According to Zias, all three of the supposed females from the western sector of the cemetery (T7, T22, T24b) exceed by 11-14 cm. the normal height range characteristic of the female population of Judea in the 1st century B.C.E. and 1st century C.E. Therefore, Zias believes that all three are adult males. In addition, based on their state of preservation and the differences in burial customs and orientation, Zias has suggested that the women and children found in the southern extension and in the southern cemetery represent relatively recent bedouin burials. These include the only burials that contained grave goods, consisting of beads, earrings, and a bronze ring. Zias has noted that whereas jewelry is rarely found in Jewish tombs of the Second Temple period, it is not uncommon in bedouin burials (including the bedouin graves that de Vaux excavated at Ein Feshkha; see below).

Another nine skeletons excavated by de Vaux were recently discovered in storage in Jerusalem and were reexamined by Susan Sheridan, a physical anthropologist from the University of Notre Dame. These skeletons come from T12, T13, T15, T16 (containing two skeletons, from T16a and T16b), T18, T19, and Tombs A and B (a box marked T17 contained pieces of wood and iron nails, but no bones). Sheridan has kindly provided me with the following information about them. The first seven skeletons, which come from graves in the western sector of the cemetery, are all adult males (including one 15- or 16-year-old "subadult" male from T15). There is some confusion regarding the location and source of the remaining two skeletons in this group. According to the markings on the boxes and on the bones themselves, they come from "Tomb A" and "Tomb B." Some scholars, including Humbert and Chambon, have equated these two graves with T9 and T10 in the northern cemetery. However, as Emile Puech has pointed out, Tombs A and B seem to represent graves that are distinct from T9 and T10. They might belong to a group of about 12 to 15 graves located to the north of the wadi at the northern end of Khirbet Qumran (that is, to the northwest of the northern cemetery). It is also possible that T9 and T10 were in the northern extension, in which case Tombs A and B should be located in the northern cemetery. According to

Sheridan, the skeleton from Tomb A is definitely an adult female, aged approximately 45-50. The skeleton from Tomb B is an old man over 60 years of age. These two graves were oriented north-south.

Sheridan has also reexamined the eight skeletons in Vallois's collection in Paris, which come from T3, T4, T5, T6, T7, T8, T10, and T11 (the remains from T3 were mixed with those from T8 and were labeled as coming from T8). All of these are located in the western sector of the cemetery, except for T10, which apparently lies in the northern cemetery (discussed above), and T11 in the central extension (to the north of the southern extension). Sheridan has kindly provided me with the following preliminary observations regarding these remains. First, all of these skeletons represent adult males. Even the skeleton from T7, which was identified by Vallois as a female, is apparently a male, although Sheridan expresses "slight reservation" over this identification because the preserved remains are fragmentary. Second, the skeleton from T4, which is located at the southern end of the western sector and is the only one in that sector with an east-west orientation, might represent a relatively recent (that is, a bedouin) burial. In this case, the jar found in the fill of this grave would already have been mixed in with the fill when the grave was dug. Sheridan notes that the male from T7 showed signs of severe arthritis in his hips and must have been in pain. The older woman from Tomb A suffered from moderate osteoporosis, and the old man buried in Tomb B suffered from severe osteoarthritis. The teenage male from T15 was apparently sick for most of his childhood. According to Sheridan, overall the population represented by the skeletons she examined suffered from neck arthritis, the build-up of hardened tartar on the teeth, and numerous tooth cavities. She also notes that the skeletons display no evidence of trauma (that is, a violent death), which contradicts one theory that these represent the burials of soldiers killed in battle (a suggestion associated with the interpretation of Qumran as a fort).

By now, many readers must be wondering how it is possible to confuse male and female skeletons, and why scientists cannot determine whether some of the burials are the remains of bedouins or 2000-year-old sectarians! The examination of ancient human remains (to determine the individual's age at the time of death, gender, physical deformities, ethnic characteristics, etc.) is done by trained physical anthropologists. In the case of Qumran, it is sometimes difficult to determine the gender due to the fragmentary state of the remains. In other words, the parts of the skeleton most indicative of gender, such as the pelvic region, are not always preserved. Various factors including local conditions such as the hot climate and the salinity of the soil have contributed to the poor state of preservation of the Qumran skeletons.

In addition, not all of the bones seem to have been collected and saved at the time of the excavations. For example, Sheridan notes that de Vaux seems to have collected mainly the cranium and the pelvis of the skeletons and left or discarded the other parts in the graves. Other excavated bones have since been lost or were stored in less than ideal conditions.

There are two main methods for determining the date of burials: (1) dating associated objects, that is, grave goods (burial gifts) or other objects (such as wooden coffins or cloth shrouds) that were placed in the graves at the time of the burial; (2) radiocarbon dating the bones themselves. As we have seen, neither of these methods has been used successfully on the Qumran material so far. In other words, due to the absence of associated grave goods, the lack of collagen in the bones, and the saturation of the wood coffin fragments with paraffin it is currently impossible to provide scientific dates for the Qumran burials. Perhaps the refinement and application of new scientific methods of analysis will provide information in the future.

Another problem with the Qumran material is the small size of the sample. Statistically, it is virtually impossible to draw any conclusions based on a sample of only 43 excavated graves out of a total of 1100-1200. In fact, Sheridan notes that the 39 skeletons which have recently been reexamined using modern anthropological methods represent only 3.5 percent of the burials in the 1100 graves. Opposition from certain sectors of the ultra-orthodox Jewish community in Israel as well as the current political situation make it unlikely that additional graves will be excavated in the foreseeable future. On the other hand, the fact that de Vaux excavated random graves distributed throughout the cemetery means there is a good chance that this sample is demographically representative of the whole.

In light of the current controversies surrounding the skeletal remains from Qumran, it is at present only possible to conclude as follows:

1. No more than two adult females (from T22, T24b) are known to be represented in the western sector of the cemetery at Qumran.
2. One more (apparently sectarian) adult female was found in Tomb A, to the north of the site (in the northern cemetery).
3. Women and children predominate in the southern extension and in the southern cemetery. I believe that Zias is correct in identifying these as recent bedouin burials. The burial in T4 at the southern end of the western sector might also represent a bedouin burial. The fact that bedouin burials are present at Qumran is indicated by de Vaux's reference to one he excavated inside the settlement (in L118, mentioned in Humbert and Chambon's volume), which was oriented east-west. De

Vaux also excavated three bedouin graves inside the main building at Ein Feshkha (in L2) and another about 100 m. to the northeast. A triangular mother of pearl pendant, 13 glass and glass paste beads belonging to a necklace, one stone bead, and a Turkish coin pierced by a hole were found in these graves. Other bedouin graves were excavated at Ein el-Ghuweir (see below).

4. Even with the females in T22 and T24b, there is a much higher proportion of males buried in the western sector of the cemetery.

Thus, the evidence from the western sector of the cemetery suggests that women were present at Qumran but represented a disproportionately small part of the population. The complete absence of infants and children among the excavated burials in the western sector is striking given the high rate of infant and child mortality in antiquity. Despite the small size of the sample, this evidence suggests that the community at Qumran did not include families. If we reject Zias's suggestion regarding the identification of the burials in the extensions as bedouins, then women and children were present in larger numbers among the sectarians (although still in a minority), but their graves were marginalized. This would also mean that female sectarians were buried with items of personal adornment (jewelry). This is important because, as we shall see, almost no jewelry or other gendered objects are recorded from the settlement at Qumran. If one argues that the absence of such items from the settlement is due to the ascetic lifestyle of the female sectarians, we should not find them in their graves. In other words, it is contradictory to argue that the absence of jewelry and other gendered objects from Qumran does not mean that women were absent from the settlement (on the basis of the assumption that ascetic women would not wear any items of personal adornment) while at the same time identifying the women buried with jewelry in the southern extension and southern cemetery as sectarians. We shall return to this issue later.

The fact that, despite differences in orientation, the bedouin burials at Qumran resemble the sectarian ones (and until now were identified as sectarian) indicates that more than just morphological criteria must be used in identifying their occupants. This problem has been highlighted by recent excavations in the 1st- to 2nd-century C.E. Nabatean cemetery at Khirbet Qazone at the southeast end of the Dead Sea. The 3500 graves at Khirbet Qazone are oriented north-south and, as at Qumran, the bodies were inhumed at the base of a shaft dug into the ground and sealed by mud bricks. There are, however, at least two major differences between these cemeteries: (1) the burials at Khirbet Qazone included proportionate numbers of men, women, and children, and (2) a few contained grave goods (mostly bracelets, earrings, and beads, but no whole pottery vessels). Five funerary stelae were discovered from disturbed graves. This evidence indicates that shaft graves with a sealed loculus at the base containing a single inhumation were not used exclusively by the sectarian population at Qumran. This means that cemeteries with graves of this type cannot automatically be assumed to contain an Essene or sectarian population.

Another example of a cemetery of this type is located at Ein el-Ghuweir, a site on the western shore of the Dead Sea that lies to the south of and is contemporary with the settlements at Qumran and Ein Feshkha (see Chapter 10). Pesach Bar-Adon, an Israeli archaeologist who conducted excavations at Ein el-Ghuweir, identified the remains as a sectarian settlement. Bar-Adon also excavated two cemeteries, one on a hill to the north of the settlement and the other on a hill to the south of the site, on the other side of a ravine. In the northern cemetery, all but two of the graves were oriented north-south (Tomb 17 was oriented northwest-southeast and Tomb 15 was oriented east-west). In the southern cemetery, which Bar-Adon identified as a bedouin cemetery, the graves were oriented east-west. The graves resembled those in the western sector at Qumran. Each contained an inhumed body covered with a disintegrated shroud, which had been laid in a sealed loculus at the base of a shaft. The 18 graves Bar-Adon excavated in the northern cemetery contained 12 men and six women, while the two he excavated in the southern cemetery contained a man and a seven-year-old child. After mentioning that the southern cemetery is bedouin, Bar-Adon makes no further differentiation between the burials in the two cemeteries. The males ranged in age from 18 to 60/70 and the women were 18 to 34 years of age. Overall they appeared to be in poorer health than the population at Qumran. Storage jars and a bowl of 1st-century C.E. date found in the fill appear to have been deliberately smashed and placed in the some of the graves. One jar was inscribed in black ink with the Hebrew name Yehohanan, indicating that the population was Jewish. As we shall see, however, it is impossible to determine whether this population was sectarian or was connected with the community at Qumran.

Other cemeteries of this type have been excavated at a site near Ein el-Ghuweir called Ḥiam el-Sagha, as well as in Jerusalem. Based on the similarity of the graves to those at Qumran, the excavators of these cemeteries have suggested that they were used by an Essene or sectarian population. This method of burial is fundamentally different from that practiced by other Jews living in Judea in the 1st century B.C.E. and 1st century C.E. Many Jews buried their dead in underground, rock-cut burial caves consisting of one or more rooms, which were used by extended families over the course of several generations. Rock-cut burial caves are found at Jericho and Ein Gedi. By the 1st century C.E., the burial caves in Jerusalem and Jericho had loculi cut into the walls to accommodate the individual bodies, which were wrapped in a shroud and sometimes placed in a wooden coffin. After a body was placed in the loculus, the opening was sealed with a stone slab. Sometimes the loculi were emptied after the flesh had decayed, and the skeletal remains were gathered and placed in small carved stone boxes called ossuaries. The ossuaries were left on the floors of the caves and in the loculi or on benches lining the walls of the burial chambers. Pottery vessels including cooking pots and perfume bottles were also placed inside the tombs. Sometimes coins were placed on the eyes or inside the mouth of the deceased. This apparently represents a custom that some Jews adopted from the Greeks; the coins were to pay Charon, who ferried the dead across the river Styx into the underworld. The entrances to the burial caves were closed with large stone slabs, or sometimes by a rolling stone. According to the Gospels, Jesus was laid to rest in a burial cave that belonged to Joseph of Arimathea.

Burying the dead in rock-cut caves used by several generations of the same family was an ancient custom among the Jews of Judea that goes back to the First Temple period. In contrast, the populations at Qumran, Ein el-Ghuweir, Hiam el-Sagha, and the cemeteries of this type in Jerusalem were buried individually instead of with their families and ancestors. No one has satisfactorily explained their peculiar orientation, although a number of suggestions have been made. As some scholars have noted, if a physical resurrection was envisioned, the bodies would be facing north. The cemetery at Khirbet Qazone indicates that this method of burial is not only associated with sectarians or even only with Jews. Perhaps, as Taylor has suggested, it represents a burial custom among the poor that was adopted by (or originated with?) the community at Qumran. Nevertheless, the fact that the western sector of the cemetery at Qumran is adjacent to the settlement (as well as the north-south orientation of the burials in that sector) indicates that those buried there represent the site's occupants.

## Gendered Objects from Qumran

Do the artifacts recovered in de Vaux's excavations provide any indication of whether women were present among the community at Qumran? As we shall see, although it is largely negative, the archaeological evidence suggests only minimal female presence at Qumran. Aside from finding the physical remains of women in the settlement (such as the female burials in the cemetery), one means of identifying women in the archaeological record is to find objects that reflect their presence, that is, objects that were used or owned *exclusively* by women. Scholars refer to these as "gendered" objects. Tampons and brassieres are modern examples of gendered objects.

Were any gendered objects found at Qumran? Unfortunately, few organic materials are preserved from de Vaux's excavations. This means that items such as hairnets, which might attest to the presence of women at Qumran, have not survived (assuming they originally existed). Taylor noted that "in a society in which many roles were clearly gendered . . . certain objects were particularly used by women: combs, mirrors, cosmetics, also jewelry (beads, necklaces, earrings, noserings) and spindle whorls or other items reflecting specific women's domestic work." The gathering and preparation of wild vegetables, dairy production, spinning, laundering, water fetching, cooking, and pottery production have traditionally been major female activities worldwide. Women in Roman Palestine also engaged in work outside the domestic sphere, for example, in pottery-making, trade, agriculture, butchery, and bread-making. As a rule, however, women were responsible for the household tasks, while men worked outside the house. Despite the chronological and interpretive problems surrounding rabbinic sources and their relationship (if any) to the community at Qumran, they are important for this discussion because they provide some information about women in Roman Palestine. According to the rabbis, "These are the kinds of labor which a woman performs for her husband: she (1) grinds flour, (2) bakes bread, (3) does laundry, (4) prepares meals, (5) feeds her child, (6) makes the bed, (7) works in wool" (Mishnah *Ketubot* 5:5). However, even work considered to be a woman's task when performed inside the house, such as baking, was usually a male profession in other contexts. This means that although women could have done some of the cooking and baking at Qumran or manufactured pottery we cannot assume that this was the case.

We must therefore identify among the archaeological finds from Qumran objects such as those mentioned by Taylor which were associated exclusively or almost exclusively with women — that is, gendered objects. Our search is hampered by the lack of a final publication of the material from de Vaux's excavations, which means that none of the conclusions presented here can be considered definitive. However, de Vaux's published field notes include lists of the objects found in each locus. Of the gendered objects that Taylor enumerates, no combs or mirrors appear in these lists (see Figs. 55, 57). Since combs and mirror cases were made of wood, their absence is not surprising (although the preserved materials could include the mirrors themselves, which were made of polished bronze, or bronze mirror cases like the one from Masada mentioned below, or other cosmetic items).

The other types of gendered objects mentioned by Taylor are jewelry and spindle whorls. Although men in the Roman world sometimes wore finger rings and fibulae (a kind of safety pin to used to fasten a cloak), Alexandra Croom has observed that "Men tended not to wear much jewellery, as those that did were considered effeminate." On the other hand, women wore a variety of jewelry including necklaces, earrings, finger rings, and bracelets. Spindle whorls are associated with spindles, which were used for spinning wool. The raw wool or linen was tied to a stick called a distaff and then teased out by hand, using a weighted stick (the spindle) to twist the raw material into thread. The spindle was a bone or wooden stick with a spindle whorl at the top to provide the weight. Spindle whorls are cone-shaped objects made of stone, bone, wood, or glass and pierced by a hole for attachment to the spindle (see Fig. 57). According to Croom, "Spinning was such a typical activity that the distaff and spindle became a symbol of womanhood." Taylor too has noted that "the association of women with spinning was one of the most definitive among gendered roles in antiquity." Even in industrial contexts at Pompeii, the spinners were apparently women whereas the weavers were men. I agree with Taylor that in the rabbinic sources "spinning does *not* appear on the list of 'banned' male employments, probably because in Graeco-Roman Palestine spinning — like midwifery — was something *men did not do.*"

There do not appear to be any references to spinning and weaving in the sectarian scrolls. In addition, despite a number of references to Essene clothing, Josephus and Philo do not mention spinning and weaving either. Although it is an argument from silence, if male members of the highly gendered Essene community engaged in spinning, presumably this activity would have been legislated (in the sectarian scrolls) or singled out for description and perhaps ridicule by Josephus, Philo, and other authors. For example, Tal Ilan has noted that, "When women are mentioned in the documents composed by the Dead Sea Sect, it is almost always in *halakhic* contexts." It thus seems safe to associate spindle whorls in Roman Palestine (including at Qumran) with the presence of women. However, the archaeological evidence does not support Taylor's assertion that "the most striking objects for engendered archaeology to be uncovered at Qumran are bone spindle whorls." In fact, only two spindle whorls are listed in de Vaux's field notes. One, described as made of alabaster, comes from L20. Since L20 belongs to Period III (and existed only in Period III), this spindle whorl is not associated with the sectarian settlement at Qumran. The other spindle whorl comes from L7. This locus represents a sounding made at the beginning of the excavations in 1951. De Vaux's notes provide no indication of the provenience of this spindle whorl in terms of the different occupation levels, although L7 appears in association with Period II in the plan illustrated in Humbert and Chambon's volume. This locus lies on the margins of the settlement to the west of the tower. Therefore, based on the material published to date, only one spindle whorl appears to have been found in association with the sectarian settlement at Qumran, and it comes from an area that lies on the margins of the settlement. For the sake of completeness, I note that one limestone spindle whorl is listed from Ein Feshkha. It comes from L18, which is located in a structure that also showed evidence of Byzantine occupation. No spindle whorls are published from Ein el-Ghuweir.

Is jewelry attested at Qumran? Without illustrations or a final publication, it is impossible to determine whether some of the objects listed in de Vaux's notes, such as "bronze rings," might represent jewelry. The only bracelet (a fragment) listed comes from a Period III locus (L43). Other objects listed, such as fibulae, were also worn or used by men. Without illustrations, it is impossible to determine whether the mother of pearl "ornament" (perhaps an inlay?) listed from L111 and the two bronze "ornaments" from L125 and L130 represent gendered objects. That leaves beads, only five of which are listed in de Vaux's notes. One comes from L43, the Period III locus with the bracelet mentioned above. A globular bead was found in L35, in the southeast corner of the central courtyard of the main building. A large glass bead comes from L41, a room on the north side of the central courtyard of the main building. The fourth bead was found "outside" L44, which is the area of the potters' workshop on the eastern edge of the settlement. The fifth bead, described as cylindrical, was found in the fill above the steps of L48, which is the miqveh on the eastern side of the settlement that was damaged in the earthquake of 31 B.C.E. In other words, only four beads were found in contexts that might be associated with the sectarian settlement, although two come from loci with evidence of later occupation (L35, L41).

The scroll caves at Qumran yielded only three beads (from Caves 11Q and B, listed in Humbert and Chambon's volume) and two fragments of a wooden comb (from Cave 1). A bronze earring or nose ring was found in Cave 24, which is located about 50 meters north of Cave 11. The comb fragments and a cooking pot found in Cave 1 point to domestic occupation on a very limited scale. No gendered objects are published from the recently excavated residential caves in the marl terrace to the north of Qumran.

To summarize, the published and identifiable gendered objects associated with the sectarian settlement at Qumran consist of one spindle whorl and no more than four beads. This evidence corresponds with that from the cemetery, which attests to the presence of women, but only very minimally. The evidence from the site is, of course, suggestive rather than definitive, for the following reasons: (1) the final publication of the material from de Vaux's excavations could reveal the presence of additional gendered objects; and (2) the conclusion that women are only minimally represented at Qumran is based on negative evidence — that is, an argument from silence. It is impossible to prove *on the basis of the archaeological evidence alone* that women were not present and active in various capacities (as bakers and cooks, potters, agricultural laborers, etc.). Nevertheless, this argument from silence is impressive, especially when we compare Qumran with contemporary sites in the Judean Desert where women were undoubtedly present. The sites we shall consider here are Masada and the Judean Desert caves. We shall also examine the archaeological evidence from the Byzantine monastery at Khirbet ed-Deir.

## Masada

According to Josephus, the Jewish rebels who occupied Masada during the First Jewish Revolt against the Romans (66/67 to 73/74 C.E.) consisted of families of men, women, and children. For example, Eleazar Ben Yair's speech, as reported by Josephus, includes the following line: "Let our wives thus die undishonoured, our children unacquainted with slavery" (*War* 7.334). In the controversial mass suicide, Josephus reports that the men killed "with their own hands their own wives and children" (*War* 7.393). The archaeological evidence from Yigael Yadin's excavations confirms Josephus's testimony that women and children were present among the rebels. The skeletons from Masada include the remains of what appears to be a rebel family, consisting of a man, woman, and child, in the area of the bathhouse on the lower terrace of the northern palace. Iron arrowheads and bronze scales of armor, a fragment of a prayer shawl *(talith)*, a potsherd inscribed with Hebrew letters, and a pair of women's sandals were found near the skeletons. According to Zias, these human remains represent Roman, not Jewish burials. However, Yadin's notes indicate that these individuals were not formally buried (one of Zias's arguments is that the Jews never buried their dead with arrows and sandals), but instead were buried when the northern palace burned and collapsed. This explains why their remains were left there and were not removed or reburied. I see no reason to doubt their identification as Jewish rebels. On the other hand, the number and identity of the skeletons that Yadin found in a cistern on the southeast side of the mountain are disputed (anywhere from five to 25 individuals who could be Jewish rebels, Roman soldiers, or Byzantine monks!). Nine ostraca from Masada bear the names of or references to women. These are Hebrew ostraca inscribed "the wife of [Ze]baida," "the wife of *Tybw*," "the daughter of N[  ]," (or perhaps, "the house of . . ."), "the wife of Jacob," "the daughter of Domli," "Shalom (or Salome) the Gali[lean]," "the daughter of Qatra," and Greek ostraca inscribed "give to Salome, . . . four . . . ," "Mariam, the daughter of Kypselos." In contrast, only a small number of ostraca was found at Qumran, and they seem to have no references to women.

Numerous examples of ancient textiles were preserved at Masada. They include fragments of sleeveless tunics and rectangular mantles of a type worn by men and women in Roman Palestine. Some of the brightly-colored clothing probably belonged to women. The Masada finds also include four fragmentary hairnets. Avigail Sheffer and Hero Granger-Taylor have noted that hairnets were associated especially with Greek-style dress and were seldom worn by Roman women. References in rabbinic sources indicate that hairnets were a standard garment worn by Jewish women in Roman Palestine. The beads and jewelry from Masada are unpublished. Three hundred eighty-four spindle whorls made of wood, ivory, bone, stone, and glass were found at Masada. In addition, ten wooden combs are listed in the catalogue of wood remains. In his popular book on Masada, Yadin illustrated examples of cosmetic equipment found in the dwellings of the Jewish rebels, including cosmetic palettes and eyeshadow sticks, and a bronze mirror case (see Fig. 56). In addition, clay loom weights belonging to warp-weighted looms were found in many of the casemate rooms, as well as the remains of at least one wooden loom (see Chapter 9). Most of these objects come from rooms in the casemate wall that were occupied by the Jewish rebels.

## The Bar Kokhba Caves in the Judean Desert

Caves in the Judean Desert that were occupied by Jewish rebels at the time of the Bar Kokhba Revolt (132-135 C.E.) have also yielded evidence for the presence of women and children. These caves served as temporary hideouts for bands of rebels who sought refuge from the Roman army. Most of the evidence comes from the Cave of Letters in Naḥal Ḥever, south of Ein Gedi. In this cave, Yadin found the skeletal remains of four men, nine women, and six children. The documents discovered include the archive of a woman named Babatha who was one of the refugees hiding inside the cave. A bundle of balls of linen thread and a wooden mirror case with a bronze mirror were found with the purse that contained Babatha's archive (in antiquity, mirrors were made of polished bronze instead of glass). A second mirror identical to the first was discovered elsewhere in the cave (see Fig. 55). Another archive from the Cave of Letters, belonging to a woman named Salome Komaïse, indicates that she too took refuge there. Other gendered objects found in the cave include five spindle whorls, fragments belonging to one or two wooden combs, a polished horn spoon for cosmetic use, a wooden cosmetic box containing rouge powder that was found with one of the mirrors, and 22 or 23 beads (17 to 18 beads, some of semi-precious stones, were found together and probably belonged to the same necklace). The numerous, well-preserved textile fragments include fringed scarves that apparently belonged to women, a woman's hairnet, and a linen child's shirt or tunic. A bundle of dyed, unspun wool and balls of woolen thread were also found in the cave.

Other caves in the Judean Desert that were occupied at the time of the Bar Kokhba Revolt have yielded similar finds, though fewer in number and more limited in type. The finds from the Cave of Horror in Naḥal Ḥever included the skeletons of five adult males, five adult females, and 10 children (including a possible fetus; one more skeleton could not be identified). At least 10 spindle whorls of wood and stone, one wooden spindle shaft, and many fragments of wooden combs were also discovered in this cave. One complete wooden comb and two fragments were found in the Cave of the Pool in Naḥal David, above Ein Gedi, as well as two wooden spindle whorls and a bead of green stone. The caves in Wadi Murabbaʿat (to the north of Ein Gedi) yielded a number of spindle whorls, most of wood and others of stone, and wooden spindle shafts. There is also a clay loom weight pierced by a hole. Other finds from the caves in Wadi Murabbaʿat included many wooden combs and a small cosmetic spoon made of iron (see Fig. 57). Among the textiles was a possible hairnet.

More recently, two caves near Jericho yielded evidence for occupation by Jewish rebels at the time of the Bar Kokhba Revolt. These caves, called the Cave of Avior and the Cave of the Sandal are located in Wadi el-Mafjar (the Cave of the Sandal is located ca. 300 meters to the south of the Cave of Avior). The Cave of Avior contained 38 disarticulated skeletons of men, women, and children (23 adults and 15 children) who apparently suffocated when the Roman army built a bonfire at the entrance to the cave. Because of their fragmentary state, the age and gender of many of the skeletons could not be determined, although they included five adult males and three adult females. The tip of a braid of human hair belonging to a woman or girl was also discovered. Ten human skeletons representing three adult males, four adult females, and three children were found in the Cave of the Sandal. Since (unlike the Cave of Avior) this cave had not been disturbed in later periods, it yielded a number of finds. These included two gold rings and a gold earring, a silver cosmetic spoon, and a wooden comb.

## The Byzantine Monastery at Khirbet ed-Deir

How does Qumran compare with a settlement that we know was inhabited by adult celibate men? Yizhar Hirschfeld recently published the final report on his excavations at the site of Khirbet ed-Deir in the Judean Desert. There is no doubt that this Byzantine (6th- to 7th-century C.E.) monastery was inhabited by a male population. It is therefore not surprising that no gendered objects are published from the site: no spindle whorls or shafts, beads or jewelry, combs, hairnets, mirrors, or cosmetic items. There are also no references to women in the four Greek inscriptions found at the site. Although a burial recess and burial chapel were excavated, no human skeletal remains were discovered. Presumably, the cooking and baking in the large kitchen attached to the refectory were done by men.

## Were There Women at Qumran?

The contrast between the finds from Qumran and the other Judean Desert sites considered here becomes even more pronounced when we compare the duration of their occupation. Whereas Qumran was occupied for about 100 to 150 years, the rebel occupation at Masada lasted no longer than six to seven years. The Judean Desert caves were probably occupied for a much shorter period than the three-and-a-half year duration of the Bar Kokhba Revolt. On the other hand, the Byzantine monastery at Khirbet ed-Deir was occupied for about 150 years. In addition, since Qumran suffered three violent destructions during the course of its existence (in 31 B.C.E., ca. 9/8 B.C.E., and 68 C.E.), we would expect the associated levels to yield finds that were in use at the time of those destructions. That this is the case is indicated by the hundreds of whole or restorable ceramic vessels found at Qumran, as well as the numerous other small finds. If women were present at the site, spindle whorls and other gendered objects should be represented in much greater numbers at Qumran than at Masada and in the Judean Desert caves. Instead, only one spindle whorl was found, on the margins of the settlement, and no more than four beads. Similarly, although female burials are present, they are greatly outnumbered by males in the western sector of the cemetery (and they are present in more proportionate numbers but spatially marginalized if the apparently bedouin burials in the southern extension and southern cemetery are included). In other words, the archaeological evidence attests to only minimal female presence at Qumran.

Taylor has suggested to me that the absence of jewelry and cosmetic

items at Qumran does not necessarily reflect the absence of women, since female Essenes presumably would have "spurned the usual female adorn-
ments." Similarly, Maxine Grossman has asked me the following question:
"Could the 'erasure of gender' in the ideology of the covenant community
('we are too pious to behave that way', 'no makeup, no dancing, no dates')
lead to an erasure of gender in their material remains? What you might have,
then, is the presence of men and women, but a different kind of men and
women than in other communities. The presence of beads may suggest the
presence of women at a site, but the absence of beads need NOT suggest the
absence of women." Taylor and Grossman are correct that the absence of
gendered objects does not necessarily indicate that women were not present
at Qumran. As I noted above, based on the absence of gendered objects alone,
it is impossible to prove that women were not present at Qumran, because
this is an argument from silence. However, I am unconvinced by Taylor's and
Grossman's argument for a number of reasons. First, this argument tries to
circumvent the archaeological evidence. Second, Josephus does not describe
female Essenes as refraining from wearing jewelry or cosmetics (although in
*War* 2.140 he mentions that the men swear never "to outshine his subordinates in his dress or by increased adornment"). In addition, there is no legislation in the sectarian scrolls prohibiting the use or wearing of these items by
women. There is also no indication that sectarian or Essene women (even the
elderly) refrained from spinning wool. In fact, I wonder whether it is anachronistic (or at least unfounded) to assume that because female Essenes were
ascetics they would have refrained from spinning wool and from using cosmetics or any items of personal adornment.

Grossman has asked me another provocative question: "Is the absence
of feminine-gendered 'personal objects' paralleled by an absence of MASCU-
LINE-gendered ones, as well? I don't know what sort of 'toys' or 'fripperies'
men would have had in antiquity (pins and decorations to hold their clothes
together, purses to carry small tools, knives or other implements with decorative handles, etc.), but do we find any of THOSE among the small finds? That
is, could it be that a community that avoids frivolousness would avoid the
very possessions that we think of as a mark of the presence of women in the
first place?" To answer Grossman's question, I reviewed de Vaux's notes and
found that there is unequivocal evidence for the presence of men in the archaeological record at Qumran. The first piece of evidence consists of the disproportionately large number of male burials in the cemetery. A second piece
of evidence is provided by two ostraca (inscribed potsherds) that were found
by James Strange in 1996, during the course of clearing the base of the east
face of the eastern boundary wall of the settlement. One ostracon mentions

that "Honi son of [. . .] gave to Elazar son of Nahmani [    ] Hisday from Holon" a house and fig trees and olive trees. The second ostracon, written in a different hand preserves the name of "Jehose]ph son of Nathan[. . . his [s]ons from En [Gedi(?).]" We have also seen that a cylindrical jar with the name "Yoḥanan Haṭla" painted in red on the shoulder was found in a basin in L34.

The third piece of evidence consists of various objects listed in de Vaux's notes among the small finds from the settlement. As I noted above, a large amount of pottery and many coins (mostly small bronze coins) as well as other small finds were recovered in the excavations, associated with the three destruction levels. These finds include the following tools and knives listed in de Vaux's notes: a tool or weapon from L2; knife blades from L4 and L34 and an iron knife from L76; a tool from L7; iron blades from L30, L31, L46, L101; three groups of bronze and iron tools from L52; an iron pick from L114; an iron sickle from L126. Other objects listed, such as bronze and iron shafts, points, and plaques could also represent tools or weapons; there are also iron knives from L15 and L16 at Ein Feshkha. Although women could have used these objects at least on some occasions, they are usually associated with men. The same is true of the industrial workshops located throughout the settlement, including a tuyere (the nozzle of a blowpipe for a furnace) in L119 *bis*.

Although the iron arrowheads and other weapons found at Qumran might belong to the Roman soldiers who destroyed the settlement in 68 C.E. and occupied it after that, some could have been used by the male members of the community. As an aside, I note that the question of whether male sectarians engaged in combat or used weapons depends on the interpretation of the literary sources. For example, Philo states that "In vain would one look among them for makers of arrows, or javelins, or swords, or helmets, or armor, or shields; in short, for makers of arms, or military machines, or any instrument of war" (*Every Good Man Is Free* 78). On the other hand, the War Scroll (which contains detailed descriptions of military formations and equipment) indicates that the sect anticipated a prolonged and bloody military engagement at the end of days. At Masada, a workshop was discovered where the Jewish rebels manufactured barbed, trilobate iron arrowheads. This demonstrates that the Jews used and produced weapons of Roman type. Because it is therefore impossible to determine whether the pieces of military equipment from Qumran (which are relatively few in number and limited in repertoire) were used only by the Romans or also by the sectarians, I exclude them from this consideration of masculine objects. The weapons listed in de Vaux's notes include a total of six iron arrowheads from L4, L19, L33, L41, L45c; bronze sheaths from L14 and L91; and a javelin point from L30. Other objects listed in de Vaux's notes could also represent military equipment.

The archaeological evidence reviewed here contradicts the identification of Qumran as a villa or manor house, where females would have been part of the population both as residents and as servants or slaves. This conclusion is supported by the discovery of female skeletal remains, spindle whorls, cosmetic spoons, and ostraca with references to women in the Herodian-period villas in Jerusalem's Jewish Quarter. The contrast between the contemporary Jewish population of Judea and the minimal female presence at Qumran (in an unknown capacity and perhaps only at certain times or occasions?) must have given the impression that the Qumran community consisted entirely of adult men, as described by Pliny, Josephus, and Philo. In other words, although the literary evidence suggests that there were female sectarians, their presence at Qumran was minimal. Geza Vermès has speculated that the few female burials at Qumran represent sectarians who attended the annual Renewal of the Covenant ceremony (which perhaps took place at Qumran), and happened to perish while there. In the sectarian calendar, this ceremony coincided with Pentecost (the Feast of Weeks). Finally, the absence of infants and children among the burials excavated in the western sector of the cemetery at Qumran (that is, among the apparently sectarian burials) indicates that the settlement was not inhabited by families. In contrast, numerous skeletons of children were found in the Judean Desert caves (and the remains of at least one rebel family with a child are represented at Masada). Thus, the archaeological evidence suggests only minimal female presence at Qumran and an absence of families with children.

## Bibliographical Notes

This chapter is a modified and updated version of Jodi Magness, "Women at Qumran?" in *What Athens Has to Do with Jerusalem: Essays on Classical, Jewish, and Early Christian Art and Archaeology in Honor of Gideon Foerster*, ed. L. V. Rutgers (Leuven: Peeters, forthcoming) (with bibliography; some of the main references are repeated here with additional bibliography).

For discussions of female Essenes and women at Qumran and in the Dead Sea Scrolls, see Mayer I. Gruber, "Women in the Religious System of Qumran," in *Judaism in Late Antiquity* 5: *The Judaism of Qumran: A Systemic Reading of the Dead Sea Scrolls* 1: *Theory of Israel*, ed. Alan J. Avery-Peck, Jacob Neusner, and Bruce D. Chilton (Leiden: E. J. Brill, 2001), 173-96; Eileen M. Schuller, "Women in the Dead Sea Scrolls," in Peter W. Flint and James C. VanderKam, *The Dead Sea Scrolls After Fifty Years*, 117-44; "Women in the Dead Sea Scrolls," in Michael O. Wise, N. Golb, John J. Collins, and Dennis G.

Pardee, *Methods of Investigation of the Dead Sea Scrolls and the Khirbet Qumran Site,* 115-31; Lawrence H. Schiffman, *Reclaiming the Dead Sea Scrolls,* 127-45; Linda Bennett Elder, "The Woman Question and Female Ascetics Among Essenes," *Biblical Archaeologist* 57 (1994): 220-34; Schiffman, "Laws Pertaining to Women in the Temple Scroll," in Devorah Dimant and Uriel Rappaport, *The Dead Sea Scrolls, Forty Years of Research,* 210-28; Tal Ilan, *Jewish Women in Greco-Roman Palestine* (Tübingen: J. C. B. Mohr, 1995) (for Ilan's quote about women mentioned in the Dead Sea Scrolls, see 36). Also see Joan Taylor's article on the Qumran cemetery below. Geza Vermès's observation about celibacy and the Community Rule is from "The Qumran Community, the Essenes, and Nascent Christianity," in Schiffman, Tov, and VanderKam, *The Dead Sea Scrolls Fifty Years After Their Discovery,* 581-86. For a discussion of spinning and Roman clothing, see Alexandra T. Croom, *Roman Clothing and Fashion* (Charleston: Tempus, 2000).

For the graves that de Vaux excavated at Qumran, see his publications (including the volume by Humbert and Chambon) in the bibliographical notes for Chapter 1. For the re-examination of the bones in the Kurth Collection, see Olav Röhrer-Ertl, Ferdinand Rohrhirsch, and Dietbert Hahn, "Über die Gräberfelder von Khirbet Qumran, insbesondere die Funde der Campagne 1956," *Revue de Qumran* 19 (1999): 3-46.

For discussions of the cemetery at Qumran, see Joseph E. Zias, "The Cemeteries of Qumran and Celibacy: Confusion Laid to Rest?" *Dead Sea Discoveries* 7 (2000): 220-53; Jürgen Zangenberg, "Bones of Contention: 'New' Bones from Qumran Help Settle Old Questions," *Qumran Chronicle* 9 (2000): 51-76; Rachel Hachlili, "The Qumran Cemetery: A Reconsideration," in Schiffman, Tov, and VanderKam, *The Dead Sea Scrolls Fifty Years After Their Discovery,* 661-72; Joan E. Taylor, "The Cemeteries of Khirbet Qumran and Women's Presence at the Site," *Dead Sea Discoveries* 6 (1999): 285-323; Émile Puech, "The Necropolises of *Khirbet* Qumrân and 'Ain el-Ghuweir and the Essene Belief in Afterlife," *Bulletin of the American Schools of Oriental Research* 312 (1998): 21-36; Zdzisław Jan Kapera, "Some Remarks on the Qumran Cemetery," in Wise, Golb, Collins, and Pardee, *Methods of Investigation of the Dead Sea Scrolls and the Khirbet Qumran Site,* 97-113; Rachel Hachlili, "Burial Practices at Qumran," *Revue de Qumran* 16(1993): 247-64.

For Solomon H. Steckoll's excavations in the cemetery at Qumran, see "Preliminary Excavation Report in the Qumran Cemetery," *Revue de Qumran* 6 (1968): 323-44; Nicu Haas and H. Nathan, "Anthropological Survey on the Human Skeletal Remains from Qumran," *Revue de Qumran* 6 (1968): 345-52.

For a recent discussion of bedouin burial customs, see Bethany J. Walker, "The Late Ottoman Cemetery in Field L, Tall Hisban," *Bulletin of the*

American Schools of Oriental Research 322 (2001): 47-65; also Lawrence E. Toombs, *Tell el-Hesi: Modern Military Trenching and Muslim Cemetery in Field I, Strata I-II* (Waterloo: Wilfred Laurier University Press, 1985).

For cemeteries in Jerusalem with burials that are similar to those at Qumran, see Boaz Zissu, "'Qumran Type' Graves in Jerusalem: Archaeological Evidence of an Essene Community?" *Dead Sea Discoveries* 5 (1998): 158-71; "Odd Tomb Out: Has Jerusalem's Essene Cemetery Been Found?" *Biblical Archaeology Review* 25/2 (1999): 50-55, 62. For the cemetery at Hiam el-Sagha, see Hanan Eshel and Zvi Greenhut, "Ḥiam el-Sagha, A Cemetery of the Qumran Type, Judaean Desert," *Revue Biblique* 100 (1993): 252-59. For the cemetery at Khirbet Qazone, see Hershel Shanks, "Who Lies Here? Jordan Tombs Match Those at Qumran," *Biblical Archaeology Review* 25/5 (1999): 49-53, 76; Konstantine D. Politis, "The Nabataean Cemetery at Khirbet Qazone," *Near Eastern Archaeology* 62 (1999): 128.

For spinning and weaving in Roman Palestine, see Miriam B. Peskowitz, *Spinning Fantasies: Rabbis, Gender, and History* (Berkeley: University of California Press, 1997). For gendered objects from Masada and the Cave of Letters, see Yigael Yadin, *Masada: Herod's Fortress and the Zealots' Last Stand*; Yadin and Joseph Naveh, "The Aramaic and Hebrew Ostraca and Jar Inscriptions," in *Masada I: The Yigael Yadin Excavations 1963-1965, Final Reports* (Jerusalem: Israel Exploration Society, 1989), 6-68; Hannah M. Cotton and Joseph Geiger, *Masada II*; Ehud Netzer, *Masada III*; Avigail Sheffer and Hero Granger-Taylor, "Textiles," in *Masada IV: The Yigael Yadin Excavations 1963-1965, Final Reports* (Jerusalem: Israel Exploration Society, 1994), 153-244; Orit Shamir, "Loomweights from Masada," in *Masada IV*, 265-81; Yadin, *The Finds from the Bar-Kokhba Period in the Cave of Letters* (Jerusalem: Israel Exploration Society, 1963). For the spindle whorls from Masada and the suggestion that some rooms were occupied by sectarians at the time of the First Jewish Revolt, see Ronny Reich, "Women and Men at Masada: Some Anthropological Observations Based on the Small Finds (Coins, Spindles)," *Zeitschrift des Deutschen Palastinas Verein* 117 (2001): 149-63. For references to gendered objects from other caves, see Magness, "Women at Qumran?" (above). For the ostraca found at Qumran in 1996, see Frank Moore Cross and Esther Eshel, "Ostraca from Khirbet Qumran," *Israel Exploration Journal* 47 (1997): 17-28; Ada Yardeni, "A Draft of a Deed on an Ostracon from Khirbet Qumran," *Israel Exploration Journal* 47 (1997): 233-37; Geza Vermès, *The Complete Dead Sea Scrolls in English*, 596-97.

CHAPTER 9

# The Temple Tax, Clothing, and the
# Anti-Hellenizing Attitude of the Sectarians

We begin this chapter by examining two separate issues relating to the archaeology of Qumran. First, we consider whether the hoard of Tyrian tetradrachmas from L120 represents a collection for the temple tax. We then discuss the archaeological and literary evidence for the clothing worn by the
sectarians. We conclude this chapter by considering sectarian practices in the
context of the Classical world in which they lived.

## The Hoard of Tyrian Tetradrachmas and the Temple Tax

In L120 (a room at the northern end of the secondary building), de Vaux discovered a hoard of 561 silver coins deposited in three pots, which contained
223, 185, and 153 pieces, respectively. The hoard consisted almost exclusively of
Tyrian tetradrachmas (sheqels). Although strictly speaking this could be considered three hoards because the coins were stored in three pots, I follow de
Vaux in referring to it as a single hoard. This is because all three pots seem to
come from the same level in the same locus and were apparently deposited at
the same time. After their discovery in 1955, the coins from the three pots were
mixed together and then arbitrarily divided into groups. Four hundred and
eight coins were sent to the Archaeological Museum in Amman and 153 remained at the Rockefeller Museum in Jerusalem. According to Marcia
Sharabani, who published the latter group, most of the coins in Jerusalem
come from one of the pots ("Hoard A"). They include 102 sheqels, 48 half-
sheqels, one Seleucid tetradrachma, and two Seleucid didrachmas. The other

coins from Hoard A, which were sent to Amman, consist of 13 tetradrachmas and 20 didrachmas of Antiochus VII and Demetrius II covering the years 176-187 (= 137/136 to 126/125 B.C.E., the last year of minting under the Seleucids in Tyre) and six Roman dinars, the earliest dating to 85/84 B.C.E. and the latest to 41 B.C.E. Henri Seyrig's notes, which are the best record of the contents of the hoard, have never been published.

We have seen that this hoard, which de Vaux assigned to the beginning of Period II, was instead deposited at the end of Period Ib, ca. 9/8 B.C.E. or shortly thereafter (see Chapter 4). Here I wish to consider the nature of this hoard. According to the excavation inventory register, a total of 1231 coins and coin fragments was recovered at Qumran, including the coins in the hoard. The only silver coins listed in de Vaux's notes from contexts outside the hoard are: one Tyrian tetradrachma of Antiochus VII from L7; a didrachma of Antiochus VII Euergetes from L9; a Roman imperial coin of Vespasian from L35; one autonomous Tyrian tetradrachma from L45; an illegible coin from L52; two didrachmas, of Demetrius II and Antiochus VII respectively, from L77; and one sigla of Antiochus Euergetes of Tyre from Trench A. From this list it appears that many of the Tyrian tetradrachmas at Qumran were deliberately collected together. The fact that some if not all of the scattered examples could come from post–Period Ib contexts suggests the possibility that all of the Tyrian tetradrachmas from Period Ib were gathered in this hoard.

Tyrian tetradrachmas were used for the annual half-sheqel tax paid by Jews to the Jerusalem temple during the Second Temple period. Two sectarian manuscripts from Cave 4 at Qumran deal with the matter of the temple tax: 4Q159 and 4Q513. These fragments have been described as a treatise that was an exposition of several biblical texts, or collections of assorted halakhot. They are legislative in nature, based on or dealing with biblical laws drawn almost exclusively from the Pentateuch. Because this legislative material was intended for practical observance by the author's audience, these texts are categorized as "Ordinances."

The evolution of the annual half-sheqel tax to the temple has been traced by Jacob Liver. The original obligation to give a half a sheqel as an offering to the Lord appears in Exodus 30:11-16 in relation to the taking of the census. This offering, which was binding on all those who were numbered, represented a once-in-a-lifetime payment. Eventually this one-time offering became linked with the annual third-of-a-sheqel payment instituted in the time of Nehemiah for the maintenance of the temple. Since the sources relating to the period prior to Roman rule in Judea do not mention the annual half-sheqel offering, it does not appear to have become an obligatory payment until the end of the Hasmonean period or later. Liver concluded that the regulation making the half-sheqel an annual offering was introduced only after the Pharisees gained ascendancy over their opponents, the Sadducees and Boethusians.

In 4Q159 the Pentateuchal regulation of the half-sheqel is understood as referring to an offering made only once in a lifetime by those included in the census. Lawrence Schiffman has noted that the absence of the notion of a one-time payment in 4Q513 suggests that these are different recensions of the same text. Similarly, in the Temple Scroll the payment of the half-sheqel seems to be a one-time obligation (39:7-8). According to Liver, the sect must have objected to the half-sheqel sanctuary offering because it was instituted as an annual obligation for all Israel only after they had separated themselves from the Jerusalem temple and the rest of Israel, and because it was a halakhah that had originated outside the sect. As other scholars have noted, opposition to the establishment of an annual temple tax may have existed in other Jewish circles, as expressed for example in Matthew 17:24-27, where Jesus rebukes Peter for indicating to the tax collectors of Capernaum that his master paid the annual tribute.

Liver also discussed the correlation between 4Q159 and 4Q513 and sectarian regulations concerning censuses in general. According to the Community Rule, the sect had an annual census that included the registration of its members. The Damascus Document, however, describes a single census of those who reach adulthood, and the Rule of the Congregation says that "at the age of twenty years he shall pass among them that are numbered" (1QSa 1.9). This accords with the minimum age mentioned in the Pentateuch. Liver suggested that the sect may have required the one-time payment when a man reached adulthood and his name was recorded for the first time in the census registers. The annual ceremony of entering the covenant and reviewing the registers was apparently not considered a census for those whose names were already recorded in the registers. Alternatively, the sect may have viewed the half-sheqel regulation as a law that was to apply to the community of Israel only at the end of days. The reference to a one-time payment of the half-sheqel by young men reaching the age of 20 in the Temple Scroll suggests that the sect envisioned it as a future obligation (although not necessarily at the end of days), but does not indicate whether it was already being practiced.

Hoards consisting mostly if not entirely of Tyrian tetradrachmas have been found at a number of sites in Palestine in contexts dating to the 1st century B.C.E. By the middle of the 1st century C.E., according to Leo Kadman, "there was only one purpose for which the exclusive use of Tyrian sheqels was prescribed: the Temple-Dues of half a Sheqel, which every male Jew of 20 years of age and above had to pay yearly to the Temple at Jerusalem." Donald

Ariel, however, has cautioned that "From the finds in Jerusalem (mostly in hoards), there is every reason to believe that Tyrian shekels would have been current in Jerusalem — even without the Temple-tax." He has noted that the absence of Roman coins from hoards in Jerusalem before 70 C.E. (although they were in circulation in Jerusalem at that time) suggests they did not become dominant until later. Ariel's observations regarding Jerusalem probably apply equally to Qumran, which was also a Judean site occupied by Jews. It is therefore possible that the hoard at Qumran has no connection with the temple tax, and instead represents a collection of the common type of valuable silver coinage that circulated in Judea in the 1st century B.C.E. In this case, the hoard could be understood as representing the collected wealth of the community at the end of Period Ib (ca. 9/8 B.C.E.), whose members were required to give up their private property and earnings when admitted to the sect.

If this hoard represents the collected wealth and private property of the members of the community, we might expect it to contain a mixture of coin types. Although Tyrian tetradrachmas were the dominant type of silver coinage circulating in 1st century B.C.E. Palestine, the hoard contained none of the common bronze issues of the Hasmoneans. On the other hand, such homogeneity is characteristic of many contemporary hoards in Palestine and elsewhere, which consist entirely of either silver or bronze coins. This homogeneity usually reflects the circumstances of the burial of the hoard. Philip Grierson has distinguished four classes of hoards: accidental losses, emergency hoards, savings hoards, and abandoned hoards. Among the differences between emergency hoards and savings hoards, which are the relevant classes to this discussion, the latter tend to be more selective; that is, they usually contain not only high value (as opposed to low value) coins, but also better (unworn) specimens of such coins. In addition, because emergency hoards were withdrawn from circulation at the time they were deposited, they usually reflect the proportions of types of coins current at that moment. Savings hoards, on the other hand, often cover a considerable span of years.

The hoard at Qumran, like many of the contemporary hoards from Palestine, may best fit the profile of a savings hoard (although it was apparently buried before the destruction of the site in ca. 9/8 B.C.E.). Ordinarily such hoards represent the savings of their owners, accumulated over a period of years. This could apply to the hoard at Qumran only if we assume that it does not represent all of the property and earnings of the members of the community, which must have included at least some bronze coins and perhaps other types of silver issues. In fact, de Vaux mentioned that the hoard contained a few coins that were not Tyrian tetradrachmas: "With a few exceptions, it includes only Tyrian coins, and these are almost exclusively tetradrachmae."

Nevertheless, the overwhelming number of Tyrian tetradrachmas in this hoard is suggestive of a deliberate selection of the coins contributed by the members of the community. This brings us back to the matter of the temple tax. De Vaux noted that "The later one proceeds in the period the more frequently all the various issues are represented, and the larger the number of new types." As Barbara Burrell pointed out to me, new coins are generally prevalent in ancient hoards, replacing older coins which drifted out of circulation. However, since a typical savings hoard reflects the resources of the owner from year to year, the composition of the hoard from Qumran could reflect the growing wealth or numbers of those joining the community over time.

Although it is much larger, a hoard from Isfiya (which contained about 4500 coins), like the one from Qumran, consisted mostly of Tyrian tetradrachmas, didrachmas, and some Roman coins. On the basis of its composition — about 3400 Tyrian sheqels, 1000 Tyrian half-sheqels, and 160 Roman denarii — Kadman argued that it represents a collection of the temple tax. He identified the Roman denarii in the hoard as the *agio,* or "kalbon," a 4-8 percent additional payment mentioned in the Mishnah as required of those who paid the temple tax with a half-sheqel. Two people making the payment with one sheqel were exempt from this additional charge. Since, according to Kadman, the 160 denarii from Isfiya are equivalent to 40 sheqels, or 8 percent of the 1000 half-sheqels in the hoard, it must represent a collection of the temple tax. There are at least two obstacles to discussing this issue in relation to Qumran. First, since not all the coins from the Qumran hoard have been published, it impossible to determine the ratio of Roman coins to Tyrian sheqels and half-sheqels. Second, the fact that the sectarian sources discussed above do not mention the *agio* means we do not know whether the sect accepted or adopted this additional payment. It is interesting to note, however, that of the 192 coins from "Hoard A" mentioned by Sharabani, 116 are tetradrachmas, 70 are didrachmas, and 6 are Roman denarii. This means that the Roman denarii are equivalent to 8.6 percent of the half-sheqels from "Hoard A." Only the publication of the rest of the coins from the hoard will indicate whether this percentage is consistent throughout. The number of coins may also provide an indication of how many members had joined the community at Qumran before its destruction in ca. 9/8 B.C.E., when the hoard was buried. Kadman calculated that the sheqels and half-sheqels in the Isfiya hoard represent the temple dues of 7800 male Jews of 20 years of age and above. If the Qumran hoard is a collection of the temple tax, the coins from "Hoard A" represent the one-time payment of about 300 men who were 20 years of age or older.

I believe that the character and composition of the hoard are best understood in connection with the sect's interpretation of the temple tax as a one-time payment made when a man reached adulthood and his name was recorded for the first time in the census registers. However, I cannot rule out the possibility that it represents the collected wealth of the community without any relation to the temple tax. Further discussion of this problem must await the full and final publication of the coins from Qumran or at least the surviving notes.

## Sectarian Clothing

In Chapter 8, the subject of spinning and spindle whorls was raised in the context of our discussion of women at Qumran. Here I would like to consider the matter of sectarian clothing, beginning with a consideration of the literary sources (all translations are from Geza Vermès and Martin Goodman). This discussion assumes that the sectarians/Qumran community were Essenes. Josephus refers to Essene clothing in seven different passages in *War:*

- They make a point . . . of being always clothed in white garments. (*War* 2.123)
- Their dress and outward behavior are like those of children whose teacher rears them in fear; they do not change their garments or shoes until they are completely torn or worn out. (*War* 2.126)
- . . . and, girded with linen loin-cloths, bathe themselves in cold water. (*War* 2.129)
- Afterwards they lay aside the garments which they have worn for the meal, since they are sacred garments . . . (*War* 2.131)
- . . . and he is given a hatchet, the loin-cloth which I have mentioned, and a white garment. (*War* 2.137)
- On other days, they dig a hole one foot deep with their mattocks. . . . They squat there, covered by their mantles so as not to offend the rays of God. (*War* 2.148)
- The women bathe wearing a dress, whereas the men wear a loin-cloth. (*War* 2.161; I have translated *endymata* as "dress" instead of "linen" as Vermès and Goodman have it)

According to a passage in *War* 2.140, ". . . He swears never to show insolence in the exercise of his duty should he ever happen to be in command himself, nor to outshine his subordinates in his dress or by increased adornment. . . ."

Josephus's points regarding Essene clothing can be summarized as follows: men were given garments when they joined the sect; the men always wore white; the men wore linen loincloths during immersion in ritual baths; Essenes did not discard their clothes until they were torn and tattered with age; and the men wore a special set of clothes during the communal meals. Pieces of clothing that are explicitly mentioned in these passages include the linen loincloth and the mantle worn by men. Female Essenes wore a dress when immersing themselves in a miqveh.

Philo emphasizes the frugality of the Essenes, who held their clothing in common: "their clothes and food are also held in common . . ." (*Every Good Man Is Free* 86); "And not only do they have a common table, but common clothes also. In fact they have at their disposition thick coats for the winter, and inexpensive tunics for the summer; so it is simple and lawful, for whoever desires to do so, to take the garment he wishes, since it is agreed that whatever belongs to each belongs to all . . ." (*Hypothetica* 11.12). This passage is nearly identical to Philo's description of the clothing worn by the Therapeutae in *The Contemplative Life* 38: "But as to their raiment, it also like the house is of a very cheap kind, by way of protection only against cold and heat; being a thick cloak of shaggy hide in winter and in summer a smock without sleeves or a linen coat." Although these different ascetic groups perhaps dressed in a similar manner, these passages appear to be formulaic.

Both Josephus and Philo emphasize the frugality of the Essenes, who held their clothes in common and wore them until they were threadbare or ragged. One of the passages in the Community Rule legislates for just such a situation: "Whoever causes his penis to come out from under his garment, or it (the garment has) holes so his nakedness is seen. . . ." Elisha Qimron and James Charlesworth have demonstrated that in Qumranic Hebrew, the term *yad* means "penis." Translating *yad* as "hand" in this passage creates an impossible situation (as for example in Vermès's translation, "Whoever has been so poorly dressed that when drawing his hand from beneath his garment his nakedness shall be seen . . ."), since the mantle was usually worn draped over the left shoulder, leaving the right arm completely free. Even if one removed the part of the mantle that covered the left arm, the tunic worn underneath it would have covered the genitalia (see below). This passage therefore seems to refer to cases where the penis was exposed because the tunic or loincloth was torn and tattered or no loincloth was worn beneath the tunic. The fact that this problem was specifically addressed in the sect's penal code suggests that the exposure of the genitalia due to the wearing of torn and tattered clothing was a common occurrence.

Josephus observed that Essene men always wore white and made a special point of describing their loincloths as linen. These two points are probably related. It is difficult to dye linen, especially with colors of decorative patterns. Therefore, I believe that sectarian men wore clothes of white (undyed) linen. The archaeological evidence indicates that this was an exceptional practice among the contemporary Jewish population of Judea, which explains why Josephus singled it out for description. This evidence consists of ancient textiles from Masada and the caves in the Judean Desert, especially the Cave of Letters.

A sleeveless tunic (Greek *chiton;* Hebrew *haluq*), covered by a large, rectangular mantle (Greek *himation;* Roman *pallium;* Hebrew *tallit* or *me'il*) were worn by both men and women in Roman Palestine (see Fig. 60). The Roman toga was analogous to a mantle but differed in having a curved hem. The tunic consisted of a large rectangular sheet woven with two parallel bands of a different color that run from selvage to selvage and were spaced widely apart. Whereas most Greek and Roman tunics were woven in a single piece, those from Masada and the Cave of Letters were woven in two pieces and sewn together at the shoulders, leaving an opening for the neck (see Fig. 58). This feature facilitated adherence to the laws of purity, for if one half of the mantle became impure it could be removed and replaced without defiling the other half.

Narrow stripes woven into the tunics so that they descended from the shoulders characterized all tunics of the Roman period (see Fig. 58). Called *clavi* in Latin and usually woven in shades of purple, these stripes defined the rank of the wearer (the broader the stripes, the higher the wearer's rank). Yigael Yadin demonstrated that the Hebrew term for *clavus* is *'imrah*. The mantles found at Masada and in the Cave of Letters are decorated with notched bands and gamma-shaped designs (see Fig. 59). The notched bands and gamma-shaped designs occur on mantles worn by both men and women. Jewish mantles were distinguished from non-Jewish ones by the attachment of *tzitzit* (tassels) to the four corners of the man's mantle. A bundle of dyed, unspun wool intended for *tzitzit* was found in the Cave of Letters. Whereas some of the mantles from the Cave of Letters were colored, none of the tunics had any colored decorative elements aside from the *clavi*. In contrast, colored tunics appear to be represented at Masada. With one exception, all of the linen textiles from Masada are undyed, whereas dyed color is found (with two exceptions) only on wool textiles. Similarly, none of the linen textiles from the Cave of Letters has colored, decorative patterns. All of the textiles found at Masada and in the Cave of Letters conform to the halakhic injunction of *shaatnez,* which prohibits mixing woolen and linen fibers in the same garment (from Deuteronomy 22:11: "Thou shalt not wear a garment of diverse kinds, of woolen and linen together") (see Fig. 63).

Except for the child's shirt from the Cave of Letters, none of the linen textiles found there or at Masada belongs to garments. In other words, the garments worn by the Jewish men and women at Masada and in the Cave of Letters were made of wool. The linen child's shirt from the Cave of Letters is made of two identical sheets that were sewn together like a tunic. The shirt is decorated with two thin bands that are not colored and were formed of several weft threads that had been thrown together. These stripes or bands, which were created by using a different weave instead of a different color, are called self-stripes (see Fig. 63). Yadin suggested that this represented an attempt to imitate the *clavi* of the larger tunics while complying with the law of *shaatnez* (created on the one hand by the difficulty of dying linen and creating decorative colored patterns, and on the other by the prohibition against adding colored woolen bands). The child's shirt was apparently some sort of inner garment. Pieces of an adult's linen tunic with the same kind of self-stripes were discovered in one of the caves in Wadi Murabba'at. Another linen fragment with self-stripes was found in the Cave of Avior near Jericho.

I believe Josephus's testimony indicates that, unlike the other Jews of Roman Judea who seem to have dressed mainly or entirely in wool, sectarian men wore only linen garments. A passage from 4QMMT indicates that the sect observed the law of *shaatnez*: "And concerning [his clothes], it is written that they shall not be of mixed material" (4QMMT 77-78). Because linen is difficult to dye, their linen garments would have been white. Even designs such as *clavi* and notched bands would presumably have been made of self-stripes like those described above instead of colored bands. The all-white linen garments of the sectarians would have contrasted with the woolen mantles and tunics customarily worn by other Jewish men on which these designs were colored even when the background was white. For this reason, Josephus was struck by the fact that Essenes always wore white, unlike the rest of the population.

Although color was not confined to women's clothes, the textiles from Masada and the Cave of Letters as well as iconographic and textual sources indicate that women's clothing was more likely than men's to be colored. In the Dura Europos synagogue paintings, for example, the Jewish men wear white or off-white mantles (with colored bands), while the women all wear colored garments. A Midrashic (interpretive) commentary on Deuteronomy (Sifre Deuteronomy 115b) states that "a woman shall not wear a man's white garments and a man shall not wear colored garments." A reinterpretation of the biblical injunction against men and women wearing each other's clothing (found in Deuteronomy 22:5: "A woman shall not wear that which pertains to a man, neither shall a man put on a woman's garment") is preserved on a scroll fragment from Cave 4 at Qumran (4Q159, frg. 2-4): "The clothing of a man may not be on a woman at all. [. . . And he may not] cover (himself) in the garments (or mantle) of a woman, and he may not wear the tunic of a woman." According to Lawrence Schiffman, this fragment probably derives from a document that was composed by the late 1st century B.C.E. He noted that the words "nor may a man wear the tunic *(ktwnt)* of a woman" represent an exegetical addition to avoid ambiguity, perhaps reflecting changes in the dress pattern. The substitution of the original singular form (man's garment) with the plural form "clothing" and the addition of the words "at all" emphasized the fact that this ordinance applied to any kind of clothing. This ordinance combined with Josephus's testimony and the passage from Sifre Deuteronomy suggest that sectarian men did not wear colored clothing.

Did sectarian women also wear white linen clothing? Although the references to all-white linen clothing in the passages cited here seem to refer to male members, I cannot rule out the possibility (suggested to me by Joan Taylor) that sectarian women wore similar garments. This possibility is supported by Hippolytus's description of the Essenes, which is very similar to Josephus's and might have been drawn from the same source or sources (for Hippolytus, see Chapter 3). One minor but perhaps significant difference between these passages is Hippolytus's statement that female Essenes immersed themselves in a ritual bath dressed in "a linen garment" (*Refutation of all Heresies* 9.28). In contrast, Josephus simply states that the women wore a dress *(endymata)* into the bath. However, in my opinion, the connection of white linen with priests and issues of purity (see below) as well as the sectarian concern with distinguishing between male and female clothing make it likely that only men wore all-white linen clothing.

Although no textiles belonging to garments were found at Qumran, the textiles from Cave 1 seem to support Josephus's testimony. All 77 textile fragments from this cave were made of linen and belonged to scroll wrappers and jar covers. Other linen fragments were found in Cave 11, and pieces of an unspecified cloth were discovered in Cave 24. The exclusive use of linen seems to be deliberate, as a well-preserved, embroidered wool wrapper, perhaps for a scroll, was found at Masada.

The highest quality linen cloths from Cave 1 were scroll wrappers decorated with blue lines (see Figs. 61, 62). These lines represent the only type of colored decoration found on any of the textiles from this cave. At least 16 separate cloths had this decoration, which was formed by simple blue lines (blue linen threads) in the weft. Grace Crowfoot noted the difficulty of weaving such a pattern because it involved both the warp and weft threads. The cloths decorated with these lines are nearly square; the most complete example measures 57 × 60 cm. If the edges of the cloth are included, the lines form a series of four concentric rectangles, though the outer two become progressively more square. The two innermost rectangles are woven in parallel, double lines. Crowfoot noted that

> The question arises whether this rectangular pattern has perhaps some religious significance. Reference has been made to the difficulty of either weaving or embroidering this pattern, and I find it hard to believe myself that people could take so much trouble over a rather uninteresting design unless it had some traditional meaning for them. The obvious suggestion is that the rectangles represent the ground plan of some religious building. The Tabernacle is represented by a simple rectangular figure in the Codex Amiatinus, but our figure does not really agree with this, or with the description of the temple, or Ezekiel's temple.

Crowfoot made this observation long before the publication of the Temple Scroll. Years later, Yadin noted that this design corresponds with the plan of the temple as conceived by this sect and described in the Temple Scroll. He questioned why the two inner rectangles are woven in double lines:

> Does the inner quadrangle stand for the temple, and the double lines mark its walls? Is this a description of the partition that surrounds the temple? If so, does the double line in the second quadrangle signify the inner stoa of the inner court? Or, possibly, were the lines only intended to emphasize the most sacred area? On the other hand, perhaps it is too much to expect accuracy in the *details* of the pattern, as the weavers set it to conventional form.

Yadin concluded that the woven plan on the cloth wrappers was intended to symbolize hiding the scrolls away in the temple, as was the practice in Jerusalem itself.

Indigo dye was used for the blue threads in these linen wrappers. Crowfoot suggested that the use of blue to create the lines in the cloths "may have some mystic value," though she cautioned against pressing any comparisons with the ritual use of *tekhelet* (blue) and *argaman* (purple) in the Hebrew Bible, since traditionally both dyes were from a murex or other shellfish and were dyed on wool. However, the purple color of the wool bundle intended for *tzitzit* from the Cave of Letters was obtained from indigo and carminic acid (kermes dye). This mixture was frequently used as a substitute for authentic Tyrian purple dye made from murex, which was much more expensive and difficult to obtain. Yadin concluded that this bundle of wool was intended for the blue cord *(ptil tekhelet)* of the *tzitzit.* Therefore, although obtained from indigo dye, the blue lines in the linen cloths from Cave 1 at Qumran were probably intended to represent the color *tekhelet.*

Could the linen cloths found in Cave 1 have been woven at Qumran? Although weaving in the Roman world is generally conceived of as a domestic activity associated with women, it was also done in industrial contexts outside the house by men. This is indicated by archaeological evidence from Pompeii as well as by rabbinic references to male weavers. Weaving therefore differs from spinning, which, as we have seen, appears to have been associated exclusively with women (see Chapter 8). The warp-weighted loom was the type used in Judea during the time of Qumran's occupation. This kind of loom was vertical and leaned against a wall or was tied to a building or tree for support. The threads hanging vertically (called the warp) had clay loom weights tied to one end to keep them taut during weaving. The vertical warp threads were held in place by loom weights attached at the bottom. This sustained the tension that allowed the weaver to move the horizontal woof thread in and out. During the 1st century C.E., the two-beam loom (or tubular loom) was introduced to Roman Palestine. In a two-beam loom, the loom weights that hung at the bottom of the earlier type were replaced by a beam across the loom's bottom. The warp threads were wrapped around two beams and worked from the bottom up. Although both types were used in the 1st century C.E. in Palestine, by the mid-2nd century the two-beam loom had completely replaced the warp-weighted loom. Because the wood of the looms disintegrates, only warp-weighted looms, which had clay loom weights generally, leave traces in the archaeological record.

At least 92 clay loom weights were found at Masada, which Orit Shamir has described as "virtually the last site in Israel where people still used the warp-weighted loom." In addition, burnt wooden beams apparently belonging to looms were discovered in three of the casemate rooms at Masada (L1103, L1108, and L1261). Nearly all of the loom weights published by Shamir were discovered in casemate rooms that were large enough to contain looms. Many additional loom weights were found in other casemate rooms. All of the loom weights from Masada are made of unfired clay and most are pyramidal, domed, conical, or doughnut-shaped. A perforation served to attach the warp threads. Unlike loom weights from other Roman period sites in Israel, which are fired, the Masada specimens are made of unbaked clay, perhaps reflecting the difficult conditions during the revolt. The loom weights published by Shamir represent assemblages (that is, groups apparently associated with looms), although individual specimens were recovered as well.

Since Qumran's occupation ended before the Roman siege at Masada, any looms used at Qumran would presumably have been of the warp-weighted type with clay loom weights (although, according to Hero Granger-Taylor, the textiles from Cave 1 show the change from the warp-weighted loom to the two-beam loom). Unfortunately, without illustrations of the objects found at Qumran and in the absence of a final report, it is impossible to determine with certainty whether any clay loom weights were found at the site. Although no objects are identified as loom weights in de Vaux's field notes, 39 objects are described as clay balls (*sphere de terre; boule d'argile*), baked clay balls (*sphere de terre cuite*), spheres, or spherical balls (*sphere; boule sphérique*). Most of these represent individual finds, except in the case of L105 (seven clay balls) which contained a large oven, and L130 (six clay balls), where the animal bone deposits were discovered. These two loci do not seem to be suitable locations for looms and weaving activity. It is possible that all or some of these clay balls were used for other purposes, such as jar stoppers. It is therefore currently impossible to determine whether there is evidence for weaving at Qumran. For the sake of completeness, I mention the inscribed cylindrical jar with two rims associated with the basins in L34 (in the court-yard of the main building), which might have been used for dyeing wool red (see Fig. 16). It has also been suggested that the industrial installation at Ein Feshkha was used for processing flax (see Chapter 10).

Needles provide another possible piece of evidence for the manufacture of cloth or clothing at Qumran. Five needles, all of bronze, are listed in de Vaux's field notes (from L12, L27, L42, L45, L75; another bronze needle was found in Cave 24). Of course, these could also have been used for mending or patching clothing or for sewing other materials (such as leather). Rabbinic sources contain references to male tailors. Needles found in some of the Judean Desert caves occupied at the time of the Bar Kokhba Revolt differ from the Qumran examples in being made of iron. No needles were found at Masada despite the evidence for weaving at the site.

Why did sectarian men wear all-white linen clothing? Was the white clothing a result of wearing linen or was linen chosen because it is white? A number of ancient sources associate clothing made of animal fur or skin with impurity. In contrast, because it is a plant product, linen was considered to be pure. This is why the Essenes and other ascetic sects like the Therapeutae and Pythagoreans reportedly preferred linen clothes. Philo describes the clothing worn by the priests officiating in the Jerusalem temple as follows: ". . . the dress which the priest must assume when he is about to carry out the sacred rites. It consists of a linen tunic and short breeches (loincloth), the latter to cover the loins, which must not be exposed at the altar. . . . The high priest is bidden to put on a similar dress when he enters the inner shrine to offer incense, because its fine linen is not, like wool, the product of creatures subject to death . . ." (*The Special Laws* 1.82-84). Several passages in the Hebrew Bible describe the clothing of the priests, which included a linen tunic *(ktwnt)* and linen breeches (Exodus 39:27-29; Leviticus 16:4; Ezekiel 44:17-18).

As we have seen, sectarian men were similarly attired with linen loincloths, tunics, and mantles. The loincloth seems to be a distinctively Essene article of dress (unlike the tunic and mantle, which were worn by the general population). It covered the genitalia and, because of the sectarian concern with modesty, was worn even during immersion in miqva'ot (and sectarian women wore dresses while immersing themselves). This concern with modesty is also expressed by the manner in which the Essenes drew their cloaks around them when defecating, as Josephus observed. As we have also seen, because of this concern, members were penalized for wearing torn clothing that exposed the penis.

The passage from Ezekiel 44:17-19 prohibits priests from wearing wool within the inner court of the Jerusalem temple:

> And it shall come to pass, that when they enter in at the gates of the inner court, they shall be clothed with linen garments; and no wool shall come upon them, whilst they minister in the gates of the inner court, and within. They shall have linen turbans upon their heads, and shall have linen breeches upon their loins; they shall not gird themselves with anything that causes sweat. And when they go out into the outer court, into the outer court to the people, they shall put off their garments in which they minister, and lay them in the holy chambers, and they shall put on other garments. . . .

Here wool is prohibited because it causes sweat. Leviticus 16:4 specifies that when the high priest enters the Holy of Holies in the Jerusalem temple once a year, he must be clothed only in linen garments: "He shall put on the holy linen coat, and he shall have the linen breeches upon his flesh, and shall be girded with a linen girdle, and with the linen mitre shall he be attired: these are holy garments; therefore shall he bathe his flesh in water, and so put them on."

This passage from Leviticus is strikingly reminiscent of Josephus's description of the communal meals of the Essenes:

> . . . they reassemble in the same place and, girded with linen loin-cloths, bathe themselves thus in cold water. After this purification they assemble in a special building to which no one is admitted who is not of the same faith;

they themselves only enter the refectory if they are pure, as though into a holy precinct. . . . Afterwards they lay aside the garments which they have worn for the meal, since they are sacred garments . . . (*War* 2.129-31)

Josephus describes the refectory as "a holy precinct" and the clothing worn by the Essenes during their communal meals as "sacred garments." This reflects the fact that they conceived of their community as a spiritual temple and apparently considered their communal meals to be a substitute for the temple sacrifices. The manner in which Josephus connects ritual immersion, changing clothes, and the communal meals of the Essenes also recalls the description of priestly attire in Leviticus 16:4: "He shall put on the holy linen coat, and he shall have the linen breeches upon his flesh, and shall be girded with a linen girdle, and with the linen mitre shall he be attired: these are holy garments; therefore shall he bathe his flesh in water, and so put them on."

A passage in the War Scroll (7.9-10) from Cave 1 indicates that the sectarians envisioned similar priestly attire: ". . . clad in garments of white byssus [linen]; a linen tunic and linen trousers, and girt with a linen girdle of twined byssus, blue, purple and scarlet, and a brocaded pattern, cunningly wrought, and turbaned headdresses on their heads, *these being* garments for battle. . . ." As Yadin noted, "the author's emphasis on 'byssus', 'white', 'linen' suggests that he wished to rule out any doubt on this matter." Although this passage describes battle attire, the same type of clothing was to be worn by the priests officiating in the temple. According to Yadin, the fact that the author of the War Scroll specified that every item was to be made of linen indicates a connection with the white clothing worn by the Essenes. This means that the white linen garments worn by sectarian men were modeled after the attire of the priests in the Jerusalem temple. This connection explains why all of the scroll wrappers from Cave 1 at Qumran are made of linen. The blue lines in these cloths recall the "twined linen and blue" mentioned in the descriptions of priestly attire in the Hebrew Bible and in the War Scroll. The all-white linen clothing worn by sectarian men must have visibly distinguished them from the other Jews in Judea, whose clothing was usually made of wool, had dark, decorative stripes and notched bands, and was sometimes colored.

## The Anti-Hellenizing Attitude of the Sectarians

I wish to conclude this chapter by considering sectarian practices in the context of the Classical world in which they lived. Although many of their practices undoubtedly result from concerns regarding the transmission of ritual impurity, I believe they also reflect an anti-Hellenizing sentiment and a preference for the biblical Hebrew tradition. In other words, the sectarians deliberately rejected the Greco-Roman culture of the world around them in favor of biblical Jewish practices. The sectarians' attitude is reflected by their obsession with modesty in dress, as expressed by their concern for toilet privacy and by the fact that sectarian men wore loincloths and the women dresses when immersing themselves in miqva'ot. Similarly, the Community Rule penalized members for wearing torn or tattered clothing that exposed their genitalia. Nudity was an accepted part of Greco-Roman culture, which glorified and celebrated the beauty of the human body. Anyone who attended athletic competitions or entered public baths was exposed to naked human bodies, which were commonly depicted in works of art and especially in sculpture.

The sectarians' communal meals also reflect an anti-Hellenizing sentiment. At Greek and Roman symposia, banqueters boisterously consumed large quantities of wine and dined while reclining on couches. Even the Therapeutae dined while reclining on couches, albeit rough couches due to their ascetic lifestyle (and they drank water instead of wine, according to Philo, *On the Contemplative Life* 69, 73). In contrast, the sectarians consumed nonintoxicating amounts of new wine and dined in silence, following the biblical Jewish practice of sitting upright instead of reclining on *klinae*.

The sectarians' avoidance of oil can be understood in a similar light. According to Josephus, "They regard oil as a defilement, and should any of them be involuntarily anointed, he wipes his body clean. They make a point of having their skin dry . . ." (*War* 2.122-23). The avoidance of oil has been explained in light of the sectarian belief that liquids transmit ritual impurity. While this may be true, I believe it is also an expression of their anti-Hellenizing tendencies. Rubbing the body with oil was an integral part of the Roman bathing experience. Oil was used as a cleansing agent like soap. Athletes also rubbed their bodies with oil before exercising or competing. A handled instrument with a curved blade called a strigil was used to scrape the oil and sweat from the skin, as depicted by Lysippos's famous statue the *Apoxyomenos* ("Youth Scraping Himself"). Roman men and women also styled their hair with oil. Cicero, for example, describes men "with their carefully combed hair, dripping with oil" (*Catiline* 2.22). In contrast, the sectarians apparently avoided oiling their bodies and hair.

Sectarian men were also visibly distinguished from the rest of the Judean population by their all-white, linen clothing, which lacked the dark stripes and notched bands that are characteristic of Roman-style tunics and mantles. Since the width of the dark stripes *(clavi)* indicated the wearer's rank in society, the sectarians' adoption of all-white clothing suggests a rejection of this society. Instead, Josephus's testimony and the evidence of the scrolls indicate that the sect had its own hierarchy centered around priests.

The language of the scrolls provides another piece of evidence for the sectarians' anti-Hellenizing attitude and preference for the Biblical Hebrew tradition. Abraham Wasserstein has noted that the Dead Sea Scrolls contain almost no Greek loanwords. Because Postbiblical Hebrew and Jewish Aramaic contain hundreds of Greek loanwords, Wasserstein has suggested that this reflects a deliberate avoidance of these words by the sectarians: "the Qumran sectarians . . . knew that these words were, by origin, not Hebrew or Aramaic but Greek, and they took great care to avoid using them." In contrast, Greek names were given to practically all of the descendants of the founders of the Hasmonean dynasty, and even some members of rabbinic circles had Greek names. According to Wasserstein, this evidence "suggests that the Qumran sectarians were not dissident rabbinic Jews but Jews of another kind, probably more different from the rabbinic Jews than were the earliest Christians. Both the latter and their contemporary fellow Jews were part of a world Aramaic in speech and tradition." In contrast to Qumran, where most of the scrolls are in Hebrew and only some 20 percent are in Aramaic, rabbinic Judaism showed a preference for the Aramaic tradition. Similarly, Emanuel Tov has noted that for the Qumran community, "Hebrew was *the* central language." The Qumran community used the Bible mainly in Hebrew instead of in Greek or Aramaic translations. In addition, the community apparently used a "Jewish" system of dating instead of a Roman one. Hanan Eshel has recently pointed out that although they rejected the temple cult, the Qumran community dated their documents according to the service of the high priests, to avoid using a calendar based on the reigns of the Roman emperors.

Only a relatively small number of scrolls from the caves around Qumran are in Greek. These come from Caves 2, 4, and 7, and include 4Q119-122, 126-127. Almost all of these texts contain Greek scripture (Septuagint). Eshel believes that the 19 scrolls from Cave 7, all of which are of papyrus and are in Greek, were brought by the cave's resident, who came from outside Palestine and spoke only Greek. None of the ostraca (inscribed potsherds) found at Qumran is in Greek. In contrast, ostraca and documents written in Greek have been found at Masada and in the Judean Desert caves outside of Qumran (for example, in Wadi Murabba'at). As Tov has noted, the fact that these Greek texts are documentary (such as marriage contracts and deeds to land) indicates that this language was in active use among the contemporary Jewish population of Judea. This does not seem to have been the case at Qumran.

I believe that many sectarian practices reviewed here reflect an anti-Hellenizing attitude and a deliberate attempt to return to the biblical Hebrew tradition. This is also expressed in the archaeology of Qumran, where there are no characteristically Hellenistic or Roman types of interior decoration such as frescoes, stucco, mosaics, or tiled floors *(opus sectile)* and no Roman-style bathing installations. The lack of these features could be due to financial constraints and indicates that Qumran could not have been a villa. In addition, the almost complete absence of fine wares (especially Eastern Sigillata A) from the ceramic corpus suggests a deliberate rejection of a world where fine, red-slipped wares were used for setting a civilized table.

Andrea Berlin has noted a similar phenomenon among the Jews of Roman Galilee. She attributes the absence of fine red-slipped table wares from Jewish sites in 1st-century C.E. Galilee (which are present at these sites in the 1st century B.C.E.) to a deliberate rejection of Roman control. These red-slipped wares were produced in Phoenicia, a region that was colonized and Latinized by the Romans during the 1st century C.E. According to Berlin, the Galilean Jews "made a political statement of solidarity and affiliation with a traditional, simple, unadorned, Jewish lifestyle, as well as demonstrated unified opposition to the newly looming Roman presence." She believes that the simple, undecorated houses and tombs of Galilean Jews suggest they "deliberately differentiated themselves from the Phoenicians (their neighbors on the coast), and the wealthy, display-oriented, Jewish aristocracy of Jerusalem."

In my opinion, a similar and perhaps more extreme rejection of the "wealthy, display-oriented" lifestyle of the Jerusalem aristocracy can be seen at Qumran. Beginning in the time of Herod, the consumption of imported wine and other goods and the acquisition of fine, red-slipped dishes became markers of status among the ruling Judean elite. These products were used by Herod and his associates and were adopted by the uppermost classes of Jerusalem society, including priestly families. This lifestyle can be seen in the elaborate interior decoration, beautiful stone furniture, and sets of Eastern Sigillata A dishes and other fine table wares are found in the 1st-century C.E. mansions in Jerusalem's Jewish Quarter, which Nahman Avigad described as follows:

> These homes were richly ornamented with frescoes, stucco work, and mosaic floors, and were equipped with complex bathing facilities, as well as containing the luxury goods and artistic objects which signify a high standard of living. This, then, was an upper class quarter, where the noble families of Jerusalem lived, with the High Priest at their head. Here they built their homes in accordance with the dominant fashion of the Hellenistic-Roman period. It is generally assumed that the Jerusalemite nobility was of the Sadducee faction, whose members included the Hellenizers; the lower

classes tended more to the Pharisee faction, which opposed foreign influ-
ences. Thus, it can be assumed that this quarter was occupied chiefly by
Sadducees.

The fact that these mansions belonged to the wealthiest members of Jerusalem's society in the late 1st century B.C.E. and 1st century C.E., including
priestly families, indicates that the Qumran community could not be Sadducees as some scholars have suggested. If these two groups shared common
roots or were originally related, by the 1st century B.C.E. they had developed
significantly different attitudes towards Greco-Roman culture. Based on an
analysis of 4QMMT, Hanan Eshel has suggested that the precipitating cause
of the Qumran community's split from the temple cult was a quarrel with the
Hellenized priesthood that was in charge of the Jerusalem temple. I believe
that the sectarians' anti-Hellenizing attitude and preference for the biblical
Hebrew tradition can be understood partly as a response or reaction to the
adoption of Greek and Roman practices by other Jewish groups, particularly
within the framework of their quarrel with the Hellenized priesthood. The
Qumran community not only differed in their interpretation and practice of
Jewish law, but physically distinguished themselves from other Jewish groups
— especially the Hellenized Jerusalem priesthood — in very visible ways, including their language and speech, their clothing and manner of dress, the
simplicity of design and lack of decoration of their buildings, their dining
customs, and their toilet practices and bathing habits. Perhaps the individual
inhumation practiced by the members of the Qumran community was
adopted as a response to and rejection of the elaborately decorated burial
caves and ossuaries used by the wealthiest members of Jerusalem (and Jericho) society, including priests.

## Bibliographical Notes

For my discussion of the coin hoard at Qumran in relation to the temple tax,
see Jodi Magness, "Two Notes on the Archaeology of Qumran," *Bulletin of the
American Schools of Oriental Research* 312 (1998): 37-44 (with bibliography;
some of the main references are repeated here with additional bibliography).
For the composition and fate of the Qumran hoard, see Marcia Sharabani,
"Monnaies de Qumrân au Musée Rockefeller de Jérusalem," *Revue Biblique* 87
(1980): 274-84; also see Robert Donceel and Pauline Donceel-Voûte, "The Archaeology of Khirbet Qumran," 1-38 (for the coins from Qumran, see 3-6).
For a general discussion of numismatics, see Philip Grierson, *Numismatics*

(Oxford: Oxford University Press, 1975). For opposition to the temple tax among the Qumran community and other Jewish groups, see William Horbury, "The Temple tax," in *Jesus and the Politics of His Day*, ed. Ernst Bammel and C. F. D. Moule (Cambridge: Cambridge University Press, 1984), 265-86; Peter Richardson, "Why Turn the Tables? Jesus' Protest in the Temple Precincts," in *Society for Biblical Literature 1992 Seminar Papers*, ed. Eugene H. Lovering, Jr. (Atlanta: Scholars, 1992), 507-23; Jacob Liver, "The Half-Shekel Offering in Biblical and Post-Biblical Literature," *Harvard Theological Review* 56 (1963): 173-98; "The Half-Shekel in the Scrolls of the Judean Desert," *Tarbiz* 31 (1961): 18-22 (Hebrew); David Flusser, "Matthew XVII,24-27 and the Dead Sea Sect," *Tarbiz* 31 (1961): 150-56 (Hebrew). Esther and Hanan Eshel have suggested that the sectarians tried to reduce the amount of money paid to the priests in Jerusalem from the temple treasury by rejecting the annual payment of the half-sheqel and by funding the *Tamid* sacrifices from the temple treasury; see "4Q471 Fragment 1 and *Ma'amadot* in the War Scroll," in *The Madrid Qumran Congress: Proceedings of the International Congress on the Dead Sea Scrolls, Madrid 18-21 March, 1991*, 2 ed. Julio Trebolle Barrera and Luis Vegas Montaner (Leiden: E. J. Brill, 1992), 611-20.

For the suggestion that Tyrian tetradrachmas (silver sheqels) were minted by Herod and his successors in Jerusalem from 9 B.C.E. to 65/66 C.E., see Ya'akov Meshorer, "One Hundred Ninety Years of Tyrian Shekels," in *Festschrift für/Studies in Honor of Leo Mildenberg*, ed. Arthur Houghton et al. (Wetteren: Editions NR, 1984), 171-79; also *Ancient Jewish Coinage 2: Herod the Great through Bar Cochba* (Dix Hills, N.Y.: Amphora, 1982), 7-9. For coin finds from Jerusalem, see Donald T. Ariel, "A Survey of Coin Finds in Jerusalem (Until the End of Byzantine Period)," *Liber Annuus* 32 (1982): 273-326. For discussions of the Isfiya hoard, the temple tax, and the *agio*, see Leo Kadman, "Temple Dues and Currency in Ancient Palestine in the Light of Recent Discovered Coin-Hoards," in *Congresso Internazionale di Numismatica, Roma 11-16 Settembre 1961: Atti* (Rome: Istituto Italiano di Numismatica, 1965), 69-76; "Temple Dues and Currency in Ancient Palestine in the Light of Recent Discovered Coin-Hoards," *Israel Numismatic Bulletin* 1 (1962): 9-11.

For a discussion of wine-drinking by the Essenes, see Magen Broshi, "Wine in Ancient Palestine — Introductory Notes," *Israel Museum Journal* 3 (1984): 21-40 (see 32, "Did the Essenes Drink Wine?").

For sectarian clothing, see Jodi Magness, "Women at Qumran?" in L. V. Rutgers, *What Athens Has to Do with Jerusalem* (with bibliography; some of the main references are repeated here with additional bibliography). For the clothing worn by the Jews in Roman Palestine, see Lucille A. Roussin, "Costume in Roman Palestine: Archaeological Remains and the Evidence from the

Mishnah," in *The World of Roman Costume,* ed. Judith L. Sebesta and Larissa Bonfante (Madison: University of Wisconsin Press, 1994), 182-90; Alexandra T. Croom, *Roman Clothing and Fashion.* For the observation that the Essenes were distinguished by their clothing, see Albert I. Baumgarten, "He Knew that He Knew that He Knew that He was an Essene," *Journal of Jewish Studies* 48 (1997): 53-61.

For the sectarian ordinances governing the payment of the half-sheqel and the prohibition against men wearing the clothing of a woman, see Lawrence H. Schiffman, "Ordinances and Rules," in *The Dead Sea Scrolls: Hebrew, Aramaic, and Greek Texts with English Translations* 1: *Rule of the Community and Related Documents,* ed. James H. Charlesworth (Louisville: Westminster John Knox, 1994), 145-75. For the Rule of the Community's punishment for exposure of the genitalia, and a discussion of the meaning of *yad* as "penis" in Qumranic Hebrew, see Elisha Qimron and Charlesworth, "Rule of the Community," in Charlesworth, *The Dead Sea Scrolls* 1:1-51 (see 33).

For the textiles from Cave 1 at Qumran, see Grace M. Crowfoot, "The Linen Textiles," in Dominique Barthélemy and J. T. Milik, *Qumran Cave I,* 18-38. For Yigael Yadin's discussion of the linen scroll wrappers with blue lines from Cave 1 at Qumran, see *The Temple Scroll* 1: *Introduction* (Jerusalem: Israel Exploration Society, 1983), 198-200; his observation regarding the plan of the temple in Jerusalem is on 199, n. 52. For textiles and loom weights from Masada and the Cave of Letters, see Avigail Sheffer and Hero Granger-Taylor, "Textiles," in *Masada IV,* 153-244; Orit Shamir, "Loomweights from Masada," in *Masada IV,* 265-81; Yadin, *The Finds from the Bar-Kokhba Period in the Cave of Letters.* For an overview of textiles from the Judean Desert with bibliography, see Avigail Sheffer, "Textiles," in Lawrence H. Schiffman and James C. VanderKam, *Encyclopedia of the Dead Sea Scrolls* 2:938-43. For other references, see the bibliographical notes to Chapter 8; also see Magness, "Women at Qumran?" (cited above). The passage from Philo, *The Special Laws,* is from the Loeb edition: Francis H. Colson, *Philo* 7 (Cambridge, Mass.: Harvard University Press, 1960), 147-49.

A detailed publication of the War Scroll is Yigael Yadin, *The Scroll of the War of the Sons of Light against the Sons of Darkness* (for the passage from War Scroll 7.9-10, see 219, 292). Yadin concluded that the army of the War Scroll was patterned after the Roman legions of Julius Caesar and Augustus. For the possibility that the War Scroll incorporates Roman military practices of the 2nd century B.C.E., see Russell Gmirkin, "The War Scroll and Roman Weaponry Reconsidered," *Dead Sea Discoveries* 3 (1996): 89-129; Bezalel Bar-Kochva, "The Battle between Ptolemy Lathyrus and Alexander Jannaeus in the Jordan Valley and the Dating of the Scroll of the War of the Sons of Light,"

*Cathedra* 93 (1999): 7-56 (Hebrew). For discussions of the Essenes' avoidance of oil, see the bibliographical notes to Chapter 7.

For Abraham Wasserstein's observations regarding the avoidance of Greek by the sectarians, see "Non-Hellenized Jews in the Semi-Hellenized East," *Scripta Classica Israelica* 14 (1995): 111-37. For Greek texts from Qumran, see Emanuel Tov, "The Nature of the Greek Texts from the Judean Desert," *Novum Testamentum* 43 (2001): 1-11; "Greek Texts from the Judaean Desert," *Qumran Chronicle* 8 (1999): 161-68. For the Qumran community's use of a dating system according to the high priests' service, see Hanan Eshel, "4Q348, 4Q343 and 4Q345: Three Economic Documents from Qumran Cave 4?" *Journal of Jewish Studies* 52 (2001): 132-35. For Andrea M. Berlin's observation that the Jews of Galilee deliberately refrained from using Eastern Sigillata A, see the Bibliographical Notes to Chapter 5. For Nahman Avigad's quote about the 1st-century C.E. mansions in Jerusalem's Jewish Quarter, see *Discovering Jerusalem*, 83. For the suggestion that the precipitating cause of the Qumran sect's split from the temple cult was a quarrel with the Hellenized priesthood, see Hanan Eshel, "4QMMT and the History of the Hasmonean Period," in *Reading 4QMMT: New Perspectives on Qumran Law and History*, ed. John Kampen and Moshe J. Bernstein (Atlanta: Scholars, 1996), 53-65.

Although I do not discuss it here, readers interested in a round stone object from Qumran that has been interpreted as a sundial should consult: George M. Hollenback, "The Qumran Roundel: An Equatorial Sundial?" *Dead Sea Discoveries* 7 (2000): 123-29; Matthias Albani, Uwe Glessmer, and Gerd Grasshoff, "An Instrument for Determining the Hours of the Day and the Seasons (Sundial)," in *A Day at Qumran: The Dead Sea Sect and Its Scrolls*, ed. Adolfo Roitman (Jerusalem: Israel Museum, 1997), 20-22; Abraham Levy, "Bad Timing," *Biblical Archaeology Review* 24/4 (1998): 18-23; Glessmer and Albani, "An Astronomical Measuring Instrument from Qumran," in Donald W. Parry and Eugene Ulrich, *The Provo International Conference on the Dead Sea Scrolls*, 407-42.

CHAPTER 10

# The Settlements at Ein Feshkha
# and Ein el-Ghuweir

Two sites located on the northwest shore of the Dead Sea have been identified as sectarian settlements related to Qumran: Ein Feshkha and Ein el-Ghuweir (see the map in Fig. 1). We begin this chapter by reviewing the archaeological remains from both sites. We then examine their chronology and consider whether they were indeed sectarian settlements.

## Ein Feshkha (see Figs. 64, 65)

Ein Feshkha (Hebrew Einot Zukim) is located by brackish springs on the shore of the Dead Sea, 3 kilometers (2 miles) south of Qumran. During his last season at Qumran in 1956, de Vaux cleared one room at Ein Feshkha. After finding pottery and coins identical with those of Period II at Qumran, he conducted large-scale excavations in 1958. The remains at Ein Feshkha include a main building, an industrial area to the north of the main building, and an enclosure with a porch or shed to the southwest.

### The Main Building

The main building is a large rectangle measuring 24 × 18 m. (76.8 × 57.6 ft.) with the same orientation as the main building at Qumran. The main building at Ein Feshkha consists of an open courtyard surrounded by rooms on all four sides. The entrance to the building was through two side-by-side doorways on the eastern side. De Vaux suggested that the northern doorway and passage (L9) provided access to the northern suite of rooms (L21-L22), while the southern doorway and passage (L11A) led into the central courtyard: "It is hardly possible to explain why these two doors should have been placed so close to one another except by presuming that the western end of the passage was originally closed so that it did not lead into the inner courtyard, since the central door already gave access to this. It can also be concluded that one of the entrances was designed for human use and the other for animals."

The rooms along the northern side of the courtyard (L21, L22, L22 *bis*) were entered through a single doorway in L22 and were separated from each other by low, narrow partition walls. These rooms yielded about a half dozen coins and some small potsherds. Jars were embedded in the floors of L21 and L22. De Vaux suggested that these rooms and those on the south side of the courtyard (L7, L10) were storerooms. L7 and L10 were paved with small stones and were separated by a poorly constructed wall that was probably a later addition. A lump of bitumen was found against the eastern wall of L7 above the floor. This room contained many potsherds and some fragments of stone vessels. There were fewer sherds in L10, and both loci yielded a total of three coins. A cylindrical weight made of white limestone was also found in L10. The letters LEB are inscribed on its flat face. De Vaux noted that L is the Greek symbol for "year," E has the numerical value of "five," and B could either have the numerical value of "two," or is an abbreviation of the Greek word for "king" *(basileus)*. Thirty-two coins were found in a room in the southeast corner of the building (L11B), which had a drain running diagonally through it to carry water away from the courtyard. A tiny room in the northwest corner of the courtyard (L6) was divided into two halves by a low bench. A jar was embedded in the floor in the western half of the room.

A staircase on the southeastern side of the building (next to L10) provided access to a roof terrace above the rooms on the northern and southern sides of the courtyard as well as to a second story of rooms on the western side (above L3 and L5). According to de Vaux, this staircase and the second-story rooms to which it provided access were added in Period II. Six stone steps belonging to the staircase were preserved. They led to a landing above L13, from which point another flight of steps would have turned 180 degrees and continued up above L12.

A square pier on the western side of the courtyard supported a balcony at the second-story level in front of L3 and L5. The upper-story rooms of L3 and L5 must have had doorways opening onto this balcony, which served as a gangway connecting the roof terraces above the rooms on the northern and southern sides of the courtyard. In L3 and L5, de Vaux found the remains of two successive ceilings (one belonging to the first-story level and the other to the second-story level), separated by a layer of debris containing potsherds that had collapsed onto the ground floor. De Vaux suggested that these rooms (L3, L5) served as residential quarters or offices. The southwestern room (L3) was paved with small stones. The lower half of a basalt grinding stone lay on the floor by the doorway. A small plastered niche was located in the northwest corner of the room and two cupboards were built into the eastern wall. One cupboard contained a small jar and a rectangular limestone basin connected to a channel. Six coins and a relatively large amount of pottery, including an inkwell, were found in this room. Bits of rounded plaster of unknown function had fallen from the second-story level.

The northwest room (L5) had a packed dirt floor and a semicircular paved area abutting the east wall. A cupboard was built into the eastern wall near the doorway. Twenty-four coins and some small fragments of pottery were found in this room. A circular column drum, 38.5 cm. high and 45 cm. in diameter, apparently came from the second-story level of L5. One quarter of it had been cut out, giving it a stepped profile. A groove was cut into the center along the inner side of the upper step. Traces of fine plaster still adhered to the outer face and the stepped part. De Vaux noted that this stone could not have served a structural purpose but was at a loss to suggest its function. He tentatively proposed that it was a sundial, though he admitted this was unconvincing.

Fragments of stone vessels were recovered in several rooms (L5, L7, L21). These include a basin and a large vase (71 cm. high) that apparently came from the roof terrace above L21. The vase has a high pedestal and was carved out of a single block of soft limestone or chalk. A Hebrew inscription is lightly incised on the side of the vase. Although mostly illegible, the words "in the first year" can be made out. Soft limestone or chalk vessels are common at Jewish sites around Palestine from the 1st century B.C.E. to the 2nd century C.E. They range in size and type from large, lathe-turned jars like the one from Ein Feshkha to small, crudely carved "measuring cups." According to rabbinic halakhah, stone vessels (unlike pottery and glass) could not become impure through contact with impure objects. They were therefore preferred by observant Jews who could afford them, as they were more expensive than pottery vessels. Stone quarries where these vessels were manufactured have been discovered in the region around Jerusalem. About 200 fragments of stone vessels were discovered at Qumran. There are 70 fragments from Ein Feshkha, and a few pieces from Ein el-Ghuweir. This evidence indicates that stone vessels are common at Qumran just as at other contemporary Jewish sites. Hanan Eshel has demonstrated that, although the sectarians used stone vessels, they differed from other Jews in believing that these vessels could be rendered impure through contact with oil. This is because, according to sectarian halakhah, oil is more susceptible to defilement than other liquids. The sectarians presumably did not use stone vessels as containers for oil.

A number of carefully cut square and triangular tiles made of white limestone or bituminous grey stone and measuring 15 and 20 cm. or less to a side were found in various loci at Ein Feshkha, especially in L11 and L21. The largest concentration was found in L28 (the open area to the north of the main building), where 28 tiles were piled outside the wall of L22. They measured 21 cm. to a side, and had been placed in pairs, with the flatter sides against each other. The limestone used for the tiles was not from the immediate vicinity of Ein Feshkha. In his notes, de Vaux hypothesized that the tiles had been brought to the site and stored there for a planned construction that was never carried out. In his preliminary report on the Ein Feshkha excavations, de Vaux noted that the tiles were too few in number to pave a floor. Other finds from L28 which are apparently associated with the main building include a basalt mortar (grinding stone) with three legs found outside L21 and a large concentration of potsherds and fragments of glass bottles from outside L5. These finds belong to the debris that was cleared out of the main building after it was reoccupied at the beginning of Period II.

De Vaux distinguished several phases of occupation at Ein Feshkha. According to him, the first two phases (Periods I and II) were contemporary with Period Ib (that is, ca. 100-31 B.C.E.) and Period II at Qumran. Unlike Qumran, however, Period I at Ein Feshkha did not end with a violent destruction. However, like Qumran, Period II at Ein Feshkha appears to have ended with the destruction of the settlement by the Romans at the time of the First Jewish Revolt. After this, the site was abandoned for 30 to 50 years. At the end of the 1st century or early in the 2nd century, the rooms along the northern side of the courtyard were reoccupied, perhaps by Jewish rebels at the time of the Bar Kokhba Revolt. After this, the main building was abandoned for good, although there was limited reoccupation of the southwest enclosure during the Byzantine period.

## The Southwest Enclosure

The area to the southwest of the main building was enclosed by walls measuring over 40 meters on each side. The north wall of the enclosure was originally attached to the southwest corner of the main building. The only structure found within the enclosed area was a row of square stone piers running parallel to the north wall which created a 30-meter wide porch or shed that was open to the south. Wooden posts placed on top of the piers (which are preserved to a height of no more than 45 cm.) would have supported the edge of the porch's roof. The foundations and lowest part of the walls are constructed of field stones while the rest of the walls were presumably of mud brick. A pavement of small stones covered much of the floor of the porch, ending neatly to the south of the row of piers at the point where the overhang of the roof would have terminated. A room at the eastern end of the porch (L20; and perhaps another room at the western end, L19) might have been used as living quarters. The porch could have provided temporary shelter for people or animals, or, as de Vaux suggested, might have been used as a drying shed for reeds or dates (which were probably cultivated in the brackish water of the springs). An enclosure with a different plan existed in this area during Period I, although its complete outline could not be determined.

The enclosure was abandoned after Period II until the Byzantine period (5th to 6th centuries), when the square room at the eastern end of the porch (L20) was rebuilt. This activity destroyed the connection between the north wall of the enclosure and the southwest corner of the main building. The limited Byzantine reoccupation is probably associated with monks from the monastery at Hyrcania (Khirbet el-Mird), which is the site of a Herodian fortified palace overlooking the Buqeia valley about 9 kilometers (6 miles) to the west of Ein Feshkha. The monks apparently cultivated vegetable gardens by the springs at Ein Feshkha.

## The Industrial Area (Northern Enclosure)

Like the area to the southwest, the area to the north of the main building was enclosed by walls. One wall of the enclosure was attached to the northwest corner of the main building. The western half of the area seems to have been empty, but the eastern half contained a system of basins and water channels. The water did not come from the existing springs, which are 3 to 5 meters lower than the basins and channels. Instead, the water apparently came from a spring at a higher level to the west which has now dried up. Because it originated at a higher level than the current springs, this water was presumably sweet, not brackish. From its point of origin, the water was brought through the north wall of the enclosure via a sluice gate with two openings separated by a stone slab (L29). From there the water flowed southeast through a channel into a small rectangular tank (L23). The overflow was carried off through a channel running to the north under the enclosure wall. Two other channels carried the water into the industrial basins to the southeast.

The more southerly of the two channels fed a large, square, plastered basin (L24) a little over 1 meter deep. The bottom of the basin was covered with a whitish deposit, and its floor sloped down slightly towards the east. The southeast wall of the basin, which is the deepest side, is pierced by a conduit formed by a stone with a smooth round hole in it. The basin could have been filled or drained by plugging or unplugging this hole. The conduit continued through the southeast wall of the basin as a trough or channel. It emptied into a rectangular pit (1.3 m. deep) that was coated with lime, plaster, and gravel (L25). The trough and pit were surrounded by a rectangular paved area that lay at a lower level than the natural ground level. Three steps led from the ground level down to the paved area around the pit. Waste water drawn from the pit would have collected in a plastered depression at the bottom of the steps. The channel that fed the plastered basin in L24 branched off and encircled it on the west, terminating at a second plastered basin (L27). This basin (L27) lies to the south of the pit in L25 and is separated from it by a wall. At the point where the water entered basin L27, it flowed down three steps into a rectangular area with a gently sloping paved and plastered floor. A plastered rectangular pit is sunk into the middle of this area, abutting the dividing wall with L25.

The second of the two channels branching off from L23 led to a rectangular plastered basin (L26, measuring 8 × 3.50 m.) to the north of L24, L25, and L27. A parapet running along the inner wall broke the flow the water at the point where the channel emptied into the basin. The western half of the area between the plastered basins and pit (L24, L25, L27) to the south and the channel that fed the rectangular basin (L26) to the north was paved with large stone slabs. To the east, the continuation of this area was paved with smaller stones. An intact jar and two large oblong stones were found lying in this area and two more oblong stones lay at the bottom of the basins in L24 and L26. The stones were carved roughly in the form of cylinders and were obviously used in the industrial activities conducted in this area.

What kind of industrial activities were carried out here? De Vaux pointed out that the shallowness of the basins indicates they were not used as cisterns, while the absence of steps rules out their use as baths. This must have been an industrial installation in which water played a major role. The nature of the industry is unknown. De Vaux suggested that it was a tannery for the curing of animal hides. The basins would have been used for the repeated washing, rinsing, and steeping of the hides, which could have been stretched and scraped on the oblong stones. The final process by which hides are turned into leather is the actual tanning, in which they are treated with tannin (a substance contained in the bark of trees, nuts, and other materials). However, an analysis of deposits taken from the pits, channels, and basins failed to turn up any traces of tannin. De Vaux suggested that the absence of tannin could be explained if parchment and not leather had been produced here, since parchment is untanned leather. In this case, some of the parchment used for the Dead Sea Scrolls might have originated in the industrial installation at Ein Feshkha.

A more serious obstacle to de Vaux's interpretation is the complete absence of animal hairs from the deposits, since hides used for parchment and leather had to be depilated. Because of these problems, Frederick Zeuner suggested that the installations were used to raise fish. However, de Vaux noted that the small size of the basins would have limited the number of fish that could be raised, while the presence of plaster on the basin walls would have inhibited the growth of algae and other plants on which fish feed. Alternatively, it has been suggested that the basins were used to soak flax, although there is no evidence to support this interpretation either. More recently, Ehud Netzer has interpreted these basins as datepresses based on their similarity to installations at Jericho. According to de Vaux, the northern enclosure and industrial area only existed during Period II at Ein Feshkha.

## Ein el-Ghuweir (see Fig. 66)

Another group of brackish springs is located by the shore of the Dead Sea to the south of Ein Feshkha. The springs at Ein el-Ghuweir (Hebrew Ein Qaneh) are located about 9 miles south of Qumran, and there is another group at Ein et-Tureibeh, 12 miles south of Qumran. Ruins dating to the Iron Age and the early Roman period lie on a narrow strip of land overlooking the springs at Ein el-Ghuweir, sandwiched between the cliffs to the west and the seashore to the east. After the Six-Day War in 1967, Israel built a highway along the western shore of the Dead Sea. In 1969, as part of this project, the Israeli archaeologist Pesach Bar-Adon conducted salvage excavations at Ein el-Ghuweir. He uncovered the remains of a large structure measuring 43 × 19.5 meters. The foundations and lower parts of the walls are of field stones, and the upper sections were presumably of mud brick. Bar-Adon used Roman numerals instead of locus numbers to designate the excavated rooms.

The main part of the structure was occupied by a large rectangular courtyard, which Bar-Adon described as a large hall (I). A row of stone pillars, some connected by low partition walls, created a long, narrow porch or room along the northern side of the courtyard (II). Because two ovens and two granaries were discovered in this room, Bar-Adon described it as a kitchen. There were also numerous fragments of cooking pots, bowls, jugs, flasks, and storage jars. Six jars surrounded by stones were found in a 25-30 cm. deep depression. Other finds from the kitchen and other areas included more pottery, oil lamps, bronze coins, and a spouted stone "measuring cup."

Bar-Adon distinguished the remains of two successive layers of paved stone floors in the kitchen, each covered with layers of ash. The layers of ash indicate that this room was originally roofed, presumably with reeds and mud. A threshold for a door was found in the middle of the north wall of kitchen. A channel constructed of two parallel rows of stones ran through or under the wall to the west of the doorway. Only small parts of two more rooms further to the east (III and IV) and one to the north (V) were uncovered. The remains were poorly preserved, and much of the structure (especially the southern part) had been washed away by flash floods. Bar-Adon also excavated a cemetery located about 800 meters to the north of this building. Although the graves resemble those at Qumran, they contained male and female burials (see Chapter 8).

## The Chronology of Ein Feshkha and Ein el-Ghuweir

The chronological sequences at Ein Feshkha and Ein el-Ghuweir are based upon Qumran, where de Vaux divided the sectarian settlement into three phases, termed Period Ia, Period Ib, and Period II. In approximate terms, de Vaux dated Period Ia at Qumran from ca. 130-100 B.C.E., Period Ib from ca. 100-31 B.C.E., and Period II from ca. 4-1 B.C.E. to 68 C.E. The first phase of occupation at Ein Feshkha and Ein el-Ghuweir was assigned by their respective excavators to the time of Period Ib at Qumran. As we have seen, however, occupation at Qumran continued after the earthquake of 31 B.C.E., which means that de Vaux's Period Ib has a pre–31 B.C.E. phase and a post–31 B.C.E. phase. The post–31 B.C.E. phase of Period Ib at Qumran ended with a destruction ca. 9/8 B.C.E. or shortly thereafter (see Chapter 4). How does this revised chronology compare with that of Ein Feshkha and Ein el-Ghuweir?

### The Chronology of Ein Feshkha

The complex at Ein Feshkha is partly contemporary with the sectarian settlement at Qumran. Although no cylindrical jars are definitely attested at Ein

Feshkha (see Chapter 5), the rest of the ceramic corpus is similar to that of Qumran. De Vaux distinguished two main occupation phases at Ein Feshkha: Period I and Period II. Period II at Ein Feshkha is contemporary with Period II at Qumran. Most of the pottery recovered in the excavations belongs to this phase, and the dating is supported by the numismatic evidence. As at Qumran, Period II at Ein Feshkha ended with a destruction by fire. The earlier occupation phase is called Period I. The only evidence for this phase came from the area of the main building, where de Vaux distinguished an earlier level in L6 (the tiny room in the northwest corner of the courtyard) and in L21 and L22 (the long room on the north side of the courtyard). Most of the pottery associated with Period I is fragmentary, and much of it comes from debris that was cleared out of the main building and discarded outside its north wall when the site was reoccupied at the beginning of Period II. Although he equated this phase with Period Ib at Qumran, de Vaux noted there is no evidence that Period I at Ein Feshkha ended with a violent destruction either by earthquake or fire. However, the fact that the building was cleared out suggests it was abandoned for some time.

The repertoire of ceramic types published from Period I contexts at Ein Feshkha is very limited. What is important, however, is that none of the types (such as the cups and bowls) has to antedate the Herodian period. Other types, such as the bag-shaped storage jars and an unguentarium (perfume bottle), should certainly be dated no earlier than the time of Herod the Great. The numismatic evidence supports this chronology. Among the coins from Period I are four coins of Alexander Jannaeus (103-76 B.C.E.), one of Mattathias Antigonus (40-37 B.C.E.), and one coin of Herod the Great. A similar picture was obtained from a house in Jerusalem's Jewish Quarter called the "Herodian Residence," which was paved over by a street during the reign of Herod the Great. Most of the coins from this house were of Alexander Jannaeus, and some were of Herod. Nahman Avigad, the excavator, noted that since the coins of Alexander Jannaeus are known to have remained in circulation even under Herod, they do not necessarily indicate a Hasmonean phase of occupation. Instead, it is the latest pottery and coins that provide the date for the associated building or level. The pottery and coins therefore indicate that Period I at Ein Feshkha dates to the Herodian period.

De Vaux was puzzled by the fact that there is no evidence for the earthquake of 31 B.C.E. at Ein Feshkha, which is just 2 miles south of Qumran. He attributed this to a different geological formation at Ein Feshkha. However, the ceramic evidence indicates that Period I at Ein Feshkha dates to the Herodian period. I believe that this settlement was first established after the earthquake of 31 B.C.E., which would account for the absence of evidence for earthquake destruction at the site. Because of the limited nature of the ceramic repertoire, it is difficult to determine whether the end of Period I at Ein Feshkha is contemporary with the end of the post–31 B.C.E. phase of Period Ib at Qumran, that is, ca. 9/8 B.C.E. At any rate, the ceramic evidence does not contradict the possibility that Ein Feshkha was abandoned (but not destroyed) at the same time as Qumran.

## The Chronology of Ein el-Ghuweir

At Ein el-Ghuweir, Bar-Adon distinguished two layers of burnt material in the hall and kitchen, which indicated that the complex had been destroyed twice by fire. Regarding the chronology of the settlement, he concluded as follows:

> The coins were identified as belonging to the time of Herod, Archelaus, and Agrippa I, i.e., from the period between 37 B.C.E. and 44 C.E. According to these limits, the settlement did not exist for long. In contrast to this, the pottery finds considerably extend the period during which the settlement existed. In accordance with the material discussed above, the types of pottery found both in the large structure at 'En el-Ghuweir and in the cemetery are similar to those found in Qumran Ib. Thus, they date from Qumran's most flourishing period — from the days of Alexander Yannai [= Jannaeus] until the beginning of the reign of Herod. The pottery types are also similar to those from Qumran II, the period ending with the Great Revolt and the destruction of the settlement in 68 C.E. It is therefore possible that the two layers of burned material at 'En el-Ghuweir parallel the double destruction of Qumran and 'En Feshkha.

Bar-Adon's chronology is not supported by the ceramic evidence, for types that clearly antedate the reign of Herod are absent from the corpus at Ein el-Ghuweir. This parallels the complete absence of pre-Herodian coins from the site. Some of the ceramic types, such as the asymmetrical flasks, have a range throughout the 1st century B.C.E. and 1st century C.E. However, most of the published types from Ein el-Ghuweir, such as the bag-shaped jars, the unguentaria, and the wheel-made ("Herodian") oil lamps, do not antedate the Herodian period. The ceramic and numismatic evidence therefore indicates that the settlement at Ein el-Ghuweir was established no earlier than the reign of Herod the Great. On the basis of the published evidence, it is impossible to determine when the fire that destroyed the earlier phase of the

THE ARCHAEOLOGY OF QUMRAN

settlement occurred and whether it is contemporary with the destruction at Qumran ca. 9/8 B.C.E. This review indicates that Qumran is the only one of the three sites with evidence for a pre-Herodian phase of occupation.

The numismatic evidence suggests that, like Qumran, Ein Feshkha was destroyed in 68 C.E., during the First Jewish Revolt. Four coins of Herod Archelaus, 32 coins of the Procurators, and 45 coins of Herod Agrippa I are among the coins associated with Period II at Ein Feshkha. The latest specimen associated with Period II, a coin of the second year of the First Jewish Revolt (67/68 C.E.), supports de Vaux's suggestion that the settlement was destroyed at the same time as Qumran. On the other hand, de Vaux noted that only seven bronze coins were found at Ein el-Ghuweir, consisting of five coins of Herod the Great, one of Herod Archelaus, and one of Herod Agrippa I (42 C.E.). He therefore suggested that the occupation of Ein el-Ghuweir ended before the outbreak of the revolt and the destruction of Qumran and Ein Feshkha in 68 C.E. On the other hand, as de Vaux noted, the fact that only seven coins were found in the excavations means this is a weak argument from silence (that is, the argument is based on the absence of certain types of coins in a very small sample).

## Were Ein Feshkha and Ein el-Ghuweir Sectarian Settlements?

According to de Vaux, the main building at Ein Feshkha was not a private dwelling but instead served the needs of a sectarian community. He concluded that, "The nature of the two phases of occupation [at Ein Feshkha] is fairly clear. They are exactly contemporaneous with Periods Ib and II of Khirbet Qumran. The installations at Feshkha are close to those at Khirbet Qumran; the architecture is similar; the ceramic material is homogeneous. All these signs point to the fact that the two were organically connected. They were inhabited by the same community, and it is this that explains their common history."

The main point of de Vaux's argument is that since the occupation phases of Qumran and Ein Feshkha are contemporary, and because they have similar architecture and pottery, they must have been inhabited by the same community. As we have seen, however, the occupation phases at Qumran and Ein Feshkha do not correspond precisely although they overlap (with the settlement at Ein Feshkha having been established 50 to 100 years later than the one at Qumran). In fact, the archaeological evidence does not enable us to determine whether the populations of these two sites were related or connected.

As I noted in Chapter 1, archaeology proves the connection between the scrolls in the caves and the settlement at Qumran. This evidence does not exist at Ein Feshkha. There are no scrolls from caves adjacent to the site. The Hebrew inscription on the stone vase (and the presence of stone vessels) indicates that the inhabitants were Jewish but does not tell us whether they were sectarian. Although the ceramic repertoire from Ein Feshkha is similar to that from Qumran, it lacks the distinctive cylindrical jars and lids. These similarities are therefore generic; in other words, these pottery types are generally characteristic of Judean sites in the 1st century c.e. The small amount of pottery published from Ein Feshkha (only 45 pieces) makes it hazardous to draw sweeping conclusions. In contrast with Qumran, where three different destruction levels yielded large numbers of whole or restorable vessels, nearly all of the pottery from Ein Feshkha appears to consist of small fragments (little of which was saved or at least illustrated by de Vaux). This limited corpus includes one painted Jerusalem bowl, a painted unguentarium, and one piece of terra sigillata — presumably Eastern Sigillata A — which is mentioned in de Vaux's notes for L16. Ein Feshkha also lacks the other distinctive features of Qumran, including the animal bone deposits, the large adjacent cemetery, and the system of miqva'ot. Because Ein Feshkha lacks these features, it is impossible to determine whether it was used or inhabited by a sectarian community.

Many ancient Palestinian houses had two stories of rooms arranged around a central courtyard. The rooms at the ground-floor level were usually used as working spaces (for cooking and related activities), for storage, and as stables for animals. The living and sleeping quarters were located upstairs, away from the dirt and noise. This arrangement is analogous to modern Western multistory houses, in which the basement (used for storage) and the den are at the bottom of the house, the kitchen, living room, and dining room (spaces for public activities) are on the ground-floor level, and the bedrooms (private areas) are upstairs.

The main building at Ein Feshkha is arranged in this manner. The ground-floor rooms were used for storage and as working spaces, as indicated by the jars sunk into the floors, the cupboards built into the walls, the stone pavements (which are often found in rooms where liquids were spilled), and the finds (such as the basalt grinding stone, the inscribed stone weight, and the numerous potsherds). The second-story rooms above L3 and L5 (which might have been one large room at the second-story level) could have been used as living (that is, sleeping) quarters. It is possible that this building was occupied by a sectarian community. For example, the inkwell from L3 (the room on the southwest side of the courtyard) is paralleled by three inkwells from the area of L30 (the "scriptorium") at Qumran. The bits of rounded plaster (mentioned by de Vaux but unfortunately nowhere illustrated) from the second-story level of L3 recall the plastered benches and tables from the second story of L30 at Qumran. It is not clear whether the inkwell from L3 also came from the second-story level. The enigmatic cut and stepped column drum comes from the second-story level of L5, and the large stone vase originally stood on the adjacent roof terrace of L21. The arrangement of the side-by-side doorways providing access into the main building at Ein Feshkha (L9 and L11A) recalls the two passages leading into the staircase in the courtyard of the main building at Qumran (L35; see Chapter 6).

De Vaux considered Ein Feshkha to be "an agricultural and industrial establishment used to benefit the community of Qumran." The southwest enclosure was a shed for drying dates raised by the springs, and parchment (presumably for the scrolls written in the "scriptorium") was produced in the industrial area. This may or may not be the case. The main building at Ein Feshkha is probably a farmhouse (as de Vaux suggested), but it is impossible to determine whether it was inhabited by a sectarian community. It is reasonable to assume that dates were cultivated by the springs, and the southwest enclosure could have been used as a drying shed. The nature of the industry in the northern enclosure is still debated, as it was in de Vaux's time.

The fact that the settlements at Qumran and Ein Feshkha are contemporary and are 2 miles from each other provides only circumstantial evidence for a connection between them. The existence of contemporary, nonsectarian settlements in the Dead Sea region means we cannot assume that Ein Feshkha was a sectarian settlement. These include the towns or villages at Jericho and Ein Gedi (which could have included sectarian populations but were not sectarian settlements), the fortress at Rujm el-Bahr at the northern end of the Dead Sea, and the Hasmonean anchorage at Qasr el-Yahud (Khirbet Mazin) at the mouth of the Kidron Valley. The Kidron Valley originates in the area of Jerusalem and empties into the Dead Sea to the south of Qumran. As an aside, I note that the presence of anchorages at Khirbet Mazin and Qasr el-Yahud and the location of the settlement at Ein Feshkha indicate that the water level in the northern basin of the Dead Sea was not much lower in the 1st century c.e. than it is today. This means that Qumran, which sits atop a plateau at a higher elevation, could not have been used as a commercial entrepot with a dock on the sea shore, as Alan Crown and Lena Cansdale have claimed.

The evidence that Ein el-Ghuweir was a sectarian settlement is even weaker because, although it is contemporary with Ein Feshkha, Ein el-Ghuweir is 9 miles from Qumran. Like Ein Feshkha, Ein el-Ghuweir has none of the distinctive features of Qumran, including no scrolls in nearby caves, no cylindrical jars, no animal bone deposits, and no system of miqva'ot. The ceramic repertoire is generally characteristic of 1st-century c.e. Judean sites, although there are no examples of terra sigillata among the 11 bowls published and no imported amphoras. In fact, neutron activation analysis has indicated that the ceramic vessels from Qumran and Ein el-Ghuweir are made of unrelated clays. The Hebrew name Yehohanan on a storage jar from one of the graves in the cemetery at Ein el-Ghuweir indicates that the inhabitants were Jewish but not that they were sectarians. Because the architectural remains were fragmentary and eroded, it is difficult to determine the original layout and function of the buildings. The recent excavations at Khirbet Qazone have demonstrated that the type of cemetery found at Ein el-Ghuweir (which includes burials of men and women) is not necessarily sectarian (see Chapter 8). Even if the cemetery at Ein el-Ghuweir is sectarian, de Vaux noted that there is no evidence for its connection with the settlement, which is located some 800 meters to the south. Although Bar-Adon believed that Ein el-Ghuweir was a "secondary settlement" of the sectarian community at Qumran, de Vaux was more cautious:

> The group involved here [at Ein el-Ghuweir], having installed themselves some 15 km. southwards from Qumran, and about 12 km. to the south of the natural barrier of Ras Feshkha, could not in any case have had any very close connection with the community centre [at Qumran]. Finally, no document of the type found at Qumran has been found either in the ruins themselves or in the caves nearby. . . . In the absence of any stronger proof it may perhaps be suggested that it is rash to apply the designation 'Essene' to the building excavated near 'Ain el-Ghuweir or to the cemetery which may have been attached to it. We should bear in mind that particularly during the second Iron Age and the Roman period the west bank of the Dead Sea was more thickly populated than we have been accustomed to imagine.

To conclude, although the settlements at Ein Feshkha and Ein el-Ghuweir were inhabited by Jews and are contemporary with Qumran, the available evidence provides no indication that their populations were related to the sectarian community at Qumran. In other words, the archaeological remains do not provide evidence that Ein Feshkha and Ein el-Ghuweir were sectarian settlements, although it is possible that they were.

## Bibliographical Notes

For de Vaux's preliminary report on his excavations at Ein Feshkha and Bar-Adon's publication of his excavations at Ein el-Ghuweir, see the bibliographical notes for Chapter 1. For my chronology of Ein Feshkha and Ein el-Ghuweir, see Jodi Magness, "The Chronology of Qumran, Ein Feshkha, and Ein el-Ghuweir," in *Mogilany 1995: Papers on the Dead Sea Scrolls offered in memory of Aleksy Klawek,* ed. Zdzladisław J. Kapera (Krakow: Enigma, 1998), 55-76 (with bibliography). For the suggestion that the arrangement of side-by-side doorways in the main building at Ein Feshkha recalls the Temple Scroll's description of the rotation of the priestly courses, see George J. Brooke, "The Temple Scroll and the Archaeology of Qumran, 'Ain Feshkha and Masada," *Revue de Qumran* 13 (1988): 225-37 (see 231-33).

For sectarian views on stone vessels and the transmission of impurity, see Hanan Eshel, "CD 12:15-17 and the Stone Vessels Found at Qumran," in *The Damascus Document: A Centennial of Discovery,* ed. Joseph M. Baumgarten, Esther G. Chazon, and Avital Pinnick (Leiden: E. J. Brill, 2000), 45-52. For a study of stone vessels, see Jane M. Cahill, "The Chalk Assemblages of the Persian/Hellenistic and Early Roman Periods," in *Excavations at the City of David 1978-1985 Directed by Yigal Shiloh* 3: *Stratigraphical, Environmental, and Other Reports.* Qedem 33, ed. Alon de Groot and Donald T. Ariel (Jerusalem: Institute of Archaeology, Hebrew University, 1992), 190-274. For a recently discovered quarry for stone vessels in the Jerusalem area, see David Amit, Jon Zeligman, and Irena Ziberbod, "A Quarry and Workshop for the Production of Stone Vessels on the Eastern Slope of Mount Scopus," *Qadmoniot* 122 (2001): 102-10 (Hebrew).

For an analysis of the sediment in the basins at Ein Feshkha and the suggestion that they were used for raising fish, see Frederick E. Zeuner, *Palestine Exploration Quarterly* 92 (1960): 27-36 (see 33-36). For the suggestion that these basins were used for soaking flax, see Magen Broshi, "Qumran: Archaeology," in Lawrence H. Schiffman and James C. VanderKam, *The Encyclopedia of the Dead Sea Scrolls,* 736. Ehud Netzer's interpretation of these basins as datepresses is forthcoming in an article in *Judea and Samaria Research Studies,* Volume 11 (in Hebrew; I thank Magen Broshi for this information). Emanuel Tov informs me that an archaeologist at the École who is working on the publication of de Vaux's material from Qumran believes the basins at Ein Feshkha were used for the production of linen. For neutron activation analysis results indicating that the pottery vessels from Qumran and Ein el-Ghuweir were made of different clays, see Broshi, "The Archaeology of Qumran," in Devorah Dimant and Uriel Rappaport, *The Dead Sea Scrolls: Forty*

*Years of Research*, 103-15 (see 114-15); Joseph Yellin, Magen Broshi, and Hanan Eshel, *Bulletin of the American Schools of Oriental Research* 321 (2001): 65-78.

For the "Herodian Residence" in Jerusalem's Jewish Quarter, and Avigad's observation regarding the coins of Alexander Jannaeus, see Nahman Avigad, *Discovering Jerusalem*, 84-88.

# Index of Authors and
## Contemporary Historical Figures

# Index of Scrolls, Biblical Books, Extrabiblical Books, and Individual Historical Figures

# INDEX OF SCROLLS, BIBLICAL BOOKS, ETC.

# Index of Sites and Place Names

# General Index

*agio,* 192, 207

amphora(s), 75, 76, 78, 82, 85, 88, 94, 97, 100, 101, 103, 161, 223

*Apoxyomenos,* 203

aqueduct(s). *Also see* Qumran, 106, 131, 137

arrowhead(s), 61, 99, 179, 184

balk. *See* baulk

baptism (Christian), 138, 160

Bar Kokhba Revolt, 28, 63, 88, 180, 181, 182, 200, 213

baulk, 6, 7

bedouin(s), 25, 26, 27, 28, 31, 79, 80, 170, 171, 172, 173, 174, 182, 186

Betsoa. *Also see* Jerusalem, Gate of Essenes, 129

bitumen, 20, 22, 211, 213

Boethusians, 43, 190

Byzantine, 63, 82, 96, 106, 162, 178, 179, 182, 213, 214

Carbon 14. *See* radiocarbon dating

Cave of Horror. *Also see* Naḥal Ḥever, 181

Cave of Letters. *Also see* Naḥal Ḥever, 180, 181, 187, 195, 196, 198, 208

Cave of the Pool. *Also see* Naḥal David, 181

Christianity, 138, 186

corpse-impurity, 87, 120, 135, 138, 140, 141, 154, 159

cylindrical jar(s), 26, 44, 52, 58, 59, 74, 79-85, 87, 88, 89, 100, 102, 123, 169, 184, 200, 217, 221, 223

Cypriot, 78, 98

datepress, 21, 30, 216, 224

dendrochronology, 10

earthquake, 6, 11, 55, 56, 57, 59, 60, 64, 65, 66, 67, 68, 69, 72, 81, 100, 106, 107, 117, 122, 123, 124, 125, 126, 128, 129, 148, 149, 150, 152, 153, 178, 217, 218, 219

Edomites, 157

Egypt, 25, 40, 107, 109, 145

Essenes, passim

fresco(es), 91, 92, 93, 94, 100, 205
    wall paintings, 157

genizah, 25

hairnet(s), 176, 180, 181, 182

*haluq. See* tunic

*hashakah,* 151